Into, Through, and Beyond Secondary School

Critical Transitions for Immigrant Youths

Printed in the United States of America
10 9 8 7 6 5 4 3 2 1

Topics in Immigrant Education 1

Editorial/production supervision: Joy Kreeft Peyton and Sonia Kundert
Copyediting: Sonia Kundert
Editorial/production assistance: Amy Fitch, Adriana Vaznaugh, and
    Lynn Fischer
Indexing: Kathleen McLane
Design and cover: SAGARTdesign

ISBN 1-887744-03-7

The writing and production of the volumes in this series were supported by a grant from The Andrew W. Mellon Foundation, as one aspect of the Program in Immigrant Education. The opinions expressed in this volume do not necessarily reflect the positions or policies of The Andrew W. Mellon Foundation.

Library of Congress Cataloging-in-Publication Data
Lucas, Tamara, 1951-
    Into, through, and beyond secondary school : Critical transitions
    for immigrant youths / Tamara Lucas.
        p.   cm. -- (Topics in immigrant education ; 1)
    Includes bibliographical references and index.
    ISBN 1-887744-03-7 (pbk.)
    1. Immigrants--Education (Secondary)--United States.
    2. Immigrants--Services for--United States.   3. School-to-work
    transition--United States.   I. Title.   II. Series.
    LC3731.L83   1997
    371.829'00973--dc21   97-15333
                                                            CIP

Into, Through, and Beyond Secondary School

Critical Transitions for Immigrant Youths

Tamara Lucas
The National Center for Restructuring Education, Schools, and Teaching
Teachers College, Columbia University

Topics in Immigrant Education Series

Series Editors:
Joy Kreeft Peyton and Donna Christian
Center for Applied Linguistics
Washington DC

Into, Through, and Beyond Secondary School:
Critical Transitions for Immigrant Youths
by Tamara Lucas

New Concepts for New Challenges:
Professional Development for Teachers of Immigrant Youth
by Josué M. González & Linda Darling-Hammond

Through the Golden Door:
Educational Approaches for Immigrant Adolescents With Limited
Schooling
by Betty J. Mace-Matluck, Rosalind Alexander-Kasparik,
& Robin M. Queen

Access and Engagement:
Program Design and Instructional Approaches for Immigrant
Students in Secondary School
by Aída Walqui

After a hiatus of half a century, a wave of immigration is once again transforming the United States. With over a million immigrants, legal and illegal, entering the United States each year, the foreign-born constitute the fastest-growing segment of our population, reaching 24.5 million in 1996, roughly 10% of the population, the highest proportion since World War II (U.S. Bureau of the Census, 1997).

Even more striking than the scale of immigration is its makeup. Since the passage of the Immigration Act of 1965, which eliminated national origin quotas, Asia and Latin America have replaced Europe as the main sources of newcomers to the United States. The largest groups come from Mexico (accounting for 27.2% of the 1996 foreign-born population), China, Cuba, India, and Vietnam.

New immigrants to the United States come with diverse languages, cultures, and experiences, even within these larger groups. Asian immigrants, for example, include people from more than 13 countries in South, Southeast, and East Asia as well as the Pacific Islands. A single nationality can include several ethnic groups, each with a distinctive language and culture. A Laotian immigrant might be an ethnic Lao or a member of the Hmong, Mien, or Khmu ethnic minorities. An Asian Indian immigrant might be a Punjabi-speaking Sikh, a Bengali-speaking Hindu, or an Urdu-speaking Moslem.

While the great majority of Latin American immigrants share a common language, and to some extent a common culture, this group also displays a great diversity that is due to the various ancestries—European, African, and Native American—and nations represented. Recent Latin American immigrants have arrived chiefly from Mexico, El Salvador, Guatemala, Nicaragua, and Honduras. Caribbeans, arriving in smaller numbers, come mostly from Haiti, the Dominican Republic, Jamaica, and Cuba.

Today's immigrants also vary in their social and educational backgrounds and personal experiences. They come from the elite as well as the most disadvantaged sectors of their societies. Some left to escape poverty; others were fleeing war or political persecution; others were attracted by the hope for better educational and economic opportunities. Some came directly to the United States; others arrived after harrowing escapes followed by years in refugee camps.

Immigrant Students in America's Schools

While immigration has affected all aspects of American life, nowhere is the changing demography of the United States more keenly felt than in education. First- and second-generation immigrant children are the fastest-growing segment of the U.S. population under age 15 (Fix & Zimmerman, 1993). The 1990 U.S. Census counted 2.1 million foreign-born children in the United States. If children born in the United States to immigrant parents are included, the total is 5 million. By 2010, if current trends continue, 9 million school-age children will be immigrants or children of immigrants, representing 22% of the school-age population (Fix & Passel, 1994).

With over 90% of recent immigrants coming from non-English-speaking countries, schools are increasingly receiving students who do not speak English at home and who have little or no proficiency in English. There has been an increase of almost 1 million English learners in U.S. public schools (grades K-12) in the last 10 years, approximately 5.5% of the public school student population (Fleischman & Hopstock, 1993). It is difficult to determine the number who are considered limited English proficient (LEP, the term used by the federal government and most states) because states determine numbers of LEP students in different ways (Gándara, 1994). However, according to the 1993-94 Schools and Staffing Survey (National Center for Education Statistics, 1997), over 2.1 million public school students in the United States are identified as LEP. They account for 5% of all public school students and 31% of all American Indian/Alaska Native, Asian/Pacific Islander, and Hispanic students enrolled in public schools. The largest proportion of this population (over 79%) are native Spanish speakers (see Goldenberg, 1996). California has been particularly affected. The number of students classified as LEP in the state's public schools more than tripled from nearly 400,000 in 1981 to nearly 1.3 million in 1995 (California Department of Education, 1995). These students were reported to speak one or more of 54 different primary languages.

Along with an increase in sheer numbers of immigrant students who are at various stages of learning English, schools are also faced with an increasing number of students needing extra academic instruction in addition to English as a second language (ESL) classes. Approximately 20% of all English language learners at the high school level and 12% at the middle school level have missed two or more years of schooling since the age of six; 27% in high school and 19% in middle school are assigned to grades at least two years lower than age/grade norms (Fleischman & Hopstock, 1993).

Because newcomers to this country tend to concentrate in certain areas, the responsibility for educating immigrant students is not evenly shared across the country. According to the 1993-94 Schools and Staffing Survey, 82% of the LEP students in K-12 public schools live in only five states—California, Texas, New York, Florida, and Illinois; more than 40% are in California. Dade County, Florida, is an example of a school system struggling to serve a sudden, relatively recent influx of immigrants. Approximately a quarter of the 330,000 students in Dade County, Florida, in Fall 1996 were born outside the United States (Schnaiberg, 1996), and the county adds an average of 1,322 foreign-born students a month to its rolls. At the same time, employment opportunities draw immigrants to smaller cities and even rural areas as well, creating new challenges for schools in those areas.

An increasingly diverse student population is hitting the schools at the same time as a record number of students in general (the *baby boom echo,* a term used by demographers referring to children of the original baby boomers) are entering school. In the fall of 1996, over 51 million children entered school, a new national record (U.S. Department of Education, 1996). The Department of Education predicts that numbers of students enrolled in school will not level off until 2006, when they reach 54.6 million, almost 3 million more than in 1996. The greatest increase over the next decade will be in high school enrollments, projected to increase by 15%. Thus, schools already struggling with the influx of immigrant students are also facing the strains of high overall enrollments.

Understanding the Immigrant Student Population

In this series, the term *immigrant* includes those students (including refugees) born outside the United States, but not those born and raised in non-English speaking homes within the United States. Within this group, the focus is on English language learners who are in ESL or bilingual classes, those who no longer have access to ESL or bilingual services but are having trouble in academic classes taught in English, and those who are literate in their native language as well as those who are not. Because the series focuses on students for whom secondary school is a reasonable placement, students' ages range from 9 to 21 years.

U.S.-born secondary school students enter school at age 5 or 6 and, if they remain in school, follow a fairly predictable sequence of coursework. Educators can, therefore, assume certain experiences and knowledge among those students. However, no such assumptions can be made about adolescent immigrant students' educational backgrounds and readiness for secondary schooling in the United States. Immigrant students arrive at all ages. They may have had an educational preparation superior to that provided by most U.S. schools, or they may have had no previous educational experience at all. Thus, different educational approaches are called for with these students—for example, a 15-year-old who immigrated from Mexico at age 13 with a strong educational background, one who immigrated at age 13 with only two years of prior schooling, and one who immigrated at age 7 and entered school immediately.

Many additional factors can affect immigrant students' adjustment to U.S. schooling and their success in the transition from adolescence to adulthood. These include individual and family characteristics, the similarities and differences between their native countries and cultures and the United States, their immigration experiences, and the contexts in which they live in the United States. (See Tamara Lucas's volume in this series, pages 18, 19, 114, and 115.) Knowledge of these factors can form the foundation upon which educators build programs and approaches that will assist these students in making their way through school and on to postsecondary school or work.

Facing the Challenges

The demographic realities described above are cause for serious concern, and many educators believe that the education system in the United States is poorly prepared to meet the needs of its linguistically and culturally diverse student population. Gándara (1994) claims that English language learners were sidelined in the first wave of reform efforts during the 1980s, and a report by the Stanford Working Group (1993) calls the nation's school systems to task for failing to provide these students with equitable educational opportunities. Moss and Puma (1995) found that English language learners receive lower grades and are judged by their teachers to have lower academic abilities than native-born students, and they score below their native-English-speaking classmates on standardized tests of reading and math.

The challenges of educating immigrant students and English language learners are especially acute at the secondary school level. As Chips (1993) argues, immigrant students of secondary school age can face major difficulties in acquiring English and succeeding in school. If they are newcomers to the United States, they have much less time than elementary age students to learn English and master the academic content required to graduate from high school. They must pass tests that require English skills that they do not have. They must study subjects such as physical science, chemistry, economics, and geometry that require high levels of English academic language. Most secondary school texts and materials require a high level of English reading ability. Few schools provide native-language support for these classes, English-language instruction tied to content, or content classes taught with adaptations of English appropriate for these students' levels of proficiency. Students learning English often find it difficult to be accepted in well-established groups of English-speaking students. Finally, students who hope to attend college or university after high school face even greater challenges, as they attempt to succeed in classes designated for college credit and to master the maze of requirements for college acceptance.

High dropout rates among language-minority secondary school students are just one indication that many schools are failing to meet the challenge. For example, Hispanic students are more likely than White students to leave school during their high school years (10% versus 4%; National Center for Education Statistics, 1996). In 1994, the number of Hispanic students aged 16–24 who had not completed high school and were not enrolled was 30%, as compared to 8% for White students (Lockwood, 1996). Certain subgroups of Asian refugee populations also have high dropout rates; a study of dropout rates in California schools found that those schools with high concentrations of Southeast Asians had the highest dropout rates (U.S. Commission on Civil Rights, 1992).

A number of factors underlie the failure of secondary schools to serve the needs of immigrant students. These include

- a school structure that does not facilitate smooth transitions from program to program, school to school, or school to college or work;
- an instructional program that fails to give them access to academic concepts and skills;
- few program and curricular alternatives for students with limited prior schooling and low literacy skills; and
- a shortage of school personnel trained to meet their specific needs.

These factors characterize an educational system that has failed to keep up with its changing population, particularly at the secondary school level. At the same time, relatively little research is available on effective approaches to educating students at this level (August & Hakuta, 1997).

The books in this series address these issues, providing profiles of immigrant students from a variety of backgrounds, critical reviews of what we know from the research that is available, and descriptions of programs that show promise.

Into, Through, and Beyond Secondary School: Critical Transitions for Immigrant Youths, **by Tamara Lucas**

Immigrant adolescents who enter U.S. schools with limited proficiency in English must negotiate a series of critical transitions in order to progress through school. At the same time that they are dealing with the difficult developmental transitions from childhood to adolescence to adulthood, they also must make the transitions from their native country to the United States, from middle to high school, from bilingual and ESL classes to content area classes, and from high school to postsecondary education or work. Typically, little academic or personal assistance is given to help students make these transitions successfully. The transition from bilingual and ESL to mainstream content classes can be particularly problematic, because students lose the support of programs designed specifically for them and may not be able to cope with the demands of classes and teachers.

The move out of high school also requires considerable attention, particularly for immigrant students who enter the U.S. school system at the secondary school level. Programs to prepare them for postsecondary education and work opportunities are generally lacking; school counselors often have neither the time nor the training to give them the attention, information, and support they need; and they may receive little guidance regarding academic and career options or strategies for pursuing them. Even if students are interested in academic preparation, they may, because of their English proficiency levels, find themselves in vocational education courses or in study halls, rather than in college preparatory courses; and neither they nor their parents may have the information or ability to make their desires known.

In this, the first book in the series, Tamara Lucas argues that in order for schools to help immigrant students make successful transitions through and beyond secondary school, we must apply the best knowledge we have about teaching, learning, and schooling in our work with these students as well as with all other students. We must reconceptualize our notions of learners and learning, teachers and teaching, and schools and schooling. Lucas discusses four specific principles that can be applied by secondary school staff to facilitate these reconceptualizations and promote students' transitions—cultivate organizational relationships; cultivate human relationships; provide access to information; and provide multiple and flexible pathways into, through, and beyond secondary school. She provides a set of questions that school staff can use to guide them in establishing effective practices within each principle, and she describes programs in which these principles have been implemented.

Access and Engagement: Program Design and Instructional Approaches for Immigrant Students in Secondary School, by Aída Walqui

In this book, Aída Walqui describes features of secondary schools in the United States that make it difficult for immigrant students to succeed. These include fragmented school days, fragmented instructional programs in which ESL and content area teachers work in separate departments and rarely interact, the complex system of courses and of graduation and college entrance requirements, the practice of placing students in grades according to their age, and the use of traditional methods of documenting student achievement. She profiles six immigrant high school students (from Brazil, El Salvador, Haiti, Mexico, Russia, and Vietnam) and the challenges they face in school; describes the philosophies, designs, and instructional approaches of four programs (in California, Iowa, and New York) attempting to address these challenges; and proposes 10 characteristics of schools and programs that can foster effective teaching and learning for immigrant youth.

Through the Golden Door: Educational Approaches for Immigrant Adolescents With Limited Schooling, **by Betty Mace-Matluck, Rosalind Alexander-Kasparik, and Robin M. Queen**

A growing number of recent immigrant students enter middle and high school with little or no prior formal schooling. Often referred to as "late-entrant" or "low-literacy," these students are between the ages of 9 and 21 and are three years or more below their age-appropriate grade level. As a result, they often do not have time to fulfill high school graduation requirements before they reach the state's maximum age for high school attendance. In this book, the authors profile five such students (from Haiti, El Salvador, and Vietnam), describe in detail four programs designed to serve them (in Illinois, Texas, and Virginia), identify critical features of secondary school programs for them, and give program contact information and resources.

New Concepts for New Challenges: Professional Development for Teachers of Immigrant Youth, **by Josué M. González and Linda Darling-Hammond (with Elsie Szecsy, Kavemuii Murangi, & David Jacobson)**

Because of immigrant students' diverse backgrounds and needs, teachers require specialized preparation to work with them. It is increasingly clear that *all* teachers with English language learners in their classes need to know about second language development, cross-cultural awareness, and methods to teach both language and academic content. However, teachers have limited opportunities to update their skills or follow rapidly changing trends and developments. In this book, the authors argue that in order to develop a teaching force that is competent to work with immigrant students (and all students), we need to move far beyond traditional notions of "inservicing" and "teacher training." They describe preservice and inservice professional growth opportunities that are intensive, long term, and considered to be a regular part of teachers' lives rather than remedial. The authors focus particularly on structures and models that value community, collegiality, and collaboration, and they describe innovative approaches to preservice and inservice professional development in California, Maryland, Minnesota, and New York.

Conclusion

New visions of learning, teaching, and schooling push us to break through the traditional boundaries of the classroom and the school to redefine who participates in teaching and learning, in what ways they participate, and where resources for teaching and learning reside. Immigrant students must be included in the population of *all* students whom school reform movements and new approaches to schooling are designed to serve. We can no longer develop programs that ignore the needs of these students and deprive them of the benefits of broad educational reforms. The education of immigrant students needs to sit squarely within the educational reform movement, so those students of secondary school age have access to high-quality programs in school and postsecondary opportunities beyond school, and the opportunity to become productive members of our society.

To do this, we need strong, responsive school programs and practices that provide opportunities for these students to learn academic content while they are learning English, that smooth their transitions through and beyond school, and that are sensitive to the special needs of students with limited prior schooling and low literacy skills. Educators of these students need to understand the principles and practices of educational reform and participate in the design and implementation of new programs and approaches. Finally, all educators must develop culturally and linguistically responsive understandings and skills to facilitate the success of all of their students.

Series Acknowledgments

The Program in Immigrant Education, begun in 1993, was funded by The Andrew W. Mellon Foundation to improve immigrant students' access to high-quality education in secondary school, their success in school, and their transitions to education and work after high school. Demonstration projects in Northern California, Southern California, Maryland, and Texas were established to implement, document, and evaluate innovative projects to accomplish these general goals.

This book series was developed to inform project staff as well as researchers and practitioners working with immigrant students about topics that are critical to this effort. After extensive conversations with project directors and staff, advisors to the program, and leaders in the field of immigrant education, priority topics were identified. For each topic, authors were asked to review what is known, document promising programs, and identify available resources.

We are grateful for the input we received on topics, authors, and book content from project staff Albert Cortez, JoAnn Crandall, Ann Jaramillo, Laurie Olsen, and David Ramírez; program advisors Keith Buchanan, Margarita Calderón, Eugene García, Victoria Jew, Eric Nadelstern, and Delia Pompa; and colleagues Michelle Brewer Byrd, Russell Campbell, Rosa Castro Feinberg, Kenji Hakuta, Tamara Lucas, Betty Mace-Matluck, Denise McKeon, and G. Richard Tucker. We extend special thanks to Tamara Lucas, who provided information included in the introduction; to Sonia Kundert, who coordinated the books' production; and to Adriana Vaznaugh for collecting information and communicating with authors. Finally, we are grateful to Stephanie Bell-Rose, program officer at The Andrew W. Mellon Foundation, for her enthusiastic support of this work.

Joy Kreeft Peyton and Donna Christian, Series Editors

References

August, D., & Hakuta, K. (1997). *Improving schooling for language-minority children: A research agenda.* Washington, DC: National Academy Press.

California Department of Education, Educational Demographics Unit. (1995). *Language census report for California public schools 1995.* Sacramento, CA: Author.

Chips, B. (1993). Using cooperative learning at the secondary level. In D.D. Holt (Ed.), *Cooperative learning: A response to linguistic and cultural diversity* (pp. 81-97). McHenry, IL and Washington, DC: Delta Systems and Center for Applied Linguistics.

Fix, M., & Passel, J.S. (1994). *Immigration and immigrants: Setting the record straight.* Washington, DC: The Urban Institute.

Fix, M., & Zimmerman, W. (1993). *Educating immigrant children: Chapter 1 in the changing city.* Washington, DC: The Urban Institute.

Fleischman, H.L., & Hopstock, P.J. (1993). *Descriptive study of services to limited English proficient students. Vol. 1: Summary of findings and conclusions.* Arlington, VA: Development Associates.

Gándara, P. (1994). The impact of the education reform movement on limited English proficient students. In B. McLeod (Ed.), *Language and learning: Educating linguistically diverse students* (pp. 45-70). Albany, NY: SUNY Press.

Goldenberg, C. (1996). Latin American immigration and U.S. schools. *Social Policy Report, 10*(1), 1-29. Ann Arbor, MI: Society for Research in Child Development.

Lockwood, A.T. (1996, Summer). Caring, community, and personalization: Strategies to combat the Hispanic dropout problem. *Advances in Hispanic Education: U.S. Department of Education/Hispanic Drop-out Project, No. 1* [Online]. Available: http://www.ncbe.gwu.edu/miscpubs/used/advances/s96no1.html [1996, November 14].

Moss, M., & Puma, M. (1995). *Prospects: The Congressionally mandated study of educational growth and opportunity.* Cambridge, MA: Abt Associates.

National Center for Education Statistics. (1996). *Dropout rates in the United States: 1994* (NCES 96-863). Washington, DC: U.S. Government Printing Office.

National Center for Education Statistics. (1997). *A profile of policies and practices for limited English proficient students: Screening methods, program support, and teacher training [SASS 1993-94]* (NCES 97-472). Washington, DC: U.S. Government Printing Office.

Schnaiberg, L. (1996, September 11). Immigration plays key supporting role in record-enrollment drama. *Education Week, 16,* 24-25.

Stanford Working Group. (1993). *Federal education programs for limited-English-proficient students: A blueprint for the second generation.* Stanford, CA: Stanford University.

U.S. Bureau of the Census. (1997). *The foreign-born population: 1996* [Online]. Available: http://www.census.gov/population/www/socdemo/foreign96.html [1997, April 15].

U.S. Commission on Civil Rights. (1992, February). *Civil rights issues facing Asian Americans in the 1990s.* Washington, DC: Author.

U.S. Department of Education. (1996, August). *A back to school special report: The baby boom echo.* Washington, DC: Author.

A project of this size owes its completion to many people beyond the author. I could not have gathered the information or made what sense of it I have without the help of many people along the way who made significant contributions to the form and substance of this volume. Joy Kreeft Peyton, Associate Director of the Program in Immigrant Education at the Center for Applied Linguistics, and Ana María Villegas, Montclair State University, have supported, questioned, and pushed me throughout the writing process. Early in the process, Hugh Mehan, University of California San Diego, and Florence Jackson, New York City Public Schools, advisors for the project, and Donna Christian, Director of the Program in Immigrant Education and President of the Center for Applied Linguistics, met with me for a day. Their suggestions and insights helped to clarify the task and set the direction for the volume. The three of them, along with Margarita Calderón, Center for Research on the Education of Students Placed at Risk (CRESPAR); Eric Nadelstern, Fund for New York City Public Education and International High School; Laurie Olsen, California Tomorrow; and Joy Kreeft Peyton and Deborah Short, Center for Applied Linguistics, reviewed the first draft of the volume, contributing their critical eyes to the revision. Adriana Vaznaugh, Program Assistant at the Center for Applied Linguistics, provided valuable assistance by doing searches and tracking down documents I needed. Sonia Kundert provided expert editorial assistance.

I am also grateful to the many people in schools and school districts who took time to meet with me personally, to talk on the phone, and to send information. I couldn't possibly mention them all here. I visited several classes at The International High School at LaGuardia Community College in Queens, New York, met with a group of students, and interviewed several faculty members. I would especially like to thank Claire Sylvan, Ruth Ellen Weiner, Charles Glassman, María Escalante, Marsha Slater, and the students I met. Thanks also to Katharine Sid at Seward Park High School in New York City and to Malula González at White Plains High School. Several people associated with the WISE program in Westchester County, New York, also gave generously of their time, especially Mary Lou Montalto and

George Castellanos at New Rochelle High School and Vic Leviatin, WISE Services Director. Five people talked with me by phone to give me their insights into issues and strategies related to the transition from ESL and bilingual programs into mainstream programs: Joan Kass, White Plains Public Schools; Estee López, Bilingual/ESL Technical Assistance Center, Southern Westchester BOCES; Joan Mason and Nancy Meyers, Phoenix Union High School District; and Nancy Weisgerber, J.E.B. Stuart High School, Fairfax County, Virginia.

Tamara Lucas

Eduardo *finished high school in the spring of 1995, having completed all his credits with a C-minus average. But to his own and his family's surprise, he did not actually receive his diploma, because he had not passed the writing portion of the state's high school competency exam. His high school counselor told him that he could take a summer school class to prepare for the October exam, so he enrolled. At this point, a friend of the family learned of Eduardo's situation when she asked him what he was going to do during the summer, and he told her about the class. This friend had immigrated to the United States from Cuba when she was eight years old and had successfully negotiated the educational system all the way through graduate school. She decided to see if she could help. When she went to speak with the summer school teacher about Eddie's chances of passing the writing exam, the teacher was not optimistic. She said that Eddie's writing was full of grammatical errors and that she was having difficulty getting him to write more than a few sentences, which meant that his essays were too short and undeveloped. Despite the teacher's efforts and his regular attendance, he had not made much progress during the first three weeks of the course.*

At the end of August, Eddie's parents called the family friend, saying that they wanted him to enroll in college for the fall and asking for information about colleges he could apply to. They were surprised to learn that he could not enroll in any four-year or two-year colleges without his high school diploma. They said that they had heard about a trade school that offered a certificate in computer repair, but the program cost $10,000 for one year of study with no guarantee of a job upon completion of the program. Though they thought this sounded like a good career for Eddie, it was out of the question for this family to come up with such a high tuition.

Eduardo's story is typical of many young people who immigrate to the United States at adolescence or later. He arrived in the United States from Colombia when he was 13, the oldest of three children. His family moved to a poor neighborhood in a poor city in the Northeast. He and his brother and sister went to urban schools that were overcrowded, understaffed, and without human or financial resources to educate the largely poor, immigrant student body. Both of his parents worked long hours, and as soon as the children were old enough, they helped their mother clean people's houses and their father do yard work and car repairs on weekends and sometimes in the evenings. The school did not reach out in any effective ways to engage Eddie's parents, so they remained unfamiliar with the system and its requirements, counting on the school and their children to do what was best. They trusted that the school system would prepare their children for college and for a better life than theirs. The school system did not help Eddie and his siblings develop their native Spanish abilities, nor did it adequately develop Eddie's English writing abilities or give him access to technological skills. While Eddie liked the idea of a career in computers, he had never actually used one, because the school had only a few and his family had none.

By the time Eddie completed his high school program, he was facing a bleak and scary future. Given the offer of tutoring to help him prepare for the high school competency test and provided with phone numbers of some community colleges that would admit him provisionally until he passed the exam, he did not respond or follow up, simply continuing in his summer job at Burger King and postponing the future. This volume is about what can be done so that other Eduardos arrive at their high school graduations with more options and more hope.

Immigration to the United States has increased significantly in the recent past. Fix & Passel (1994) estimate that the United States receives approximately 1.1 million newcomers per year—about 800,000 documented and 200,000–300,000 undocumented. Although neither federal nor state governments report the number of immigrant students in the education system (McDonnell & Hill, 1993), the impact of immigration is clearly evident in the public schools, which enroll increasing numbers of language minority students, many of whom are newcomers to this country. Using figures from the 1980 U.S. Census, the National Coalition of Advocates for Students (1988) calculated that foreign-born students accounted for at least 6% of elementary and secondary enrollments in this country. More recently, Fix and Passel

used data from the 1990 U.S. Census and from Immigration and Natu-
ralization Service sources to estimate that immigrants will represent
about 22% of the school-age population by 2010 (1994, p. 43).

School systems, schools, and individual teachers are challenged to educate increasing numbers of students who do not share the experiences
and assumptions of the majority of children whom schools have served
in the recent past. The educational system must develop the capacity
to prepare immigrant students along with native-born students for
productive lives. While our understanding of immigrant education in
general is limited, insight into the educational experiences and possibilities of secondary-school-age immigrants is particularly lacking. The
goal of this volume is to help address this gap in our knowledge. Specifically, the volume examines critical transitions that adolescent and
young adult immigrants undergo in the process of becoming integrated into the United States—initial entry into U.S. culture and
schools, movement through school, and movement beyond high
school—and presents principles and strategies for facilitating those
transitions.

In this volume, I use the term *immigrant* in an experiential sense rather
than a legal one, including anyone who was born or has spent his or her
childhood years in a country outside the United States and who then
moved to the United States to live for some period of time (beyond
simply traveling as a tourist). While I acknowledge that people who are
born and raised in non-English-speaking contexts within the United
States may share many experiences with immigrants, I am not including them in my definition. I am including those who have moved to the
United States from other countries seeking better economic and educational opportunities for themselves and their families (the "pull" factors of the United States) and those who have come fleeing political
turmoil, war, and extreme economic hardship in their own countries
(the "push" factors within their native countries) (Olsen, 1988, p. 18).
Thus, I am considering refugees as well as immigrants.

Immigrant students arrive in the United States at all ages and may bring with them educational preparation that is far superior to that provided by most U.S. schools, may have had no previous educational experience at all, or, more likely, may have had educational experiences that fall somewhere between these two extremes. Because age of arrival in the United States and previous educational experience have an especially important influence on older immigrants, I am limiting the scope of this volume to immigrant students in secondary schools who arrived in the United States at age 11 or older and those who have had enough previous educational background to make secondary school a reasonable placement. (See the volume in this series by Mace-Matluck, Alexander-Kasparik, and Queen [in press] addressing the needs of immigrant students with little prior school.) Because of the importance of language in education and the special challenges faced by those not proficient in the language of the educational system, I am excluding immigrants who arrive already fluent in standard English.

Overview of the Volume

In this volume, I examine four principles that can be applied in facilitating transitions into, through, and beyond school for immigrant youths in secondary schools. I start with what is, then attempt to develop a vision of what is possible. I include descriptions of well-established practices in educating immigrant students and learners of English as a second language and provide points of departure for grounding the education of immigrant students within new conceptions of teaching, learning, and schooling.

Transitions permeate the lives of secondary immigrant students. Immigrant youths face the sociocultural transition from their home country and culture into a new country and culture, which includes entering a new school system. Simultaneous with these changes, and along with all secondary-age students, they go through the developmental transitions from childhood to adolescence to adulthood and through institutional transitions as they enter the new educational system, make their way through it, then move beyond secondary school into work, higher education, or both. This volume focuses on the institutional transitions of secondary-school-age immigrant students—especially the transitions into U.S. culture and schooling and beyond high school. It also examines—though in less depth—the transition out of special programs and classes (usually designed for learners of English as a second language rather than for immigrant students) into regular, or mainstream, programs or classes. Experienced only by learners of English as a second language, this transition is key to the successful progress of such students through school in the United States. In another volume in this series, Aída Walqui addresses ways that curricular and instructional practices can facilitate the success of immigrant students through secondary schooling when they are developing the knowledge and skills to carry them into their adult lives.

Transitions can be conceived either as points in time (e.g., the day a young person graduates from high school) or as periods of time leading up to and following a change of status or situation (e.g., the senior year in high school and the freshman year in college). In this volume, I take the latter perspective. However, because my purpose is to provide information and ideas that can assist educators in developing strategies for facilitating transitions for immigrant youths in secondary school, I concentrate on the period of time when they are in secondary school, not the time before or after.

The numerous examples of approaches and strategies presented as ways to facilitate immigrant youths' transitions into, through, and beyond school in the United States should suggest many possibilities for educators. However, the overriding message I hope to convey is that we must match the immigrant students we have in our particular schools and classrooms, considering all the complexities that make them who they are, with the various possibilities in order to determine which of those possibilities will serve them best. I cannot do the matching myself; I cannot suggest the best approaches or strategies, because what is best depends on the students themselves and the context in which they live and go to school. There is no way to package the process of learning about the immigrant experience, learning about the particular immigrant youths in particular schools and classes, giving careful consideration to which opportunities for learning and growth will support them best, and enacting those opportunities in real schools and classes. Rather, I offer a framework for this process and some concrete directions for educators in schools and districts to pursue.

While some parts of the discussion are relevant for teachers, counselors, and others who work with immigrant students, this volume is primarily intended for people whose job it is to take the broader view beyond individual classrooms or programs. Thus, I am speaking primarily to administrators and policy makers—those who set policy, establish procedures, and provide leadership in establishing the values and philosophy of a district or a school, as well as those who are responsible for designing, overseeing, and monitoring overall strategies for educating young people, including immigrants. If the matching of immigrant students with the possibilities is to take place in a school or district, policy makers must make it a priority and support the processes involved. If the possibilities are to become realities, someone must be responsible for overseeing all the complex steps and stages of the process. These people will gain the most from what is presented here.

This book is a hybrid, both a review of theoretical and research-based literature and a description of programs and approaches that have not been formally studied through research. I used two distinct sources of information: available literature, including research and written descriptions of programs and approaches, and data I personally collected through visits to selected programs that assist immigrant students making the transitions into, through, and beyond secondary school. I reviewed research and practical literature examining the process of acculturation; the experiences of secondary-age immigrant students and the state of immigrant education in U.S. schools in the past decade; approaches designed to assist secondary immigrant students in adjusting to U.S. culture and the U.S. school system; the nature of adolescence; current conceptions of teaching and learning; approaches designed to help students move from high school into the world of work (the so-called school-to-work literature, which includes virtually no discussion of immigrant students per se); and issues in immigrant students' access to higher education and approaches designed to provide such access.

To provide concrete and detailed illustrations of some of the approaches described in the literature, I also visited selected sites and gathered first-hand information. I was limited in this endeavor to visiting those schools and programs that were close at hand; fortunately, I had access to several sites that exemplify approaches described in the literature, to which I refer throughout the volume. One school and one program provide many illustrations and are more fully described than others: The International High School at LaGuardia Community College, in Queens, New York, and the WISE Individualized Senior Experience (WISE) program, in Westchester County, New York. The former, a four-year comprehensive high school enrolling only recent immigrants, is well established as a successful school. It is a Title VII Academic Excellence Program; it was identified and examined as an exemplary Special Alternative Instructional Program in a study of such programs in 1990 (Tikunoff et al., 1991); its approach to authentic assessment has been described at length and glowingly (Ancess & Darling-Hammond, 1994). International High School also exemplifies many approaches that assist secondary immigrant students in the transitions into and beyond school, for which I provide ample illustrations. The WISE program, a senior-year experiential learning program, is more limited in scope than International and less well known, but it, too, illustrates many of the features of desirable approaches identified in the literature, especially with respect to the transition beyond high school. It also brings to life the particular kinds of adaptations that can be made in a progressive, mainstream program that can render it responsive to immigrant students.

This volume is organized into six chapters. In chapter 1, I examine the complex role that transitions play in the lives of secondary immigrant students, exploring the transitional nature of immigration itself and the developmental and institutional changes secondary immigrant students experience. In chapter 2, I examine changing conceptions of learning, teaching, and schooling in order to situate immigrant education within the context of mainstream education reform. In chapters 3 through 6, I present principles for facilitating secondary immigrant students' transitions into, through, and beyond school, giving examples from projects in which these principles are implemented. (Information about how to contact these programs is provided at the end of the book.) These principles are stated as four directives: (1) Cultivate organizational relationships. (2) Provide access to information. (3) Cultivate human relationships. (4) Provide multiple and flexible pathways for immigrant students moving into, through, and beyond secondary school. In an attempt to offer some concrete guidance for carrying out these principles, I provide a series of questions for each principle that can be used to interrogate practices to determine whether, in applying them, educators are incorporating the perspectives, needs, and strengths of immigrant students. In the conclusion, I summarize the central themes of the volume and offer recommendations for policy and for practice.

PART I

Immigrant Students and the Educational Context

Immigrant Students in Secondary School: Complex Lives in Transition

Immigrant youths in the United States go through a complex set of transitional experiences. Immigration is itself a sociocultural transition, as immigrants encounter a new culture. At the same time, secondary immigrant youths are making developmental transitions as they move from childhood to adolescence and from adolescence to young adulthood. In addition, these young people go through institutional transitions as they enter a new system of schooling, work their way through the system, and move beyond it into work and higher education (see Figure 1). Depending upon the age at which immigrant youths arrive in the United States, these sociocultural, developmental, and institutional transitions may interact in ways that complicate their lives considerably.

Figure 1. Transitions in the Lives of Secondary School Immigrant Students

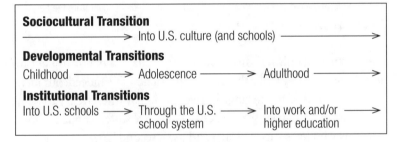

Immigration as a Sociocultural Transition

Immigration is itself a transitional experience. Immigrants enter a new culture with customs, assumptions, expectations, institutions, laws, and language that differ from those of their native culture. Their own roles within the new culture and others' perceptions of them differ from those of their native culture, but they may not be aware of the new roles and perceptions. The previously respected patriarch, for example, may not be seen or treated as such within the new culture. The mother who worked only at home in her native land may be forced to seek employment outside the home in the United States. These differences in roles often lead to intergenerational conflict as the younger generation adopts the ways of the new culture. Many current immigrants to the

United States not only share these transitional experiences common to immigrants throughout the world, but also find themselves categorized and treated as ethnic and racial minority group members, a new identity for many who come from more homogeneous countries than the United States (see, for example, Olsen, in press). Such treatment frequently involves prejudice, racism, and violence, at worst, and patronizing paternalism, at best.

The task of the immigrant in establishing an identity in the new culture is complex:

The immigrant needs to make comprehensible a whole new culture and language and to create a new self-concept which embraces both the old and the new. This process of acculturation involves painful, sometimes unconscious decisions, such as what is to be saved or sacrificed from the old, evaluating what one wants and needs to adopt from the new, and integrating these into a comfortable sense of self. (Olsen, 1988, p. 30)

Linguistic and cultural disorientation can have a major impact on immigrants as they make the transition to a new life. Indeed, our identities are so linked to the language we speak that when we try to communicate in a language we are not fluent in, we suffer language shock. All of us who have tried to learn and use a second language as adolescents or adults know the embarrassment and humiliation of talking like a child in a grown-up body, of having to simplify our language so much that our ideas become diluted and childish. We feel disconnected from others, unable to confidently express our ideas and feelings in language. Parts of our personalities are stifled, hidden from others, because we no longer have the means to let them out into the world.

Anne Tyler (1980) gives fictional expression to some of these feelings of language shock in her short story, *Your Place is Empty.* Mrs. Ardavi, an elderly Persian woman visiting the United States, feels acutely the loss of herself in her lack of language:

She grew impatient with the woodenness of the dictionary words. What she wanted was the language to display her personality, her famous courtesy, and her magical intuition about the inside lives of other people. Nightly she learned *salt*, *bread*, *spoon*, but with an inner sense of dullness, and every morning when she woke her English was once again confined to *thank you* and *NBC*.

Less eloquently, but no less effectively, one of my former students expressed the same frustration at being unable to express herself linguistically in a short (unedited) essay:

I am from Afghanistan. I like the united States.
put the food vary different in Afgh.
pecuse en Afg. don't have any Macdond
our dit did and I like en the united States
the arm and I like en Afg. any tank
and I like food en my country
and I can't tell you whay
peciuse I don't have any Sentences.

Just as language and identity are thoroughly interwoven, so are culture and identity. Encountering customs, assumptions, and expectations that are not our own, we are bound to feel confused, anxious, angry, and alienated at times. We feel especially disoriented when our previously successful logic or problem-solving methods do not help us function in a new culture or if what we accept as natural or basic facts or customs are offensive, humorous, or meaningless to people in our new culture. Anne Tyler's fictional Mrs. Ardavi suffers from culture shock, just as she does from language shock:

Mrs. Ardavi had to remind herself constantly not to kiss her granddaughter too much, not to reach out for a hug, not to offer her lap. In this country people kept more separated. They kept so separate that at times she felt hurt. They tried to be subtle, so undemonstrative. She would never understand this place.

Another student of mine, this one from Vietnam, described in an essay her "extreme shyness" as a serious problem partly because of the customs and expectations in the United States:

I consider this a very serious problem in my life because: In a classroom, if I don't speak up who will know whether I understand or not. In a group of people, if I keep quiet all the time, who will understand that what type of person I am. So this is an easy way to loose a lot of friends. In front of a boy, my hands keep shaking, may be a boy should think I am up-normal girl, because in this country no difference between a girl and a boy. This is a country where it has a lot of freedom. I cannot live by the way in my own country.

For many immigrants, suddenly being labeled and treated as a member of a racial or ethnic minority group is another shocking transition. Few countries are as racially and ethnically diverse as the United States, so few immigrants have had contact with people from as many different ethnicities as they do here. Coming from more homogeneous contexts, many immigrants have not had the experience of being a member of an ethnic minority group themselves. Cummins (1989) argues that the educational system "disempowers" ethnic and racial minority communities and students through its racist structures, sending the message that "to survive in this society your identity must be eradicated and your community must not threaten the power and privilege of the dominant group" (p. 56). The educational system reflects this racism when it (1) fails to incorporate minority students' languages and cultures into the school program; (2) excludes minority communities from participation in schools; (3) assumes a "transmission" approach to pedagogy, which relegates students to a passive role; and (4) approaches assessment in such a way that it "legitimizes the location of the 'problem' within students" rather than seeing it as a function of the interaction of students with the educational context (p. 58ff).

In addition to these more subtle forms of racism in the educational system, immigrants face more overt ethnic conflicts. For some, this is a bitter disappointment. Immigrants who have experienced discrimination and stigmatization in their home countries, such as Amerasians in Vietnam, expect to escape such prejudice in the United States and are disillusioned when they have similar experiences here. Racial and ethnic tensions among immigrant groups as well as between immigrants and native-born U.S. citizens have increased in recent years as the economy has weakened and more groups are competing for fewer resources. Growing anti-immigrant feelings resulted in the passage of Proposition 187 in California in 1994, which if enacted would deny education, health, and social services to undocumented immigrants and place educators in the position of asking their students to produce documentation of their legal status in this country. This legislation reflects the prejudice that immigrants are increasingly encountering.

Developmental Transitions

While learning to adjust to a new language and culture and to their minority status in the United States, secondary-school-age immigrants also must contend with profound developmental changes—the transition from childhood to adolescence and from adolescence to adulthood. Although transitions between different phases in human development are all challenging in their own ways, the passage from childhood to adolescence is particularly demanding. As children move into adolescence, they

are faced with a host of psychosocial changes cohering around puberty, increased cognitive capacity, the acquisition of new skills and competencies, as well as the formulation of an identity and establishment of successful relationships with peers and adults, ... changes [which] occur within social contexts—in families, communities, institutions, and societies. (Camino, 1992, p. 53)

Early adolescence (from 9 to 14 years of age) is "unmatched in the juxtaposition of simultaneous changes—cognitive, biological, social, and emotional—by any other period in the life span" (Takanishi, 1993, p. 3). Throughout the teenage years, young people "tackle two major tasks.... identity formation and development of self-worth and self-efficacy" (Nightingale & Wolverton, 1993, p. 14), both of which are shaped by contextual as well as individual factors (Petersen & Epstein, 1991). The "task of constructing a sense of self takes on a variety of dimensions for students of different gender, racial, and ethnic groups" (Wheelock, 1993, p. 7). For immigrant youths, these tasks are particularly challenging because they are defining themselves as individuals, but also learning what it means to be a member of a nondominant group in the United States. To negotiate successfully the demands of this developmental phase, immigrants must strike a balance between two value systems—that of their native culture, ever present in the home, and that of the dominant American culture, which prevails in school. Learning how to balance the cultural tug between home and school inherent in this identity formation process is painful (Spenser & Dornbusch, 1990).

Along with their age cohorts in the United States, older adolescent immigrants must make the transition that occurs after high school. At that point, students must choose a path into their future—to continue their education, to go to work, or to do both—with the ultimate goal of productive employment. In the United States, this is seen as the beginning of adulthood, "marked in part by movement from those roles that signify dependency to those roles that signify independence" (Pallas, 1993, p. 413). The emphasis here is on getting teenagers to become independent from their families and to assume responsibility for themselves. During this time, they are encouraged to define themselves and to choose a career or employment path that suits them.

This sense of individualism and independence is not valued universally, however. In some other cultures, for example, the family—often in its extended form—is valued above the individual. In keeping with this world view, many adolescent immigrants are socialized at home into valuing collective achievement more than individual accomplishment. Decisions about long-term career or employment goals are more tightly influenced by family circumstances and tradition than is generally true for those who are already assimilated into the American cultural mainstream. The pressure to act collectively rather than individually is especially strong among immigrant families that have recently arrived in the United States and are struggling to survive and establish themselves economically in this country. Such differences in expectations between their families and their new culture can lead to severe cultural clashes for adolescent immigrants making the transition into young adulthood.

The extended period of youth and adolescence is also foreign to people from many other cultures and situations, especially those who live in poverty. Many children must take on adult responsibilities at very young ages in their home countries and in the United States. For most Mexican youth, for example, "adolescence ... is a short span between childhood and the grinding responsibilities of adulthood" (Saragoza, 1989, p. 13). Children who have witnessed violence also do not experience the extended youth and adolescence that most U.S.-born children take for granted.

Institutional Transitions

Immigrant youths must also navigate a whole set of institutional transitions. The school is an institution within their new culture that plays a central role in their new lives. Just as they must learn how to integrate their own ways of thinking, talking, and behaving with the ways of their new culture in order to be successful, they must also learn new daily routines and functions, new rules and regulations, and new unwritten expectations and assumptions of the school system. They can no longer count on their own or their families' experiences to guide their behavior and to help them gauge their educational progress. Because many of the expectations and conventions of schooling are unstated, newcomers to the system have a very difficult time finding out what they need to know. Yet few schools give more than cursory attention to orienting immigrant students and their families to the school system. For the most part, students and their families must rely on their social networks rather than the educational system to learn what they can about the system in order to ensure the students' success. This transition process may last throughout a young person's secondary school years, because there are always new and more subtle elements of schooling to be understood. Thus, the transition into U.S. schools continues even as immigrant students are moving through the system, learning how to gain access to the kinds of classes and support services that will give them the best preparation for the future they envision for themselves.

A final institutional transition for secondary students is the move from secondary school into work and/or higher education. The period at the end of high school and the beginning of whatever comes next is a difficult time in the life course of all youths in the United States, especially for those who do not follow the preferred path into higher education. "The United States does very little to smooth the transition from school to work for high school graduates, while it spends large sums on those who continue their educations" (Barton, 1990, p. 27). This "non-system of school-to-work transition … fails minority youth dramatically" (Kazis, 1993, p. 5), including immigrant youths. Because of poverty, the inability to complete high school on time or with sufficient credits to go directly to college, or the need to continue improving their English proficiency, most students who immigrate to the United States at age 11 or older must go to work prior to or concurrently with pursuing a higher education.

Whether they are going on to higher education or directly into the workforce, immigrant students must maneuver this transition into young adulthood without many of the support systems to which their native-born, middle-class peers have access. These middle-class youths can look to the adults they know for examples of the possibilities open to them. The adults that recently arrived immigrant youths know who could serve as role models may not have achieved success within the U.S. system themselves; in fact, the young people may have adapted more successfully to the new culture than the adults in their families. Likewise, immigrant youths are unlikely to know adults who can help them get jobs at all, much less jobs that offer possibilities for future growth and stability. If they want to go to college, they are less likely than their middle-class, native-born peers to know adults who have themselves gone to college or who can help them prepare for, select, and apply to a college in the United States. If they are undocumented, they face even greater obstacles in their efforts to make it to higher education. While some states (e.g., New York, Illinois, and Arizona) charge resident tuition to undocumented immigrants who can show that they have lived in the state for a certain period of time, others, notably California, charge out-of-state tuition (Stewart, 1993). This is an insurmountable financial obstacle for most and is exacerbated by the federal prohibition on financial aid for undocumented immigrants. Lacking built-in supports and facing major obstacles, many immigrant youths must fend for themselves as they move beyond school, taking whatever opportunities they can seize.

Thus, change and transition permeate the lives of recently arrived immigrant students in secondary schools. Everything is in flux. They must negotiate their entrance into U.S. culture and schooling while adjusting to the physical, psychological, and social changes of adolescence, and they must move beyond high school and enter the world of early adulthood within their new culture and language. Considering the challenges they face, it is a wonder that any of them successfully make it into and beyond secondary schools in this country.

Immigrant Youths and Education reform

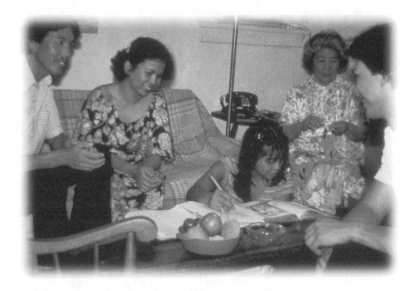

Our conceptions of teaching, learning, and schooling have changed radically in recent years, and these changing conceptions are inspiring fundamental changes in U.S. educational practices. Schools are being redesigned to reflect innovative structures and processes, and teachers are developing new instructional approaches that incorporate shared decision making, collaboration, and active learning. These reforms have grown out of changing theories of learning (Resnick, 1989; Vygotsky, 1962, 1978), demands on the educational system to prepare students differently for the information-based society of the 21st century (Barton, 1993; Darling-Hammond, 1993; Drucker, 1994; Marshall & Glover, 1996), and the recognition that changing demographics require new approaches to ensure that the growing numbers of students of diverse racial, ethnic, linguistic, and socioeconomic backgrounds learn to high levels. Federal, state, and local policies are pushing these changes along. In New York, for example, the New Compact for Learning (New York State Department of Education, 1991) makes fundamental changes in curriculum, assessments, school organization, school governance, and school–community linkages that reflect the changing conceptions discussed below.

While these approaches to teaching, learning, and schooling are not yet in place in most schools, they are grounded in theory and are increasingly supported by educational policies. They also have the potential to empower educators, families, communities, and students—including immigrant students. Therefore, they can productively inform and influence practices at classroom, school, district, and community levels even without radical transformations in an entire educational system.

Unfortunately, when these innovations are applied, they generally do not include immigrant students (Olsen et al., 1994). When educators of native-English-speaking students restructure schools and classrooms, they tend not to take immigrant students into account, because (1) they do not have the experience and preparation that would make them sensitive to and knowledgeable of the needs of such students, and (2) they assume that because learners of English as a second language are enrolled in special programs that address their need to learn English, they will not be part of the regular school program that is being reconfigured until they are fully proficient in academic English and fully assimilated into U.S. culture. Until more teachers are prepared to work with immigrant students, such special programs provide the only context in which they can have access to professionals with the expertise to teach them. For recently arrived students with no English proficiency, such programs will always be necessary.

As we incorporate these practices into schooling, we must find ways to ensure that immigrant students and educators of immigrant students do not remain peripheral to education reform and restructuring. Educators of immigrant students have the knowledge and understanding to help build responsiveness throughout the system without resorting to a "one-size-fits-all" approach (Reyes, 1992, p. 435). They need to be knowledgeable of the major principles and practices of reform efforts, apply that knowledge to the design of special programs for immigrant students, and make sure that they are included in the design and implementation of new programs and approaches for the larger school.

Figure 2. Changing Conceptions of Learning, Teaching, and Schooling

Reconceptualizations of Learners and Learning
Students as: Active constructors of knowledge
              Collaborators
              Decision makers

Reconceptualizations of Teachers and Teaching
Teachers as: Learners
              Collaborators
              Facilitators
              Cultural and linguistic mediators

Reconceptualizations of Schools and Schooling
Schools as: Communities
              Learner-centered communities
              Part of a larger situational and chronological context
              Mediators between home culture and mainstream culture

The discussion that follows presents changing conceptions of learning, teaching, and schooling (presented in Figure 2 and expanded in Figure 3 on pages 58 and 59) and examines implications for immigrant students. The difficulties initially posed for immigrant students by some innovations reflecting these conceptions should not lead us to exclude immigrant students from classes and initiatives that incorporate the new conceptions. Instead, they should lead us to examine such initiatives critically to see how they can be adapted so that immigrant students can participate to their advantage.

Reconceptualizations of Learners and Learning

The metaphor of the learner as an empty vessel, symbolizing the inert container passively taking in information and knowledge as "the one who does not know" from "the one who knows" (Freire, 1985, p. 114), has been replaced by the metaphor of the builder who "constructs" knowledge by actively using all the materials at his or her disposal, including prior knowledge and experience, newly encountered knowledge and experience, the elements of the learning context, and social interaction (see Moll & Greenberg, 1990; Tharp & Gallimore, 1990; Vygotsky, 1962, 1978). Learning is now seen as "active" and "contextual" (see, e.g., Kazis, 1993, p.14).

If learning involves active construction of knowledge and understanding through connections among past, current, and new experiences and knowledge, then learners must do more than sit at a desk and listen or read or write. They must be actively engaged in exploration and search. Instead of being "sorted, managed, [and] trained," children and youths must be "regarded ... as persons with the right and responsibility to reflect upon themselves, to construct knowledge, ... to engage in the cultural conversation, ... to articulate purposes for themselves [and] to find a meaning for their lives" (Greene, 1992, p. 41). Students' roles are being redefined to reflect this new conception of learning.

Students as Active Constructors of Knowledge

Students are no longer expected to learn only by taking in information and knowledge. They are expected to make meaning for themselves from their encounters with knowledge, experience, and ideas, rather than simply memorizing information to display it. No longer engaged primarily in listening, reading, and reciting, they are involved in hands-on activities inside and outside of classrooms. They are active physically as well as mentally, moving around within the classroom, school, and community to gain access to information, ideas, and experiences. Many of the approaches designed to help students through the transition from school to work, for example, involve experiential learning components in workplaces (e.g., Tech Prep programs, career academies, cooperative education, youth apprenticeship; see descriptions in chapter 6 under *Pathways Beyond Secondary School*).

At International High School in Queens, New York, active learning is central to the immigrant student experience for reasons that the school's literature explains:

When students are actively engaged in problem solving, the chances of meeting their needs are greater than when they are passive learners under the transmission model of pedagogy. They have the opportunity to study a problem in depth, and to work in an environment in which variety is expected. Part of their obligation is to include others as they continue to meet high expectations. (International High School, n.d., p. 3)

Students in the WISE program also actively engage in experiential learning and knowledge building inside and outside the traditional classroom and the school. In a letter written in 1995, a participant from 1977 recalled how she used her prior experiences and expectations as well as the people, information, and experiences she encountered to develop both personal and academic knowledge.

For my WISE project I was a member of the Square Block Project [a collaborative effort involving several students] which documented in video, photography, and written word the life and culture of one square block in New York City (97th and 98th Street between Madison and Fifth Aves.).... Each visit to the neighborhood would bring about new contacts and connections with people who lived and worked there. These developing webs of contacts eventually painted a portrait of several communities within one area, and the idea jelled for me to represent those "communities" through interviews with a person from each of those "communities." The project gave me a taste of sociological and anthropological field work, background on Urban Planning issues, and allowed me to learn basic skills in video documentary production. Also, in the course of the project I became acutely aware of my own privilege in being able to dance in and out of different worlds that inhabited the "square block," from wealthy Fifth Avenue Penthouse dwellers, to the local bar owner, to members of a Puerto Rican social club. Probably the most valuable thing I gained was a deeper understanding of how lives are shaped by class and culture. (PC, WISE student at Woodlands High School, 1977; project: video documentary as part of the Square Block Project; career: documentary film maker)

Active participation in constructing their own knowledge works to the benefit of immigrant students in several ways. It supports and values learning through different means, including hands-on projects. This allows students to learn in different ways, rather than forcing them all to conform to the traditional, more passive memorizing of text-based information. Active learning through multiple means also reduces the reliance on language as the sole medium for learning, an obvious benefit for students who are not fully fluent in the language of the classroom.

At the same time, expecting students to engage actively in constructing knowledge, rather than simply to sit and take in what the teacher presents, can pose two challenges for immigrant students. First, the view of learning upon which it is based is culturally constructed, having arisen within the context of modern European thinking. Students from more traditional and non-European cultures are unlikely to share the suspicion that many North American educators have of paper-and-pencil, teacher-directed, passive approaches to teaching and learning. Indeed, *not* having students engage in such traditional activities may be interpreted as poor teaching by many immigrant students and their parents.

Second, it can be difficult and threatening to be asked to do something when you don't know how to do it or you don't speak the language in which it is expected to be done. Immigrant students participating in experiential activities such as internships or group projects may need extra assistance and support to overcome cultural and linguistic obstacles and uncertainties. Such assistance and support require special sensitivity to and knowledge of language acquisition, affective factors in language learning, and students' proficiency in English. In the early stages of second-language learning, for example, learners may go through a silent period, when they speak very little. Thoughtlessly placing such students in situations in which they must use their second language may be counterproductive.

Students as Collaborators

Education reformers no longer see learning as a solitary activity; instead, they see it as growing out of social interaction. Students are now expected to be collaborators and team members in a community of learners. This new role reflects both the theoretical centrality of interaction in learning (Vygotsky, 1962, 1978) and the practical need to prepare future adults for the increased teamwork required in the workplace (Glover & Marshall, 1993; Kazis, 1993). Collaboration may, in fact, be more culturally compatible for many immigrant students, whose home cultures support cooperation and collaboration over competition and individualism.

The increasing division of secondary schools into smaller "houses" or "clusters," in which a relatively small group of students stays together throughout the day, provides a structure that offers more opportunities for collaboration among students. Collaboration is also encouraged and required through the use of a variety of instructional approaches. Cooperative learning, for example, is a formal system for group work in which each participant has a role to play (see Holt, 1993; Johnson & Johnson, 1987; Kagan, 1986). Less formalized group projects run the gamut from pairs of students working in class to measure the size and shape of an apple, to groups of students going to a retirement home to interview elderly residents, to several students collaborating to write a letter to a pen pal in another city. A common strategy for supporting newly arrived immigrant students that establishes a context for collaboration is the pairing of two students as "buddies," one of whom is more experienced in U.S. culture and school and more fluent in English than the other.

Collaboration has several benefits for immigrant students. First, it promotes language use in the classroom. Students must use language to work together, while they can sit without ever speaking in a more traditional, teacher-centered classroom. This gives nonnative-English-speaking students more opportunity to develop their English skills. Collaboration also promotes cross-cultural learning and communication. Students can sit in a more traditional classroom for a year and never speak to each other, because the teacher does most of the talking and most of the interacting with students. When students of different cultural backgrounds collaborate, they have opportunities to learn about each other and learn to respect their different perspectives and experiences. Collaborative learning is also consistent with the collectivist social orientation of many non-European cultures. It may indeed be more compatible with the culturally influenced learning styles of many immigrant students than the more traditional solitary, competitive learning that has been expected of learners in U.S. schools.

On the other hand, like active learning, collaboration can pose special challenges for immigrant students. Because the patterns of social interaction vary across cultures, students of different backgrounds have different expectations for ways of relating, both inside and outside of school. While misunderstandings can arise among any group of students trying to work together productively, the difficulties are exacerbated when the groups include students from very different cultures. In addition, collaboration requires verbal communication, which, of course, may be difficult and demoralizing for immigrants who are not yet fluent in English, especially if their classmates are not sensitive to the fact that they are learning a second language. Thus, all involved must be sensitive to different ways of communicating and to the challenges faced by learners of a second language.

Students as Decision Makers

As schools and classrooms become less teacher centered and more student centered, students are called upon to make more decisions for themselves, just as adults in various roles within schools—that is, not just administrators—are making more decisions. As students "articulate purposes for themselves" (Greene, 1992, p. 41), they must choose among various paths for achieving those purposes. In schools, this means that, within certain limitations (e.g., curriculum frameworks, safety concerns, respect for others), they are making decisions about how they will learn, what they will learn, and when they will learn it. Only in schools organized to give primacy to individual needs and styles is it possible to give such rights and responsibilities to students, as Greene suggests.

The International High School environment promotes student decision making. As the assistant principal reports,

From the minute they walk in, kids start to deal with decision making in instructional and noninstructional situations—in the courses they take, in dealing in groups with other students, in deciding how teachers are going to be useful and how they are not going to be useful, in looking at careers, in selecting internships, in taking advantage of LaGuardia Community College. (R. Wiener, personal communication, October 28, 1994)

On a recent visit to the school, I observed several situations in which students were encouraged and expected to make decisions about their own learning. In one class, a student who had missed the previous day of school arrived late and was told by the teacher that she should decide whether it would be better for her to stay in the class to work on what she had missed the day before or go to the lab to work with her team on a joint writing project. The teacher then turned to talk with me. The student looked at her notebook for a couple of minutes, then decided to stay in the class rather than go to the lab. In another situation, a student needed help with an essay about his interests and abilities that would lead to his choosing an internship. One of the two teachers of the course asked, "Do you want to stay here and work with me or go upstairs and work with [the other teacher]? You decide." The boy decided to go upstairs. The teacher gave him a pass and he left the room.

The following description by a physics teacher at the school captures the degree to which student decision making is an essential value:

Over the past three years, I have radically changed what I do with students each day. Students come into the room. They record their own attendance. They choose an activity for the day, sign up for that activity, pick up their class folder, and begin work. They may listen to audio tapes of the textbook. They may work on textbook related activities, or they may choose one of several experiments. They may work on the computer, or they may go to the library. They choose their activity. They choose their partners. I create the written guidelines for each activity, make equipment available for the experiments, answer questions, talk to small groups, determine when tasks are completed, and give students credit. (Hirschy, 1990, p.17)

Treating learners as decision makers may work to the benefit of those immigrant youths who are already playing the decision-making role in their families. Many immigrant students, especially those who have faced financial or personal hardships, take on adult roles earlier than U.S.-born youths. For those students, being expected to make decisions about their own learning can allow them to use a strength they have developed and may help them feel less alienated from school than treating them as if they cannot make their own decisions. Expecting students to make decisions can also cause conflict for immigrant students. The degree to which teenagers are expected and prepared to make decisions for themselves varies across cultures. They may perceive it as the teacher's role to tell them what to do in school and may have difficulty making decisions for themselves. Again, few cultures value individual will and action as highly as does the dominant culture in the United States. Educators who are culturally and linguistically responsive to immigrant students' perceptions and experiences will be better able both to predict the difficulties the students may have with the new roles they are expected to play in U.S. schools and to provide support for them in reconciling their own expectations with those of their new contexts (see discussion below in *Teachers as Cultural and Linguistic Mediators*).

Reconceptualizations of Teachers and Teaching

Since our conception of learning has changed, so must our conception of teaching. If learners do not learn by passively ingesting information, teachers cannot teach by simply feeding them information. We now believe that "effective teaching entails assisting students to build connections between what is familiar to them and the new content and skills to be learned" (Villegas, in press, p. 306). This changing conception requires a redefinition of the roles of both educators and students.

Teachers as Learners

Learning has come to be seen as a lifelong process. Like students, teachers must continuously create their own knowledge and understandings. In particular, they must "have opportunities ... to construct their understandings of what it means to practice in a way that attends, respectfully yet purposefully, to the needs, interests, and development of learners" (Darling-Hammond, 1992, p. 22). They are learners, too. Indeed, "you cannot have students as continuous learners and effective collaborators, without teachers having these same characteristics" (Fullan, 1993, p. 46).

The changing conceptions of and approaches to teaching and learning require educators to examine their understandings of education and their strategies as educators. Such examination, of course, requires new structures that provide time and opportunities for educators to read, think, and discuss. A teacher at The International High School explained:

We have a common philosophy of education, of teaching and learning here.... The key ingredient is time for conversation among faculty. It takes place over time and helps teachers develop a philosophy of learning. Here, we have time for that.... We build in time to have professional conversations with faculty. Other schools could do what we do if they would build in this time. (C. Glassman, personal communication, October 28, 1994)

Even if conceptions of teaching and learning were not changing, the transformation in the student population, especially the growing number of immigrant students, would require new learning for educators. Teacher education programs have a long way to go to prepare their graduates to work effectively with the diversity they encounter among their students.

The narrow exposure to racial and ethnic minority cultures on the part of most preservice candidates makes it doubtful they will develop the necessary cultural expertise within the existing structure of teacher education. (Villegas, in press, p. 309)

Educators are being called upon to engage in "reflective practice" (e.g., Burbules & Rice, 1991; National Coalition of Advocates for Students, 1994, p. 127) and dialogue (e.g., Apple, 1979, 1982; Cummins, 1989; Freire, 1971, 1973, 1985; Giroux, 1981; Weiler, 1988), to examine their own biases and assumptions (e.g., Henze, Lucas, & Scott, 1993; Tatum, 1992), and to learn more about the cultural backgrounds and experiences of their students (e.g., Lucas, Henze, & Donato, 1990; McGroarty, 1986; National Coalition of Advocates for Students, 1994; Sleeter & Grant, 1987; Villegas, 1991). Many of them are actively constructing new understandings of themselves and their roles as educators, as they develop the capacity to teach students from diverse cultural and linguistic backgrounds (see below, *Teachers as Cultural and Linguistic Mediators*).

Such learning and the establishment of contexts that support it can benefit immigrant students greatly. When the system expects teachers to know everything they need to know, they cannot admit that they are ill equipped to provide excellent educational opportunities for all their students. In such a system, teachers make themselves vulnerable to criticism by admitting that they need to learn more to be effective teachers, even when the students they are teaching are radically different from the students they have been teaching before. When the system supports teachers as learners, it allows them to learn what they need without jeopardizing their professional status or making it seem as if they have deficits to be remedied, and it provides support for such learning. Thus, teachers can actively pursue professional development to learn about approaches and strategies for educating immigrant students. (See the volume in this series by González and Darling-Hammond [in press] focusing on professional development for teachers of immigrant students.)

Teachers as Collaborators

Just as collaboration and cooperation have come to be regular parts of the learning environment for students, educators are also more frequently working in teams. Traditional secondary schools are characterized by a high degree of isolation among staff. One of the 11 "workplace conditions" found in an examination of four teacher surveys was that "teachers have too few opportunities for interaction with their colleagues" (Corcoran, 1990, p. 145). The fragmentation of time and subject areas of the traditional secondary school supports an environment in which individuals have little time, incentive, or support for collaborating with each other. New secondary school structures such as minischools, clusters, and teams require and allow more interaction, joint planning, and collaborative work among faculty. Such structures are increasingly common and can be found, for example, in Fort Worth Independent School District (Lucas, 1993a, 1993b; Tikunoff et al., 1991); South Shore High School, Brooklyn; Horace Mann Middle School, San Francisco; Newcomer High School, San Francisco; Nyack (New York) High School; New Rochelle (New York) High School; The International High School, Queens; and Theodore Roosevelt High School, The Bronx—to name just a few of the schools about which I have personal knowledge.

The International High School has eliminated the traditional schedule and curriculum altogether and replaced it with 12 interdisciplinary clusters, each linking four subjects around a theme. Students graduate with all 48 credits necessary, but they don't take separate courses called "English" or "social studies." Instead, they sign up each trimester for 1 of 12 clusters called *Beginnings, Structures, Conflict/Resolution, It's Your World, Motion, Visibility, The 21st Century, Crime and Punishment, The World of Money, The World Around Us, The American Dream,* and *The American Reality.* Each cluster involves approximately 75 students and teams of four or five teachers and support personnel. The teachers design the structure, organization, and activities of the trimester-long clusters. The time is divided into 70-minute periods, but these are "arbitrary," according to a teacher in the Beginnings cluster. The teachers negotiate how to use the time and may vary it, depending on the needs of the students. For example, students may stay with one teacher for 140 minutes one day to continue to work on a project and double up with another teacher the following day. Because the teams of teachers make all the decisions about curriculum and instruction, intensive collaboration is involved.

A teacher at the school reflected on the benefits of collaboration with her colleagues:

An American education is one which fosters competition. Competition leads to hostility, isolation, secretiveness, and shame. Collaboration, on the other hand, provides many benefits.... First and foremost, it promotes a feeling of self confidence. It provides a supportive environment to help me feel secure not only in presenting what I know is good, but also in allowing me to feel secure in examining my weaknesses on my own and with others. The secretiveness and shame slip away in the process of sharing. Collaboration furnishes recognition for everybody, because each party naturally acknowledges the contributions of the others. It helps me to think because I receive input from others and am exposed to a greater variety of ideas and information. So it also broadens the scope of what I can produce. It provides a feeling of community, which I haven't experienced in other work environments. I have learned all of this at The International High School ... not only because the institution encourages collaboration, but because it provides a carefully thought out environment in which each member of the community plays a vital role. Experiencing that environment myself makes it possible for me to provide it to my students. (Dunetz, 1990, p. 5)

When administrators—the only presumed educational leaders in the old model of schooling—become collaborators, they face particular challenges:

How to be the hub and be central to all aspects of the school while not being in the center, how to be the spokesperson for all the constituencies without demanding compliance to a singular view. (Lieberman, Falk, & Alexander, 1994, p. 16)

[How to] establish an environment conducive to risk taking by trusting the faculty and encouraging teachers to assume leadership roles. (Kilgore & Webb, 1994, p. 30)

When administrators are successful collaborators, the professional status of teachers and the other adults in the school is elevated. When I visited The International High School in the fall of 1994, one of the teachers was going to another school later that day to observe interdisciplinary instruction. He had informed the principal that he was going, but he did not ask permission. The people he had to answer to about his actions were his fellow cluster team members, and he had arranged with them to be away that afternoon. In reporting this, he said, "I feel like a professional."

Teacher collaboration can strengthen the capacity of the school to educate immigrant students successfully when it involves teachers with expertise, experience, and sensitivity in working with those students. When ESL and bilingual teachers collaborate with mainstream teachers, both teachers and students reap the benefits. The ESL teacher gains insight into the mainstream curriculum, the mainstream teacher learns about immigrant students' needs and strategies for teaching them, and the student has access to the expertise and experience of both. At J.E.B. Stuart High School in Fairfax County, Virginia, ESL teachers have teamed with math, science, and social studies teachers to help give students learning English as a second language more access to academic content.

Teacher collaboration can also help immigrant students by increasing the personalization of schooling. When teams of teachers work with the same group of students in a collaborative way, they discuss progress and problems of individual students more regularly and therefore "may be able to respond more quickly, personally, and consistently to the needs of individual students" (MacIver, 1990, p. 460). This can be especially important for immigrant students who are in mainstream classes, where teachers are not likely to be as sensitive to their needs as in ESL and bilingual classes.

Teachers as Facilitators

In schools that are being redesigned to reflect the changing views of teaching, learning, and schooling, and especially in such schools with immigrant and other students from nondominant groups, words like *facilitator, guide, advisor,* and *mentor* are used increasingly to describe the roles of educators. If we learn by actively engaging with ideas and people, then the educators' role is to facilitate that engagement for their students, not to "deliver" instruction (see Darling-Hammond, 1992, p. 22). If we learn by applying our previous knowledge and experience to new knowledge and experience, then the educators' role is to help students make the connections that allow that application. In the classroom context, new roles for teachers require new instructional approaches—less lecture, less seatwork, less standardization of curriculum content, more interaction among students and between students and teachers, more experiential activities, more connection between the classroom and the world outside it, and more decision making by students and less by teachers.

In the WISE program, the key adult role is that of mentor. All students work closely with a mentor whom they choose. The mentors act as facilitators for the students, helping them to define their goals, plan their projects, identify contacts and resources needed, make connections with people, get placements for internships and other types of projects, and prepare their final presentations. One student captured several of these roles in describing how her mentor helped. She wrote,

"Mr. [P] got me the internship, let me borrow his camera, xeroxed my journal, and he talked with me about the WISE project throughout my internship."

WISE teacher–mentors are forced to step out of their usual role in front of the class and work more closely with individual students supporting their process of learning. Mentors are usually chosen not for their expertise in a subject matter but for their more human, relational qualities. Seventy-nine percent (26) of the students at New Rochelle High School who completed surveys about their WISE experiences in the spring of 1995 reported that they chose their mentors because of such qualities. They chose mentors who were caring, trustworthy, dependable, accessible, understanding, and willing to listen. Only six students cited teachers' subject matter knowledge as the reason they chose them as mentors. The importance of relationships in the mentoring process was also reflected in the surveys completed by mentors in 1995. Twenty of the 28 respondents (71%) said that one of the key differences between their experience as a mentor and their experience as a teacher was that mentor and mentee had a closer relationship. One mentor wrote, "Nothing compares to the experience of working closely and on a personal basis with these students. I learned from them to be more human and flexible!" Another wrote, "You develop a close relationship with your mentee, and it enables you to provide individual guidance."

Outside the classroom, teachers have changing roles with students as well. Teaching and learning occur as part of a relationship that does not end at the classroom door. Teachers who recognize that fact devote time and attention to the student as a person through conversation, participation in student activities and organizations, involvement with community groups, providing extra help with schoolwork, and advocacy at the personal and political levels. In fact, for students, having contact with educators who care about them is of paramount importance (Lucas et al., 1990; Poplin & Weeres, 1992). One structure that supports teachers in playing a facilitator role is the advisory period (see Carnegie Council on Adolescent Development, 1989; MacIver, 1990; Maeroff, 1990). Adults in various roles within the school meet regularly with a small group of students throughout a year. They provide each student with guidance and "the support of a caring adult who knows that student well" (Carnegie Council, 1989, p. 41). Bilingual teachers are not exempt from the need to take on this new role. Simply teaching in the language that the student knows best does not mean that students will make the necessary connections to their knowledge and experience. In fact, one of the more discouraging findings of the longitudinal study of elementary bilingual programs carried out in the late 1980s was that a "passive learning environment" characterized virtually all of the classes observed (Ramírez, 1992, p. 10).

When teachers act as facilitators, guides, advisors, and mentors, the resulting sense of community and trust can help immigrant students feel at home in their new environment and can alleviate feelings of linguistic and cultural displacement and alienation. The increased personalization associated with such teacher roles gives teachers the opportunity to learn about individual students' perceptions, feelings, opinions, and experiences, rather than to make assumptions based on generalizations, stereotypes, or hunches. For facilitators, every student, including every immigrant student, is humanized; each has a history and context, which the teacher-as-giver-of-information rarely has the luxury of learning about. On the other hand, givers-of-information are exactly what teachers are expected to be in many cultures. Students may interpret the less authoritarian relationship between the teacher and students as an indication that the teacher is not skilled, not serious about teaching, or not able to maintain discipline. Teachers need to recognize that immigrant students have to adjust to new kinds of teacher–student relationships just as they're adjusting to other aspects of U.S. culture and schooling.

Teachers as Cultural and Linguistic Mediators

Part of the role of facilitator involves helping students make connections between their existing knowledge and experience and new knowledge and experience. In that sense, all educators are mediators between the culture and language that students bring with them to school and the culture and language of the school.

Responsive teachers respect cultural differences ..., understand that culture plays a critical role in teaching and learning ..., [have] extensive knowledge about students' out-of-school experiences ..., [and know how to translate this knowledge into] their pedagogical practices. (Villegas, in press, pp. 306-307)

Educators of immigrant students need to be not only culturally responsive, but also linguistically responsive. They need to have a positive attitude toward linguistic differences, acknowledge the value of bi- and multilingualism, understand language development and second language learning, and possess the skills to guide students in developing bilingual fluency while they learn language (their native language and English) and learn through language (their native language and English).

Again, the International High School staff and curriculum stand as an illustration of linguistic responsiveness. The teachers in the school have come to view themselves as "teachers of language rather than teachers of English" (Sylvan, 1994, p. 35). Indeed, between 1990, when I first visited the school, and 1994, when I visited again, a radical change had occurred in attitudes toward native language use in the school. During my earlier visit, I was told that all instruction was conducted in English. While students did speak in their native languages with each other, I heard little native language use by teachers and no discussion of or references to students' native language use in interviews and discussions with staff. In my day at the school in 1994, I observed teachers speaking Spanish with students and encouraging students to communicate in their native languages. I was told that a course in one cluster gave credit for native language development and that this approach would "certainly expand to other courses" (R. Wiener, personal communication, October 28, 1994). Because "the locus of control for learning and language is the student" (Sylvan, 1994, p. 36), and the "teacher" is not necessarily the teacher but can be the learner him/herself, peers, or others outside the school, the "language of instruction is not necessarily English"; the language of instruction is the language that the students use for any given activity or interaction (C. Sylvan, personal communication, November 14, 1994).

Indeed, if learning draws upon learners' knowledge and strengths, if it comes from within learners rather than being imposed from outside, then the language of learning must come from the learners as well, as part of their knowledge, expertise, and experience. Imposing a language-for-learning upon students may not provide the most supportive learning environment. Such an imposition contributes to "robbing students of their culture, language, history, and values" (Bartolomé, 1994, p. 176). If native language ability is one of a student's strengths, and we want students to have all their strengths at their disposal to facilitate learning, we need to allow them to use that native language strength rather than force them to adopt a language that reduces their capacity to learn. Teaching in this way

works when teachers use their professional expertise, not principally as providers of knowledge, but as facilitators of a process which enables students and faculty to learn while making language choices to accomplish meaningful activities. It involves change from a teacher-centered, content-based, test-driven curriculum and pedagogy to a student-centered and mediated, activity-based, and project-driven approach. (Sylvan, 1994, p. 36)

This approach does not negate the necessity to learn English. To participate fully in U.S. business, government, and education, all residents, must have a command of English. However, by becoming "teachers of language rather than [just] teachers of English," the International High School faculty are both promoting student-centered learning and contributing to the development of a bilingual, bicultural citizenry, which is sorely needed to carry us successfully into the global economy of the future. Not to cultivate the native language abilities of immigrants in this country is not only unresponsive, it is foolish.

To address the real complexities of immigrant students' lives productively and appropriately, educators must know about those complexities and must apply what they know with a sensitivity to the students and their experiences. Educators who are themselves immigrants bring that knowledge and sensitivity with them to their work. They themselves struggled to learn English and balance pressures from home with pressures to adopt the ways of American culture. Educators who are not themselves immigrants, however, must at some point develop this knowledge and sensitivity, because they cannot know and feel the lives of their students firsthand. A number of professionals in bilingual and second language education, in fact, came to this field because of personal experiences working and traveling on their own, in the Peace Corps, or in similar enterprises in various countries, cultures, and languages. They developed some knowledge and sensitivity through their own experiences and through contact with people from different cultures, which led them to want to work with immigrants here in the United States.

Most educators, however, whether they are immigrants or not, work with some students who do not share their cultures and languages. They need to learn about their students' backgrounds and lives. In particular, recent immigrants of secondary school age are going through multiple transitions to which educators can best respond if they have examined and reflected upon them: adjusting to a new culture, entering adolescence, moving through adolescence to young adulthood, preparing for life after school, moving into the workforce, and moving into higher education. Various means are available for developing knowledge of and sensitivity to immigrant students' lives and experiences: for example, reading fiction and nonfiction, going to films, attending lectures and performances, seeking out knowledgeable people to talk to, or making friends with immigrants. The formal means through which educators develop their knowledge and expertise, however, is professional development. There is an urgent need in this country for high-quality professional development that can provide the foundation of knowledge and sensitivity required of educators of immigrant students (see González & Darling-Hammond, in press).

Unfortunately, immigrant students in U.S. schools suffer, because many educators are not culturally and linguistically responsive and know little about the immigrant experience. A two-year study of immigrants in U.S. schools found that

> one of the most serious barriers to equal opportunity for educational excellence for immigrant students is a lack of school personnel who are
> • equipped with language and other skills needed to teach these students effectively;
> • sensitive and well-informed about different cultures;
> • reflective of the ethnic and cultural diversity apparent in the student population, so they can serve as guides and role models; and
> • committed to the school success of immigrant children.
>
> (National Coalition of Advocates for Students, 1988, p. 56)

Available data indicate that the vast majority of teachers in the United States are European American (female) monolingual English speakers, whereas a growing number of students—in some places an overwhelming majority—are not (see American Association of Colleges for Teacher Education, 1994; Fleischman, Arterburn, & Wiens, 1995; Gold, 1993; Knoff & Otuya, 1995). In addition, because of the diversity of many schools and districts, even educators of non-European heritage are likely to have students whose cultures and languages do not reflect their own. What this means is that educators in this country, with few exceptions, need some education to increase their sensitivity to and knowledge of their students' cultures and languages. In addition to understanding and putting into practice the new conceptions of teaching and learning and participating in the new structures of schooling, "new and different kinds of teachers" are needed who

> • have a repertoire of approaches that upholds [sic] high expectations of all students, while affirming differences among students;
> • [are] knowledgeable about issues of acculturation and second language acquisition;
> • [are able to] teach with multicultural materials that reflect a diversity of experiences and perspectives;
> • establish the classroom as a safe place to explore issues of difference and prejudice;
> • have the capacity to work together across differences of race and ethnicity;

- work well with individuals and groups from a variety of cultural backgrounds and communities;
- develop a greater understanding of all kinds of difference; and
- teach their students to appreciate diversity.

(National Coalition of Advocates for Students, 1994, pp. 126-128)

To the above list I would add that such teachers need also to

- have the pedagogical skill to adapt instruction in culturally and linguistically appropriate ways to facilitate academic learning.

Educators of the same cultural and linguistic backgrounds as their students have a special role to play as cultural and linguistic mediators. They are more likely to have the knowledge, experience, sensitivity, and commitment that can effectively support the success of disenfranchised students. They can make some safe assumptions about what the students are bringing to their learning. "Cultural congruence" between teachers and students makes it more likely that teachers can help students build cultural bridges between their experiences in and out of school, thereby engaging the student more actively and productively in classroom activities (Villegas, in press, p. 306). Symbolically, the presence of these teachers in schools offers role models for students who may rarely see people like themselves in positions of authority in the United States and shows students that their languages and cultures are valued (see Lucas et al., 1990). Given the current status of education and the barriers to recruitment and retention of members of minority groups in higher education and specifically in teacher education, it is unrealistic to think that the proportion of non-European bilingual educators will ever reach parity with the student population. Still, every individual offers hope and assistance to some children.

At the same time, simply sharing a student's language and culture does not make an educator an effective cultural and linguistic mediator:

Knowledge about the out-of-school experiences of students of color does not automatically make one a responsive teacher.... It would be unfair to hold minority individuals accountable for developing culturally [and linguistically] responsive teaching strategies without the benefit of professional growth experiences to support this. [Teacher education, as well as K-12 education, must be] restructured for diversity. (Villegas, in press, p. 309)

When teachers of any background have and apply the knowledge, sensitivity, and pedagogical skill that it takes to mediate between immigrant students' existing knowledge, experiences, interests, and abilities and the new knowledge, experiences, interests, and abilities they need to make their way successfully through and beyond secondary school in the United States, they can directly address the students' needs and build upon their strengths and experiences. They can help students to develop pride in their own cultures while giving them access to what Delpit (1988, 1995) has called the "culture of power" that prevails in U.S. society and is reflected in U.S. schools.

Reconceptualizations of Schools and Schooling

Given the changing conceptions of teaching and learning and the roles of teachers and learners, a rethinking of secondary schooling itself is inevitable. Typically, secondary schools are portrayed as dreary places (see, e.g., Boyer, 1983; Corcoran, 1990; Goodlad, 1984; National Center on Effective Secondary Schools, 1991; Powell, Farrar, & Cohen, 1985; Sizer, 1992). Many, if not most, people who come into intimate contact with secondary schools (whether as teachers, parents, students, or researchers) would no doubt agree that "most American high schools still have a long way to go to substantially improve the engagement and achievement of their students" (National Center on Effective Secondary Schools, 1991, p. 19). Traditional secondary schools have a high degree of fragmentation, isolation, stratification of students and of educators, passive learning, and irrelevance to students' lives.

The picture of the secondary school experiences of immigrant students is equally gloomy. Despite some examples to the contrary (see, e.g., Lucas et al., 1990), too many secondary language minority students "find themselves struggling to understand a minimum of academic material with little effective assistance" (Lucas, 1993a, pp. 113-114). An exploratory study of 27 secondary schools in California (Minicucci & Olsen, 1991) found that, in addition to the obstacles to learning faced by all students in secondary schools, limited-English-proficient (LEP) students in particular were inadequately served because of their

diverse and complex needs ..., a shortage of teachers willing and trained to teach LEP courses, a lack of comprehensive program planning, difficulties in obtaining appropriate textbooks and materials, and the rigid departmental structure of secondary schools. (p. 45)

The biggest difference across these 27 schools was in their approaches to academic content instruction. Many of the schools offered only partial programs for English language learners in academic subject areas.

The recognition of this depressing state of secondary schooling along with the new conceptions of teaching and learning discussed above have led to a movement toward secondary school reform. Effective secondary schools are now conceived as more complex and more humane than the factories they were modeled after.

Schools as Communities

The stratified, fragmented, specialized nature of the typical secondary school reflects a "rational-bureaucratic perspective" of schools as "formal organizations." The "personal-communal" perspective, on the other hand, sees "schools as 'small societies,' organizations that emphasize informal and enduring social relationships and are driven by a common ethos" and shared values (Lee, Bryk, & Smith, 1993, pp. 173, 209; see also Barth, 1990; Newmann, 1981; Newmann & Oliver, 1967). Greater emphasis is being placed on developing relationships among all who have a stake in the educational system, including those inside and outside of the formal system. At the same time, we are cautioned not to embrace the idea of a community to such an extent that we forget the cognitive/academic role of schools: "The vision of a school as a community ... must be integrated with a view of the school as a formal organization that seeks to rationally, effectively, and efficiently promote student learning" (Lee et al., 1993, p. 229; see also Braddock & McPartland, 1993; McPartland, 1990).

When schools are conceived as "communities of learners" (Barth, 1990), this integration is made explicit. In such schools, everyone is openly and continuously engaged in learning. Greater value is placed on "learning, participation, and cooperation" than on "prescription, production, and competition" (p. 43). An example provided by Barth illustrates how an entire school became a community of learners to the benefit of all concerned, including a group of immigrant students and their families:

An all-white, fully English-speaking elementary school learned during February that a large number of Cambodian children would enroll in the school in the fall…. The parents, teachers, and principal … made a decision that it was critical for *everyone* in the school—children, parents, teachers, custodians, administrators, secretaries, lunch workers—to know who these Cambodian children were, where they had come from, and why there were coming. At the outset, no one knew anything, so for the next four months, *getting ready for the Cambodian children* became the curriculum—in reading, social studies, language arts, science, and art programs. Community was real, and as a result, the experience was vital. Learning had an important purpose. Everyone learned how to say something to the Cambodian children in their own language and also gained considerable knowledge about their cultural patterns and their suffering. As part of their preparation, those in the school learned about prejudice and the harm that prejudice brings to persons who seem different. They also learned how prejudice disrupts communities—in schools and neighborhoods. Their learning had meaning and it made a visible difference. The school had helped the Cambodian families belong. The Cambodians, in turn, had helped this school become a community of learners. (Barth, 1990, p. 44)

Many of the reforms recently being enacted in secondary schools reflect the view of schools as communities. Reductions in the degree of departmentalization facilitate the development of collegial communities through teacher collaboration. After reviewing available research, Lee et al. (1993) argued that "it seems plausible that there is a causal link between departmentalization and a lack of community" (p. 214).

When teachers work together in interdisciplinary teams in which they are responsible for the same group of students, when they have common planning times, and when they teach together, they have opportunities to develop shared goals, values, perspectives, and strategies. These reforms also increase the possibilities for relationships to develop between students and teachers, as do school structures that provide formal time for personal interaction, such as houses—in which a relatively small group of students stays together throughout the day—and advisories, in which each student has an ongoing relationship with an adult advocate and advisor. Efforts to promote student collaboration through instructional approaches such as cooperative learning, group projects, clusters of students, and block scheduling can likewise build community among students. Such reforms reflect the argument put forth by Newmann in the early 1980s:

Trusting relationships are more likely to develop if students spend sustained time with teachers on an individual basis or in small groups, and if they engage together in a range of activities such as recreation, counseling, dining, housekeeping, or even the study of more than one subject.... More constructive forms of communality could be promoted if students were expected to listen to, counsel, and lend support to one another.... Extended contact generates a greater sense of communality, mutual caring and responsibility, than conventional transient and fragmented roles. (1981, pp. 553-554)

The decreased focus on specialization for staff further reflects the desire to build a school community. Interdisciplinary instruction—whether by separate subject-area teachers working together or by an individual teacher teaching more than one content area—breaks down traditional barriers. Teachers and other school personnel are increasingly playing a greater variety of roles, as the school "seeks to influence students' social and personal development as well as their intellectual development" (Lee et al., 1993, p. 216). Adults in different roles inside and outside of schools may act as student advisors, teachers, mentors, and facilitators (MacIver, 1990; Maeroff, 1990; McPartland & Nettles, 1991).

The flattened hierarchy and shared authority in many secondary schools is another way in which community is built within schools. Adults and students may participate in various types of decision making that traditionally came under the authority of administrators. This gives these groups a common purpose and context and promotes their concept of themselves as part of a larger community. It requires that principals become " 'reflective practitioners,' capable of learning while they lead" (Barth, 1990, p. 67) and that teachers develop a stronger sense of their roles outside their classrooms.

If schools are truly committed to functioning as communities, they cannot marginalize immigrant students. They must work to integrate all students into the community in ways that promote their personal, social, and intellectual development, and that means personalizing education enough so that students can develop in different ways and at different paces. Members of the school community must learn about each other, as the school described above learned about Cambodian culture and experience in order to understand their new community members. Teachers must develop relationships with individual students rather than simply seeing them and 30 other students for 42 minutes per day. If schools do this, immigrant students stand to benefit greatly by being brought into the daily life of the school rather than being only nominal members of the community.

Schools as Learner-Centered Communities

The school is seen as a particular kind of community—one in which the focus is on the students. While everyone in the school community should be a learner, the students are the most important learners. The concept of learner-centered schooling incorporates the view that learning arises out of active student engagement:

Learner-centered schools focus on students' needs, interests, and talents as the basis for organizing schoolwork and school organization, building curriculum and learning opportunities, and developing relationships between and among students, educators, and parents. (Darling-Hammond, 1992, p. 19)

Rather than continuing to assume that all students will be equally well educated if we can only devise the right system, educators are now arguing that education should be more personalized and should give more attention to the individual within the system than to the system itself (see Anson, 1994). The increased diversity in the student population has been an important factor in this conception. When students were apparently more similar to each other and to their teachers and when fewer of them had access to schooling, one monolithic system was, no doubt, more effective than it is today.

Several practices reflect this learner-centered conception of schools. They include attempts to make schools smaller by developing schools-within-schools, alternative schools, and interdisciplinary clusters; efforts to provide a home base where students' personal as well as academic needs can be addressed through advisories, houses, and families; academic and personal support systems for those who need them; and flexible instructional and curricular practices that allow for independent, experiential learning. The ultimate learner-centered strategy is to design curriculum, instruction, and extracurricular activities so that they build upon what students bring to learning. This requires educators to incorporate the understandings, sensitivities, and skills described above in *Reconceptualizations of Teachers and Teaching* in order to mediate between the expectations of the school and the students' home cultures, socioeconomic backgrounds, languages, and experiences.

For immigrant students and others who do not match the middle-class, White, U.S.-born, English-speaking student for whom the educational system is designed, it is essential that schools design curriculum, instruction, and other activities around the students. If only one curriculum or one approach to instruction is used, it is unlikely that it will be one that is most appropriate for immigrant students. If schoolwork is really organized around "students' needs, interests, and talents," as Darling-Hammond suggests, then immigrant students will find the information, the academic content, the teachers, and the personal and academic support that they need in order to learn.

Schools as Part of a Larger Situational and Chronological Context

Educators are being urged to think systemically and to see schools and schooling as integral to a situational context that includes the school district, the surrounding business community, health and social service agencies, families of school-age children, and area residents without children—all of which may reflect socioeconomic, racial, ethnic, and linguistic diversity. Schools are no longer perceived as autonomous entities. As we become more connected to each other and the world through technology, we see schools—central institutions in our lives—as more intertwined with other institutions and as benefiting from and contributing to a concerted effort to prepare young people to be future productive citizens.

The school is also no longer seen as the locus and source of all education. Indeed, the adage that it takes a whole village to educate a child has become a cliché. A school "must be dynamically plugged into its environment if it is to have any chance at all of surviving" (Fullan, 1993, p. 42). In attempting to reform schools, many educators now acknowledge that they must have the agreement and participation of people from all the components of the educational system and the broader community, if real change is to take place (see Fullan, 1993, 1994; Fullan & Miles, 1992). Students are encouraged to extend their learning outside the school through community service, internships, and extended projects. Calls to extend the boundaries of schools through collaboration and linkages with families, businesses, community-based organizations, social service agencies, health agencies, youth organizations, and adult and higher education institutions increasingly come from individuals and organizations with very different perspectives (e.g., ASPIRA Association, Inc. [ASPIRA], 1994; Barton, 1993; California Department of Education, 1992; Darling-Hammond, 1992; Heath & McLaughlin, 1994; National Coalition of Advocates for Students, 1988, 1993, 1994; New York State Department of Education, 1991). The "full-service school" is now accepted as a good idea, even if it rarely becomes a reality.

Immigrant students and their families can benefit greatly from this new conception of schooling. As people in schools see more reasons to extend the school into the community and bring the community into the school, they are developing ways to engage the multiple groups that populate school districts, including immigrant communities. Rather than remaining the closed societies they have been, schools are opening their doors and reaching out, often in ways that will make them more accessible to all, even to those who do not speak English fluently. In addition, immigrant students and families benefit from the increased collaboration between schools and community agencies, which, in many cases, are already playing important roles in immigrant communities, providing information and various kinds of assistance. Such collaborations bring together multiple support systems for immigrant families.

Just as schools are seen as part of a larger community context and multifaceted system, they are also conceived as integral to the life course of young people in the United States (Pallas, 1993). Schools are increasingly seen as mediators for students as they make the developmental transition into adulthood, moving beyond school into the world of work and higher education. Schools are expected to prepare young people for the next stage in their lives. Considerable attention has been given in recent years to the role that secondary schools can and should play in facilitating youths' transitions beyond schooling. Schools are now expected to provide information to youths about careers and higher education opportunities and to facilitate their access to college and work experiences during the time they are in high school—often as part of their formal secondary education.

Traditionally, secondary schools have had a limited role in preparing youths for the future; they have mainly prepared middle class male students for higher education. With the increased complexity of life and work in the late 20th century, schools have come to be less and less relevant to the kinds of learning and employment to which young people will need to gain access in order to be successful. It remains to be seen whether the many strategies for making connections between secondary school and life beyond will be effective for any students and especially whether they will be appropriately adapted to incorporate immigrant students into mainstream culture (see the discussion in chapter 6 under *Pathways Beyond Secondary School).*

Schools as Mediators Between Students' Homes and Mainstream Culture

A central function of schooling is acculturation. With more or less success, schools attempt to shape students into the mainstream image of productive citizens—an image that varies according to the socioeconomic and racial group to which students belong. This is not a new conception of schooling. Though it is not always acknowledged (Apple, 1979, 1982; Bowles & Gintis, 1976; Cummins, 1989), schools have always served an acculturative purpose, and they continue to do so. However, schools can take radically different approaches in acculturating students. The more traditional approach is subtractive (Cummins, 1989) in that it requires students to abandon ways of talking, thinking, and behaving that deviate from the mainstream norm. A more additive approach is for schools to value and build on what learners bring with them to school and to learning, but at the same time give them the skills and knowledge necessary to gain access to the culture of power (Delpit, 1988, 1995). This makes it more likely that they can integrate their home cultures with the mainstream culture and can learn to make choices about how to talk, think, and behave in any particular context.

Although many educators espouse the additive approach for students with racial, ethnic, linguistic, and socioeconomic profiles that deviate from the norm, this conception remains largely unrealized in U.S. schools. Nonmainstream students have less access than mainstream students to the skills and knowledge needed to be successful in the larger culture, and few educators have the will or the ability to build on students' ways of talking, thinking, and behaving when those depart from the mainstream. Indeed, minority and poor children receive less of many resources than other children.

These children get
- less in the way of experienced and well-trained teachers;
- less in the way of a rich and well-balanced curriculum;
- less actual instructional time;
- less well-equipped laboratories and libraries; and
- less of what makes the biggest difference of all: a belief that they can really learn.

(Haycock, 1995, p. 226)

Thus, disproportionate numbers of nonmainstream students find themselves in low-track classes where their opportunities to learn are greatly reduced (see Lee et al., 1993; Oakes, 1985). They often do not receive the extra help they may need to succeed academically, do not find adults in schools who can give them the caring attention they need, and find little connection to life beyond high school (Natriello, McDill, & Pallas, 1990).

Nevertheless, some notable attempts are being made to mediate between students' homes and the mainstream culture rather than to eradicate nonmainstream ways of talking, thinking, and behaving. Some schools have organized their schedules and curricula so that students spend some portion of their day in heterogeneous groups rather than in tracked classes, providing more access to rigorous academic learning to those who are otherwise in low-track classes. As discussed above, some schools provide academic and personal support systems for those who need them. Some use flexible and personalized instructional and curricular practices, which allow for more diversity among learners and draw on strengths rather than emphasize weaknesses. Efforts to build a school community can help students, families, and educators of all backgrounds understand and communicate with each other and develop shared purposes. Some schools are making it a priority for all staff to develop sensitivity, knowledge, and skills to see all students as they are, without relying on assumptions and stereotypes. When schools do take an additive approach in actively mediating between students' home cultures and the mainstream culture, immigrant students gain valuable access to information about U.S. schooling and culture, learn to value their own cultures and experiences as well as those of other students, and develop their academic knowledge and abilities.

Conclusion

Immigrant students must be included in the population of "all" students, whom the new approaches to schooling are designed to serve, but only some of whom actually have access to educational innovations (see Olsen et al., 1994). We can no longer concentrate our energies on designing and supporting programs that effectively deprive immigrant students of the benefits of the broader education reforms and that allow many educators to avoid developing culturally and linguistically responsive understandings and skills. We need to "shift the focus from *creating more programs* to *improving whole schools*" (Haycock, 1995, p. 231). Neither can we afford to place immigrant students in mainstream classes and abandon them there without special assistance. We need to situate the education of immigrant students squarely within the education reform movement. Educators of immigrant students need to learn about the principles and practices of education reform and make sure that those principles and practices are included when their colleagues design and implement new programs and approaches. The more access immigrant students have to educational innovations and the more integrated they are into the broader educational system, the better it will be for them—provided, of course, that the innovations and the system are responsive to their particular experiences, strengths, and needs.

The changing visions of learning, teaching, and schooling push us to break through the traditional boundaries of the classroom and the school to redefine who participates in teaching and learning, in what ways they participate, and where resources for teaching and learning reside. They offer many benefits for immigrant students, provided that educators consider their implications and make needed adjustments rather than simply apply them and expect immigrant students to conform.

Figure 3. Reconceptualizations of Learners, Teachers, and Schools and Their Implications for Immigrant Students

Reconceptualizations of Learners as . . .	Implications for Immigrant Students
Active constructors of knowledge	• Supports and values learning through various means, thus acknowledging different learning styles. • Reduces reliance on language as the medium for learning. • Conflicts with the views of many other cultures, which hold that learners take in what teachers deliver. • May require more language use and cultural knowledge than some immigrants have attained.
Collaborators	• Promotes language use in the classroom. • Promotes cross-cultural learning and communication. • Is consistent with learning strategies in cultures with a collective orientation, which traditional U.S. competitive learning is not. • May require more language use and cultural knowledge than some immigrants have attained. • Requires cross-cultural sensitivity for all involved.
Decision makers	• Draws on strengths of students who play decision-making roles. • Conflicts with collective orientation in emphasizing individual will, action, and responsibility. • May conflict with adolescent roles in other cultures.
Reconceptualizations of Teachers as . . .	**Implications for Immigrant Students**
Learners	• Allows teachers to admit that they need to learn about educating immigrant students. • Provides support for learning about educating immigrant students. • Allows the pooling of expertise from more than one person in working with immigrant students. • Can increase personalization, which benefits immigrant students as nonmainstream learners.

Figure 3. Reconceptualizations of Learners, Teachers, and Schools and Their Implications for Immigrant Students (continued)

Facilitators	• Increases personalization, which benefits immigrant students as nonmainstream learners. • Conflicts with the views of many other cultures, which hold that teachers should deliver information.
Cultural and linguistic mediators	• Directly addresses the needs and builds on the linguistic, cultural, and personal strengths of immigrant students. • Helps students develop pride in their own backgrounds. • Gives students access to the "culture of power" by developing their academic skills and knowledge.
Reconceptualizations of Schools as . . .	**Implications for Immigrant Students**
Communities	• Encourages everyone to learn about immigrant students and families in order to integrate them into the community. • Requires personalization of schooling.
Learner centered	• Encourages everyone to learn about immigrant students and families in order to design schooling with learners at the center. • Requires personalization of schooling.
Part of a larger situational and chronological context	• Encourages schools to find ways to engage immigrant families in schooling. • Brings together multiple providers of service and assistance for immigrant families. • May eventually lead schools to provide assistance for immigrant students as they move beyond high school into work and higher education.
Mediators between home culture and mainstream culture	• Makes information about U.S. culture and schooling accessible to immigrant students. • Shows immigrant students that their cultures and experiences are valued. • Gives immigrant students access to academic knowledge and abilities.

Figure 3 presents some of these implications as a summary of the previous discussion. It is offered, not as a prescription for what teachers should do or know when they apply these principles to schooling immigrant students, but as an illustration of the kinds of issues they need to consider to ensure that reform makes sense for immigrant students.

Part II

Principles for Facilitating Immigrant Students' Transitions Into, Through, and Beyond Secondary School

Introduction

As educators, we cannot throw up our hands, overwhelmed by the complexities of immigrant youths' lives and too set in our ways to give serious thought to new conceptions of learning, teaching, and schooling that challenge our familiar ways of teaching and of organizing schools. We are challenged to face head-on those complexities that make our students who they are, to make sure that we are up-to-date on learning theories and teaching practices, and to design schools and instruction to take into account the differences among students. We are challenged to educate immigrant students so that they can realize their high aspirations. In order to do that, we must help secondary immigrant students successfully navigate through the multiple transitions discussed above. Four broad principles for facilitating these transitions into, through, and beyond secondary school are presented in the next four chapters. These principles are grounded in the emerging views that educational practice should be contextualized and personalized, as indicated in Figure 4.

The principles reflect the complexities of the immigrant experience and embrace new conceptions of teaching, learning, and schooling. They are also important for supporting the educational progress and facilitating key transitions in the lives of all students, and especially of students who do not fit the White, middle-class, U.S.-born norm. However, the particulars of applying these principles vary for different individual students and for different groups of students. To apply them

Figure 4. Principles for Facilitating Immigrant Students' Transitions

Contextualized Education

Principle 1: Cultivate organizational relationships.

Principle 2: Provide access to information.

Personalized Education

Principle 3: Cultivate human relationships.

Principle 4: Provide multiple and flexible pathways into, through, and beyond school.

for immigrant students who arrived in the United States at or after age 11 and who are not fluent in English, we must give special consideration to some factors that are less relevant for other students. We must ask questions about each student to ensure that we have the information we need to make decisions that will facilitate the transitions he or she is going through. In formulating these questions, we should consider the multitude of factors that influence the educational experiences of secondary immigrant students. We must also interrogate our practices to ensure that we have designed and adapted them in ways that make them responsive to the particular students for whom we are applying them.

The growing diversity in the U.S. population has led to a greater need for contextualization of education:

Traditional North American education … [has] relied on the family and community experiences of majority-culture adults to provide the activity, the conversation, the language development and the shared context upon which the schools could depend. This is no longer true, in culturally and linguistically diverse nations. The schools must now provide the common experience, activity, language, and conversation that learners require, both for individual development and the development of a common, shared and mutually endorsed community. (Tharp, 1994, p. 191)

Students who depart from the middle-class, U.S.-born standard for which the educational system is designed do not come to school with the "cultural capital" or the "social capital" (Bourdieu, 1986) that students who fit that standard bring with them simply because they grew up in their particular homes and communities. The cultural knowledge that these latter students bring with them "maps onto the knowledge expected of them in school, whereas the knowledge passed on" by other families does not (Mehan, Hubbard, Lintz, & Villanueva, 1994, p. 9). Similarly, "networks of relationships … enable resources to accrue to people because they belong to and participate in certain groups. This social capital enables … [middle-class, U.S.-born] families to assist their children" in ways that others cannot (p. 9)—for example, by helping them prepare for, select, and apply to colleges and by coaching them through the process of applying for jobs. Immigrant students and other nonmainstream students do not have access to the culture of power without explicitly being given some additional information, knowledge, and assistance (Delpit, 1988, 1995).

Schooling must be contextualized on many different levels in order to make it accessible and powerful for students who "have not been immersed in the implicit socialization process that accrues social and cultural capital to the sons and daughters" of middle-class, U.S.-born families (Mehan et al., 1994, p. 10). One way to do this is through connections between schools and other institutions. Educators are being urged to think systemically. As discussed above, schools are coming to be seen as part of a larger social and institutional context that includes the school district, the surrounding business community, health and social service agencies, community-based organizations, youth organizations, adult and higher education institutions, families of school-age children, and area residents without children. Schools are no longer perceived as autonomous entities, nor as the locus and source of all education. The transitions of immigrant students into, through, and beyond secondary school are facilitated by the cultivation of organizational relationships (Principle 1), both those that already serve immigrant families and communities (e.g., community-based organizations) and those that should serve them better (e.g., businesses and institutions of higher education). Such organizational relationships bring together multiple support systems for immigrant students.

Schools are also more contextualized for immigrant students when they provide explicit access to information that mainstream students have and that nonmainstream students need (see Delpit, 1988, 1995; Mehan, Hubbard, Okamoto, & Villanueva, 1993; Mehan et al., 1994). More specifically, schools can facilitate the transitions that secondary immigrant students encounter by providing explicit information about U.S. schooling, U.S. culture, higher education, and the world of work (Principle 2). Immigrant students need information and "experiences of how rules, abstractions, and verbal descriptions are drawn from the everyday world, and how they are applied again to it" (Tharp, 1994, p.

187). Greater contextualization of schooling is also supported through active and meaningful engagement of parents and other family members in reciprocal learning and community-building relationships (see Principle 3).

As discussed in chapter 3, the "personal-communal" or communitarian perspective of schools emphasizes the personalization of education. In this view, schools are seen as "organizations that emphasize informal and enduring social relationships" (Lee et al., 1993, pp. 173, 209; see also Barth, 1990; Newmann, 1981; Newmann & Oliver, 1967). The people within schools and their relationships with each other and with those outside of schools are more important than the structures or organization of schooling. Relationships between students and teachers are especially potent in developing a sense of community, caring, and responsibility, but all sorts of human relationships make a school a community of learners (Barth, 1990). The cultivation of human relationships can provide critical support for secondary immigrant students to successfully move through the transitions they will encounter (Principle 3).

The move to personalize education reflects the understanding of "the importance of students' being able to bring their own perspectives and experience to the learning moment" (Anson, 1994, p. 5). Rather than continuing to assume that all students will be equally well educated if we can only devise the right system—as the factory model of education assumed—educators are now arguing that education should be more personalized, that students will learn best if more attention is given to the individual within the system than to the system itself. Indeed, the U.S. educational system is designed for an imaginary student who might be described as a White, middle-class, native-English-speaking, U.S.-born, Christian, heterosexual male who is a linear thinker and has two parents who are happily married to each other, only one of whom (the father) works outside the home. Personalizing education requires giving serious thought to the extent to which students depart from this norm and designing schooling so that it takes these differences into account. Given the diversity among U.S. students today, schools must provide multiple opportunities for students to gain the academic, personal, and social knowledge and skills they need to lead productive adult lives. More specifically, secondary immigrant students must have access to multiple and flexible pathways that can facilitate their transitions into, through, and beyond school in the United States (Principle 4).

After elaborating on each of these four principles, I present a set of questions to ask in applying the principles to ensure that the key issues of language, educational backgrounds of students and families, the immigration experience, culture and cultural context, and social background and social context are considered in attempts to design schooling so that it facilitates transitions for secondary immigrant students.

Principle 1: Cultivate Organizational Relationships

Educators of all students, especially of immigrant students, need to build and strengthen relationships throughout the educational system and beyond the traditional boundaries of the system into the community. "Neither top-down nor bottom-up strategies for education reform work" (Fullan, 1994, p. 7). In order to bring about real change, we must focus on "the development and interrelationships of all the *components* of the system simultaneously ... not just on structure, policy, and regulations, but on deeper issues of the *culture* of the system" (Fullan & Miles, 1992, p. 751). This means that we need to cultivate relationships among institutions as well as among people. It is through such collaborations that individual educators and educational institutions can have an impact on those aspects of students' lives that can make or break their educational success but that are not easily addressed within the context of school alone. Relationships between the educational system and health and social service agencies, community-based organizations, businesses, and institutions of higher education can help focus attention on many of the issues that can impede students' progress into, through, and beyond secondary school. Such issues include, for example, their economic resources, race and ethnicity and the concomitant racism and prejudice, immigration status, gender, physical health, mental health, experience of life disruption and displacement, intergenerational relationships, and preparation for life beyond high school.

There is a call throughout the country for linkages among various agencies and organizations serving youths and their families (see Ascher, 1988a, 1988b; Dryfoos, 1993; Institute for Educational Leadership, 1994; National Coalition of Advocates for Students, 1994; Olsen et al., 1994; Price, Cioci, Penner, & Trautlein, 1993; Wang, Haertel, & Walberg, 1995). These linkages are especially crucial for immigrants, given their multitude of needs for information and services and their lack of familiarity with the complex and varied social, health, employment, and educational services in the United States. Collaborations among health and social service agencies, businesses, and educational institutions can help immigrant students and their families in their transition into U.S. culture and schooling and beyond high school into college and employment (as shown in Figure 5). Reciprocal relationships between schools and community-based organizations with strong connections to immigrant communities can support the inclusion of immigrant perspectives in schooling.

Communication across the differences in philosophies, goals, operating procedures, funding sources, eligibility requirements, time schedules, and perspectives of organizations as different as grass-roots community groups, public schools, teaching and research universities, and Fortune 500 companies presents many challenges. To succeed at forging productive collaborations, individuals within these disparate agencies must be committed to do what is necessary to make them succeed. Indeed, relationships among agencies are built upon relationships among people within those agencies and depend upon their finding ways to communicate in meaningful and ongoing ways. Behind every successful cross-agency collaboration, a few key individuals have succeeded at making connections with each other. Collaborations "aimed at bringing about real school change can demand that a number of people spend a great deal of time together" (Ascher, 1988b, p. 7). Figure 5 presents key organizations with which the educational system must build relationships.

Health and Social Service Agencies

"In disadvantaged communities, schools cannot address the challenge of raising the quality of education and at the same time attend to the problems of young people and their families without a substantial mobilization of health and social services resources" (Dryfoos, 1993, p. 101). If we conceive of students as whole human beings, rather than only as learners of school subjects, then we must take into account a host of nonacademic needs and influences. These influences can include hunger; fear for their safety in school, at home, and in their communities; fatigue from after-school and weekend jobs; posttraumatic stress from war and violence in their home countries; and loss of family and friends. Educators recognize the difficulty in trying to teach social studies to students who are abused or hungry or worried about their

Figure 5. Organizational Relationships Essential to Facilitating Transitions

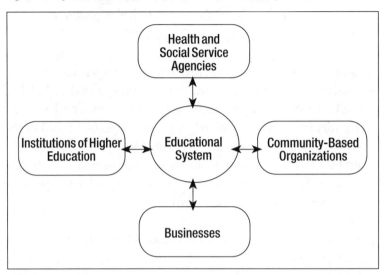

family's legal status in the United States, and they are advocating for coordinated services to address students' multiple needs.

The O'Farrell Community School in San Diego has set aside an entire wing of the school for Family Support Services, funded by the Department of Social Services, SB620 Healthy Start, and district money (Olsen et al., 1994, pp. 154-158). Staff provide crisis intervention, short-term counseling, support groups, referrals to other agencies, and consultations with school staff and families. They have developed relationships with several other agencies providing a host of services for multiethnic, multilingual families and communities. Some districts hire social workers who can make referrals to community social service agencies. In a New Jersey district, for example, the district bilingual social worker performs such roles as determining eligibility and arranging appointments and referrals for medical services, helping homeless students find housing, intervening for families who have been evicted, and making referrals to the Hispanic Association for immigrants who want to legalize their residency status in the United States (Villegas, 1992, p. 92). A New Jersey high school has established a Social Concerns Committee, composed of a bilingual assistant principal and members of the faculty and staff, which makes referrals to community agencies (Villegas, 1992, pp. 92-93).

A collaboration between schools and social service agencies specifically focused on supporting the transition from school to work is the Oklahoma City Job Training Partnership Act (JTPA) Bilingual Summer Academies for Asian and Latino bilingual students (described in National Coalition of Advocates for Students, 1994, pp. 57-66). The program balances the focus on academics and pre-employment skills, providing ESL and math courses in the morning and paid jobs in the afternoon for those old enough to work.

A more comprehensive effort at linking schools with health and social service agencies is described by the Institute for Educational Leadership (1994). In a project called *New Beginnings*, the County of San Diego (including the Department of Social Services), the City of San Diego, San Diego City Schools, the San Diego Community College District, the University of San Diego Medical Center, Children's Hospital, and the San Diego Housing Commission are collaborating to "serve the needs of low-income children, youth and families" (p. 3). The group selected as a test site Hamilton Elementary School, in "a densely populated, highly transient, and ethnically mixed neighborhood" (p. 4), where more than half the students did not speak English as their native language and more than 90% were eligible for free or reduced-price lunches. They compiled various kinds of data about the school and had a social worker conduct action research from his position within the school. They found that

families must carry their life stories around to several places and give each agency a different part of the story. Eligibility procedures were complex and specific to each agency. And agencies didn't have ways to share data. (p. 6)

In 1991, New Beginnings designated Hamilton Elementary School "a learning laboratory" where they would try to develop "a long-term strategy for changing systems that provide services to children and families" (pp. 6-7). It is too early to tell how successful the approach is, but Tom Payzant, then Superintendent of San Diego City Schools, expressed optimism that it would influence the institutions involved to "change the way they do business" (p. 8). This approach would need to be adapted to be implemented in secondary education contexts, which have traditionally been less welcoming to parents and which have offered fewer services to families than elementary schools.

Community-Based Organizations

Because community-based organizations (CBOs) are likely to be located in immigrant communities and staffed by people from those communities, they "are strategically positioned to mediate and fortify relationships between families and schools" (National Coalition of Advocates for Students, 1994, p. 95). School efforts to address the multiple needs of immigrant students are greatly enhanced through collaboration with CBOs, which provide many services for immigrants, including counseling, health screening, referral to other agencies and services, tutoring, recreation, English language classes, orientation to U.S. culture, and job preparation. Because of their advocacy role, CBOs also address many of the social issues that can influence immigrant students' adjustment to U.S. schools and their successful movement beyond school to work and higher education—issues such as racism and prejudice, development of racial and ethnic pride, interethnic communication and understanding, and access to health care and economic resources (see Camino, 1992).

ACCESS (The Arab Community Center of Economic and Social Services), a CBO in Dearborn, Michigan, where the school population is approximately 40% Arab American, has collaborated with and supplemented the efforts of the public schools in a number of projects, services, and activities, including an after-school homework and tutoring program, parent education, a bilingual library, adult education, a vocational training program, a summer academic enrichment program, a teen health clinic, a conflict resolution program, and inservice teacher training (see National Coalition of Advocates for Students, 1994, pp. 106-112).

Touchstones, an alliance of smaller community groups in Washington state, was founded in 1989 to "advocate for the needs of immigrant/refugee children and to assist them in transition from their prior experiences in their homeland to life in America by enabling them to become self-sufficient, productive members of society while maintaining their cultural and ethnic identity" (National Coalition of Advocates for Students, 1994, p. 99). Touchstones provides "one-source access to health, nutrition, social, and transportation services and assistance" (p. 100). One of Touchstones' programs is the Multi-Cultural Youth Action Council (MC-YAC), "formed by teens and young adults to serve as a voice, body, and forum for their needs and issues" (p. 104). MC-YAC's 75 members serve as tutors, instructional aides, mentors, coaches, peer counselors, advocates, and trainers working with other youths and with adults in the schools and the community.

These two examples illustrate the array of academic and nonacademic needs that CBOs can and do address with and without collaboration with schools. Collaboration can only make their impact stronger and enhance the school's role in educating the whole child.

Businesses

Unfortunately, relationships between schools and workplaces in the United States are rare, as Barton (1990) describes:

In the United States, the institutions of school and those of work are separate and most always far apart.... The school can gain knowledge of deficiencies in the preparation of students for work by being in communication with their employers. Schools can also help students learn from their work experiences by discussing these experiences with them. Employers could have the opportunity to tell schools what they perceive the educational deficiencies of these students to be. It is a chance for them to have a say in improving their prospective labor force in general; in specific they may improve the abilities of young people they may want to hire full-time after graduation. Such communication would be one element in creating a much needed dialogue between schools and employers (pp. 4, 7).

Schools and employers are increasingly called upon to establish better links in order to prepare students for the future of global business, which it is predicted will be characterized by technological sophistication, rapid changes, collaborative structures, and a plethora of information that must be managed efficiently (e.g., Ascher, 1988b; ASPIRA, 1994; Barton, 1990; Charner & Fraser, 1994; Flaxman, Ascher, Berryman, & Unger, 1995; Glover & Marshall, 1993; Kazis, 1993; Marshall & Glover, 1996; Stone, 1991). The lack of communication between schools and workplaces has meant that few schools have changed to reflect the changing needs and expectations of the workplace of the future, where employees will need to "analyze data, communicate with precision, deal with ambiguity, learn rapidly, participate in what were considered management decisions in hierarchical management systems and work well in teams" (Glover & Marshall, 1993, pp. 133-134). It has also meant that schools have lacked information and connections to assist youths who intend to go to work after high school graduation rather than to college (Barton, 1990; Kazis, 1993). Indeed, "the world of work is nearly absent from the curriculum" in U.S. schools (Flaxman, Ascher, Berryman, & Unger, 1995, p. 145).

Some initiatives do require and facilitate the development of relationships between schools and employers. Some require minimal direct collaboration, such as most adopt-a-school programs, which "may simply mean that a business provides athletic equipment or computers" to schools (Ascher, 1988b, p. 7). Others involve greater amounts of personal and institutional interaction. Many of the so-called school-to-work approaches also require collaboration between workplaces and schools.

The key to the "system" ... by which youth move from the school world to the work world ... *is a collaborative approach between the school and employers.... School systems and employers* ... *must jointly design approaches in which they share responsibilities for preparing youth for entry into employment in the primary market.* (Barton, 1993, pp. 26, 27-28)

Approaches that bring schools and employers together include cooperative education, youth apprenticeships, mentoring programs that involve business people as mentors, and career and vocational academies (see the discussion in chapter 6 under *Pathways Beyond Secondary School* for more details about these approaches). The WISE program, discussed in the same chapter under *Pathways to the World of Work*, requires WISE mentors and students to discuss expectations when students opt for internships. The International High School career education program, also described in *Pathways to the World of Work*, requires school faculty to visit potential internship sites and discuss expectations and strategies for working with students with possible sponsors. When students are immigrants, these discussions must address issues of language and culture in the workplace.

A more comprehensive collaboration, the Los Angeles Area Business/ Education Partnership Cooperative, brings together the Los Angeles area schools, the Los Angeles Technical College, California State University at Los Angeles, the East San Gabriel Valley Regional Occupational Program, more than 300 businesses, and more than 20 public and nonprofit community agencies to provide coordinated academic and vocational instruction and social services to "predominantly minority, LEP and other high risk [youths]" (described in Adler & Cragin, 1993, p. 12ff). Business and industry representatives review the curriculum to ensure that it is relevant to employment needs. They also act as tutors, mentors, and job coaches, provide "up-to-date labor market information," and help with job placement for students completing the program (p. 17).

While the number of such initiatives is growing, few schools and employers have broken through the barriers to communication. And when they make the attempt, the differences in their philosophies and goals make understanding difficult to achieve. In fact, the unquestioned acceptance of business's critique of education and the highly influential roles that some businesses and business people are playing in education pose both opportunities and dangers to public education (Mickelson, 1996). Mickelson acknowledges that financial resources, increased attention to educational issues and to the needs of families and children, new ideas from those outside the educational establishment, and the potential for a smoother transition from school to work offer benefits to schools and students. However, she warns that dangers of increased business involvement in education include the publishing of influential "ideological treatise[s] in support of market-based reforms and privatisation" with little data to support them (p. 7); deflection of responsibility away from business for the social and economic problems facing many communities; "eroding support for education as a public good" (p. 8); and decreasing value placed on equity in education, as market principles increasingly guide educational decisions.

The challenge to educators is to find ways to build on the resources and opportunities offered by relationships with businesses without losing sight of the values and principles of public education, which may not always be consistent with those of the corporate world. While this challenge is great, finding innovative ways to build such relationships between schools and workplaces can serve as bridges to immigrant students as they move beyond high school to work.

Institutions of Higher Education

Relationships between high schools and universities are stronger than those between schools and social service agencies, community-based organizations, or workplaces. The ideal high school student goes on to college before entering the workforce and does not need help from outside agencies along the way. Educators of this ideal student provide academic preparation for college. They know what is expected of students in college from personal experience and from the ongoing contact between high schools and colleges, primarily through the guidance office. The educational system is designed to support this ideal. Therefore, U.S. schools do "a whole lot more to link high school students to college than to work" (Barton, 1990, p. 22) or to other agencies.

"For students from good public or private schools, with the benefit of well-educated middle-class parents, this crossing [from high school to college] may be fraught with anxiety, but it is generally successful" (Ascher, 1988a, p. 1). But few students conform to this ideal, and certainly the lives and needs of most immigrant students are more complex than the ideal assumes. Relationships that do exist between high schools and institutions of higher education must be reconsidered and reconfigured and new types of relationships established to ensure that they work to the benefit of real students.

While school-college collaboratives serve a variety of purposes, they "have become one of the main reform measures directed at improving the school-college transition" (Ascher, 1988a, p. 5). Types of collaboration that can benefit immigrant as well as other low-income minority students include the following:

- college-level study in high school (such as the courses that students at The International High School take at LaGuardia Community College);
- academic counseling for precollege courses;
- college counseling, including college admissions information, orientation sessions, parent conferences, and career information;
- tutoring, mentoring, and skills building provided by college faculty or students;
- campus tours and contact with college students;
- summer remedial or college programs;
- financial aid programs;
- parent involvement programs to encourage support for students going to college;
- teacher development for preparing immigrant and other nontraditional students for college; and
- curriculum development at college and high school levels to facilitate the transition into higher education for immigrant and other nontraditional students.

(Ascher, 1988a; Ascher & Schwartz, 1989)

I describe a number of specific contexts and initiatives in which these types of collaborations take place for the benefit of immigrant students in chapter 6 under *Pathways to Higher Education.*

Conclusion

Given the complexities of secondary immigrant students' lives and educational experiences, the integration of approaches, people, agencies, and resources that can result from building relationships among institutions offers the best possibility for guiding students through the transitions into, through, and beyond U.S. schools. Educators, schools, and school systems must come up with creative ways to build collaborations with health and social service agencies, community-based organizations, businesses, and institutions of higher education. Such collaborations bring together multiple support systems for immigrant families.

To provide guidance to institutions and organizations in developing the kinds of relationships advocated above, Payzant offers the following guidelines for working toward coordinated services:

1. Collaborative efforts should be school-linked, but not necessarily school-governed.
2. The focus should be on the family, not individual family members.
3. Shift as many resources as possible to prevention (rather than remediation).
4. Find ways to fund services with existing resources.
5. There is no one best way.
6. There has to be a catalyst for change.... The leaders need to make their personal involvement a top priority.
7. The people at the table must know a lot about children and families.
8. Focus on where you're going, on long-term results.
9. Don't underestimate the time institutional collaboration takes.
10. Integrating services means changing the whole system, not just one or two agencies.
11. Do not let one (or even two) agencies end up with the bulk of responsibility.

(Institute for Educational Leadership, 1994, pp. 11-13, 21-24)

Obstacles to coordinating services include:

1. Difficulty focusing on prevention when you are in crisis.
2. The lack of clear communication and a common philosophy.
3. Inflexible staff, rigid roles, and limited training.
4. Confidentiality concerns that make it hard to share information.
5. Multiple eligibility requirements.
6. High student mobility.
7. Finding and blending funding across agencies.

(Institute for Educational Leadership, 1994, pp. 15-19)

8. System vs. site-based decision-making (especially in the context of restructuring).
9. Budget cuts that "fuel the sense of urgency to bring in supports from outside agencies" into schools at the same time that they reduce staff in those outside agencies.
10. Lack of clarity in administration of outside agency personnel and programs inside schools.
11. Lack of understanding of how various programs operate.

(Olsen et al., 1994, pp. 144-150)

To increase the likelihood that organizational relationships will support immigrant students in making transitions, educators need to ask the following questions and take steps to adjust practices when the answers indicate that immigrant students are not being well served.

Questions to ask in applying Principle 1: Cultivate organizational relationships.

Language:

1. Do the organizations the school is collaborating with have easy access to people (e.g., staff, volunteers) who can speak immigrant students' languages?

2. Does language have a formal (through rules or policies) or informal (through customs, staffing, unconscious behavior) impact on whether immigrant students and their families can benefit from collaborations between schools and other organizations?

3. Have steps been taken to include immigrants and their families who are not fluent in English in activities associated with the organizations and with the collaborations between them and schools?

4. Do the activities associated with the collaboration support youths in using and learning English without placing them in situations in which they will be judged inadequate or, worse, be harassed because they are not yet fully fluent?

5. Do the activities associated with the collaboration value and build upon immigrant youths' native language abilities?

Educational backgrounds of students and families:

1. Do the organizations and activities associated with them assume that participants have had particular educational experiences (e.g., formal schooling, extensive experience with printed texts, independent learning activities, mentor relationships with teachers)?

2. Are assistance and information provided for those who have not had such experiences?

Immigration experience:

1. Do the organizations have personnel who are knowledgeable about the experiences associated with immigration?

2. Do activities incorporate and value the perspectives of those who have had the experience of immigrating?

3. Are participants in activities required to show proof of citizenship or other formal papers? If so, is this consistent with the law?

Culture and cultural context:

1. Do the organizations have easy access to people (e.g., staff, volunteers) who are from or are familiar with immigrant students' cultures?

2. Do the organizations and activities associated with them incorporate different cultural perspectives and customs?

3. Is the collaboration embedded in formal or informal formats, contexts, or processes that assume familiarity with and understanding of particular customs, expectations, and assumptions that people from other cultures might not be aware of?

4. Does the collaboration incorporate certain expectations with regard to gender roles, family relationships and expectations, age groups, individuality and collectivity, or other culturally variable roles, relationships, and values?

5. Have steps been taken to value and include ways of thinking and behaving that depart from those of the U.S. mainstream in activities associated with the organizations and with the collaborations between them and schools?

Social background and social context:

1. Has the school made serious efforts to build relationships with health and social service agencies, community-based organizations, businesses, institutions of higher education, and other institutions that have a history of working with immigrant communities?

2. Does socioeconomic status have an impact on students' ability to participate in activities (e.g., enrollment or participation fees)?

3. Are activities associated with the collaboration accessible to students who have to work or who have other responsibilities outside of school (e.g., jobs or family responsibilities)?

4. Have steps been taken to value and include ways of talking, thinking, and behaving that depart from those of U.S. natives in activities associated with the organizations and with the collaborations between them and schools?

5. Have steps been taken to include members of the immigrant community in the collaborative activities, when appropriate?

Principle 2: Provide Access to Information

In order to make the transitions into U.S. schools and culture and beyond school to work and higher education, immigrant students and their families must have the information that they need to make the best decisions and to avoid misunderstandings that can impede their progress. In designing schooling and support services for immigrant students and their families, we sometimes overlook the simple and basic fact that they need to be told explicitly about expectations, procedures, customs, and resources that middle-class U.S.-born families take for granted. In fact, access to information gives access to power, as Lisa Delpit has articulated (1988):

If you are not already a participant in the culture of power, being told explicitly the rules of that culture makes acquiring power easier.... When I lived in several Papua New Guinea villages for extended periods to collect data, and when I go to Alaskan villages for work with Alaskan Native communities, I have found it unquestionably easier—psychologically and pragmatically—when some kind soul has directly informed me about such matters as appropriate dress, interactional styles, embedded meanings, and taboo words or actions. I contend that it is much the same for anyone seeking to learn the rules of the culture of power. Unless one has the leisure of a lifetime of "immersion" to learn them, explicit presentation makes learning immeasurably easier. (p. 283)

In other words, we do a great service for people who are unfamiliar with a culture or system—such as immigrants—when we simply tell them what they need to know. Of course, we may not always know what they need to know if we are true insiders to a system that is strange to them. Those who have direct contacts with both insiders and outsiders may be the most effective at deciding what needs to be communicated and how to communicate it—another important role for educators with the same linguistic and cultural backgrounds as the students and families with whom they work.

To make the transitions successfully into their new culture, through the secondary school system, and beyond high school, immigrant students need specific information about U.S. schools and culture, available resources and support services, U.S. workplaces and career preparation, and higher education in the United States.

Information About U.S. Schools and Culture

When they enter the United States and enroll in school, immigrant students are likely to feel lost and confused. They must learn everything, from the daily routines and functions of the school, to the written rules and regulations, to the unwritten expectations and assumptions. Their families have less access to information about schooling than the students themselves, which they need if they are to be productively involved in helping their children move successfully through the educational system. Immigrant students and their parents also need to understand their new culture, both as it relates specifically to schooling and as the backdrop for their new lives in general.

Immigrant students and their families especially need information that will help them make the most of the educational opportunities available to them and keep future options open. They do not have the cultural or social capital to understand the long-range implications of various educational options or to know how best to negotiate the educational system. Immigrant students and their families must be told about the complexities and implications of the tracking system and program options within the system such as vocational education, the honors program, Advanced Placement courses, and career academies. They need to understand how placement decisions are made and by whom. Because it is rarely discussed openly with students, recent immigrants may not realize, for example, that a tracking system exists. In a high-school-based ethnography, which included case studies of four immigrant students from Taiwan and Hong Kong, Harklau (1994c) found that "as newcomers and cultural novices to a school practice that was somewhat covert, individual students varied greatly in their ability to detect and interpret the nature of tracking practices at the school" (p. 233). If the students did come to realize that such a system existed and that their learning opportunities would be improved in higher track classes, they had to undertake "highly strategic negotiations in which they prompted or cajoled school personnel" to move them to higher tracks—negotiations that required "keen observational skills and finesse on the part of students" (p. 235). Few recent immigrant students have such skills in their second language.

Secondary schools and school districts use a number of approaches for providing orientation to and information about U.S. schooling and culture for immigrant students and their families. They include the following:

• Intake and parent information centers;

• Orientation workshops for families;

• Translations of written school documents and orientation materials;

• Ongoing parent workshops and seminars;

• Special orientation classes;

• A transition coordinator or counselor for immigrant students;

• Integration of orientation information into ESL or content classes for immigrant students;

• Field trips;

• Pairing recent immigrant students with other students.

Each of these approaches is briefly described below.

A school or district **intake center** or **parent information center** "can be an effective first point of contact with the school system" for immigrant students and their families (Violand-Sánchez, Sutton, & Ware, 1991, p. 8). Bilingual staff can assist with registration, assessment, and placement of students and can provide oral and written information to parents when they first enter the school system and on an ongoing basis. Center staff can perform a variety of functions, including translating and interpreting, conducting workshops and programs for parents and students, and making referrals to other agencies and individuals.

Whether conducted by intake center staff or other bilingual staff, **orientation workshops for families** can provide information that they have no other way of obtaining. Workshops held in the summer before school starts, at the beginning of the school year, and throughout a school year can inform families about school rules, procedures, and expectations regarding such issues as discipline, attendance, homework, grading, extracurricular activities, special support services, and ways the families can work together with the school. Organizations such as META (Multicultural Education Training and Advocacy), which has offices in several states, can conduct workshops on parents' rights in the United States. Family English literacy projects (described in chapter 5 under *Relationships Between Educators and Families*) include such workshops in their design.

Translations of written school documents and orientation materials into the languages of immigrant students and their families serve as another medium for providing information. Because some students and their parents may not be literate in their native language, schools should not rely solely on the translation of written documents for transmitting information, however. An orientation video in the home languages of students and their families provides another medium through which parents can learn about procedures, expectations, and opportunities. Prince George's County, Maryland, has made a video that is presented in several different languages, which parents can watch while their children are going through the intake center process.

Parents can learn a lot about school and schooling through **ongoing parent workshops and seminars**, such as family English literacy projects (discussed in chapter 5 under *Relationships Between Educators and Families*). Most family literacy projects include information to help parents learn about and adapt to U.S. culture and schooling while familiarizing them with ways to help their children succeed in school and promoting the development of relationships between parents and school staff.

Some schools, especially newcomer schools, offer **special orientation classes** to acquaint recent immigrant students with the school and the community. Topics such classes typically cover include the following (Chang, 1990, p. 12):

- School Environment: the classroom, the playground, the cafeteria, the library, using the restroom, testing and grading procedures, class schedules, the school calendar, graduation requirements, school personnel
- Foods/Nutrition
- Weather/Seasons/Holidays
- Home/Family
- The Community: parks, medical services, stores, restaurants
- Transportation: riding the bus, using public transportation, driving a car
- Career Options

Dade County's (Florida) New Beginnings Program, for teenage immigrants "without basic skills," offers orientation to the "history, key institutions, main geographic features, labor market, and transportation opportunities" in the local community. Students visit locations and practice using public transportation and other services (McDonnell & Hill, 1993, p. 78).

Having **a transition coordinator or counselor** at a high school can give recent immigrants access to information when they arrive through one person whose job it is to facilitate this difficult transition. After failing to receive funding for a Title VII newcomer school, the district office and ESL coordinators in White Plains (New York) decided that hiring a person to coordinate the initial transition of immigrant students into the high school would at least provide some assistance that the newcomer school was intended to provide. The coordinator meets with entering newcomer students to give them an orientation to the school and the educational system and continues to provide support during their first months at the school.

Rather than offering special classes, some schools **integrate orientation information into ESL or content classes**. An ESL class may be organized around content that provides information about the school, the community, and the larger society. A social studies class may focus on local and regional current events as a way of informing students.

Field trips to learn about aspects of U.S. culture and the local community may be conducted as part of a particular course or as a separate school activity for newcomers.

Pairing recent immigrant students with bilingual peers, peers who are studying their native language as a foreign language (e.g., English-speaking students in Spanish foreign language classes)**, and with other English-speaking students** can be effective ways to ensure access to information. In addition, these approaches can promote cross-cultural understanding and facilitate the development of relationships among students. Through such a buddy system, newcomer students can get information quickly, from the point of view of someone closer to their own experience, in a context that may be less threatening than asking an adult. The U.S.-born buddies must be carefully selected and prepared to ensure that they are sensitive to the uncertainties, confusions, and needs of immigrant students. If not, they can exacerbate immigrant students' feelings of alienation.

• *Pairing newly arrived students with more experienced bilingual immigrant students* has several advantages. Language differences do not interfere with communication. The more experienced students have been immigrants themselves and can therefore empathize with new students and anticipate many of their questions and problems. The similarity of experiences may help new students feel more comfortable asking questions. A connection with bilingual immigrant peers may reduce the feelings and the fact of isolation for newly arrived students.

• *Pairing immigrant students with English-speaking students who are studying their native language* has the advantage of providing both participants with one-on-one opportunities to speak the language that they are learning. The benefit is clear for the English-speaking students, who generally have little opportunity to speak with native speakers of whatever language they are studying. Immigrant students also benefit from the opportunity to interact with an English-speaking peer, because they may be in few classes with English-speaking students, and, even in those classes where they do encounter English speakers, they may rarely speak directly with them.

• It is advisable to *pair only those recent immigrants who are more proficient in English with monolingual English-speaking peers,* because difficulties in communicating may cause frustration and isolation.

These approaches can promote cross-cultural understanding as well as provide immigrant students with access to information. Such buddy systems can involve ongoing contact between the students or can take place on a more limited basis. For example, through a cultural exchange program involving San Francisco's Newcomer High School and four other high schools in Northern California, students attend a seminar "exploring cultural diversity, pluralism, and discrimination," then spend a day at each other's schools, homes, and communities (Chang, 1990, p. 14).

Information About Resources and Support Services Available

Information about resources and support services available in the school and the community can also facilitate the transitions into, through, and beyond school. "Parents [and other family members] unfamiliar with the community and unable to speak English find navigating the system tremendously difficult," observes Chang (1990, p. 14). They need information about what services and assistance are available and how to gain access to them. Most communities have agencies and organizations that provide assistance to immigrants. These groups can help to demystify the complex system that immigrants are encountering for the first time and provide crucial assistance for many as they adjust to their new lives.

Social service agencies, public hospitals, community health centers, and migrant health centers provide mental and physical health services for immigrants and refugees (see Dunlap & Hutchinson, 1994), who may be especially vulnerable to mental and physical health problems if they have lived in poverty, led traumatic lives before immigrating, and encountered difficulties during immigration. Federal, state, and local employment agencies and some community-based organizations (CBOs) provide job training and placement. While federal funding for social services of all sorts has been drastically reduced in recent years, federal programs that continue to provide some job training for immigrants and refugees include the Job Training and Partnership Act (JTPA), Job Opportunities and Basic Skills Training Program (JOBS), and the domestic resettlement assistance program administered through the Office of Refugee Resettlement (see Morse, 1994). Nonprofit groups such as META provide legal assistance to immigrants about the processes and pitfalls of immigration. Schools, adult education programs, churches, and other organizations provide tutoring, ESL, and other special courses to students and families.

Schools can make information about these resources and services available through many of the mechanisms described above. Educators can include such information in intake center interviews, orientation workshops, and seminars. They can take students on field trips to visit such agencies. They can make directories and brochures available to students and families in English and in other languages. Perhaps the most effective way to get the information across is through collaborations with the agencies and organizations that provide the services, as described in chapter 3. When immigrants have had contact with people in the agencies rather than simply hearing or reading about their services, they are more likely to approach the agency for assistance and information. When school personnel have direct contact with people from other agencies, they learn what assistance is available and how to help families gain access to it (see Olsen et al., 1994).

Information About U.S. Workplaces and Career Preparation

Immigrant students need information not only to support their transition into U.S. schooling and culture, but also to assist them in making the transition to the world of work after high school. While all U.S. students, especially those who do not plan to pursue higher education, would benefit from more assistance in preparing for employment after high school, immigrant students are especially lacking in information. Specifically, they need to know about expectations of employers in the United States (e.g., uses of time, standards of dress, norms of interaction); possible careers and preparation needed for each; and processes for finding and applying for jobs, including filling out job applications, preparing a resume, and being interviewed.

While school-to-work programs of all sorts give students some information about U.S. workplaces, strategies designed specifically for providing this information to immigrant students include the following:

- workshops;
- field trips;
- career guidance programs; and
- career education programs.

Workshops can be offered by counseling departments to acquaint students with careers and provide assistance in preparing for the workforce. To be most effective with immigrant students, counselors conducting such workshops should be bilingual and aware of the special obstacles immigrants face, such as lack of familiarity with cultural expectations and lack of proficiency in English.

Just as **field trips** can help students learn about U.S. culture, they can also help them gain information about careers. Visiting a work site, observing people at work, and having a chance to ask questions gives immigrants a firsthand look at real workplaces they are not likely to get any other way.

Career guidance "seeks to help individuals learn about their options, explore their interests, and develop a plan to achieve their occupational goals" (U.S. Department of Labor, 1993, p. 1). One of the goals of a career guidance program is to provide "easily accessible, current, relevant and unbiased" information, which can "provide a solid framework on which to base decisions" (p. 6). Effective career guidance programs are (1) comprehensive (including development of self-knowledge and self-awareness, exploration of careers through gathering of information and experience, and decision-making and career planning); (2) developmental (offering age- and grade-appropriate guidance); (3) competency based (building on what participants know and can do as they develop competency; (4) integrated (connecting education and work); and (5) experiential (p. 44). Unfortunately, few such career guidance programs exist—partly because of the greater emphasis placed on college counseling in secondary schools and partly because of the insufficient numbers of counselors in most schools.

A formal program in career education offers the opportunity for students to devote time within the curriculum and therefore the school day to learning about careers and preparing for work. Project MAINE (Maine Assists Innovators in Nurturing Excellence), a Title VII Academic Excellence program, is an example of a career awareness curriculum. The program "combines a career awareness curriculum with English as a Second Language (ESL) and native language materials" in six languages (National Coalition of Advocates for Students, 1994, p. 32). Secondary bilingual students are introduced to a variety of careers and engaged in activities to learn about those careers and to explore their interests and skills related to each. Students attend classes three times a week and receive additional counseling and assistance as needed. The career education component of The International High School curriculum, which illustrates another such approach, is described in detail in chapter 6 under *Pathways to the World of Work*.

Information About Higher Education

The college preparation, selection, application, and matriculation process can be daunting to all young people and their families. Even U.S.-born, educated, middle-class families spend a great deal of time and effort (not to mention money) in ensuring that their children have access to relevant and necessary information and assistance. Many native-born students as well as immigrants need greater access to information about higher education.

Many middle and high school students … see little connection between their school behavior and later opportunities for college. In this case the problem is more likely to be an absence of knowledge by students of college admissions processes than a need for better information by colleges about their student applicants. Students often do not know the required courses they need to take during the middle and high school grades to qualify for college admissions in major fields that can lead to a chosen career. Students in these grades may also discount entrance into many more selective colleges because they are unaware of available sources of financial aid. Such lack of knowledge prevents students from seeing the current relevance of working hard in challenging courses to earn admission to more selective colleges or to preferred major fields. (Legters et al., 1993, p. 76)

Immigrants need such information and assistance all the more. Because higher education systems differ markedly in different countries, even educated immigrants must learn how to prepare their children to go to universities in this country and to enroll them. For those who are not educated themselves, who do not speak English, and who have few economic resources, the system has traditionally been even more opaque and unfriendly. With likely decreases in financial support from student loans and other programs of financial assistance, immigrant students will find the cost of higher education in the United States an ever greater obstacle.

Approaches must be developed, first to reach those who most need the information, then to inform them about

• the educational system in this country;

- the various options that families and youths have and where those options will lead them (e.g., the community college system vs. the university system);
- the preparation required to gain access to the various options;
- strategies for getting that preparation (e.g., how to negotiate the tracking system; see Harklau, 1994b); and
- all the details and complexities of selecting a college and applying for higher education.

As with information about the world of work, all U.S. youths would benefit from such explicit information about higher education. But immigrants and their families are especially vulnerable to being locked out of the system without such information.

Some programs for immigrants and other underrepresented students incorporate such information in their activities. The Advancement Via Individual Determination (AVID) program places "underachieving" linguistic and ethnic minority students in college preparatory programs and provides them the academic and social support necessary for them to succeed (see Mehan et al., 1992; Mehan et al., 1993; Swanson, Mehan, & Hubbard, 1995). Making sure that students know what they need to know to get into college is a central feature of the program: "By far the most prevalent activity in the four AVID classes we studied during the 1991-92 school year revolved around the college application process" (Mehan et al., 1993, pp. 27-28). This is part of AVID's "explicit socialization process" in which staff explicitly teach "the implicit culture of the classroom and overtly expose students to the hidden curriculum of the school" (Mehan et al., 1992, p. 12).

AVID and many other such programs

- take students to colleges and universities to familiarize them with the context, people, and activities there;

- bring in college representatives, often minority young people themselves, to talk to students;
- assist students in selecting and applying for college and financial aid; and
- follow up on students for some period of time after they enter college to provide support in the initial period of adjustment.

I describe some of these programs in more detail in chapter 6 under *Pathways to Higher Education.*

Conclusion

The strategies described above provide various means for giving newly arrived immigrant students and their families much of the information they need to become successfully integrated into the U.S. school system and to make their way through and beyond secondary school. In determining what approaches to use, educators would do well to assume that immigrants know very little about the complex educational system in the United States, that they are eager to learn all they can, and that the more opportunities and the more varied the opportunities available, the more likely they will get the information they need. Because immigrants differ with respect to educational background, degree of familiarity with U.S. schools and culture, native language, native culture, and many other factors, schools and school districts need to develop multiple strategies for getting information across. Thus, having an intake center where parents receive an orientation to the school system does not preclude having parent workshops, establishing a family literacy project, and translating all materials into other languages. Nor does sending out all announcements in Spanish assure that all Spanish speakers get the information they need.

Without access to information, immigrant students and their families must spend unnecessary energy trying to accomplish what could be simpler tasks, and they miss out on important services and events that could support their educational and personal progress. They are, in effect, denied the access to the culture of power that invisibly paves the way for the children of native-born, middle-class, educated people through the educational and employment systems. The simple principle of making explicit the implicit and unfamiliar can have far-reaching effects on immigrants' adjustment to U.S. culture and schooling and on their progress through and beyond high school. By explicitly socializing immigrant students into the ways of the United States, we can demystify many confusing and opaque systems and processes, giving students the power to make choices for their own lives.

The following questions can help to ensure that issues of special relevance to immigrant youths and their families are taken into account in designing strategies for providing information to them.

Questions to ask in applying Principle 2: Provide access to information.

Language:

1. Does language have a formal (through rules or policies) or informal (through customs, staffing, unconscious behavior) impact on whether immigrant students and their families have access to information?

2. Is information provided in the native languages of students and their families?

3. Are suggestions made for ways students and their families can gain access to further information in their native languages?

4. Is information provided about the role that language can play in students' progress into, through, and beyond school (e.g., professions in which a non-English accent would be a barrier)?

5. Is information provided about ways students can capitalize on their native language in making transitions into, through, and beyond school (e.g., studying international relations or international business in college)?

Educational backgrounds of students and families:

1. Does the format in which information is provided make it accessible to students and family members who may not have completed many years of schooling (e.g., in video as well as written formats; through personal interactions)?

2. Is information provided about the educational expectations and requirements in making transitions into, through, and beyond school?

3. Is information provided about alternative ways for secondary students and their families to gain further education?

4. Is information provided about alternative pathways beyond school for those whose educational preparation does not allow them to take the most common routes (e.g., information about the GED, adult education programs, vocational schools)?

Immigration experience:

1. Is information available to help immigrants in the process of immigration and adjustment to their new country?

2. Is information provided about special benefits available for immigrants (e.g., scholarships) and obstacles that immigrants face (e.g., citizenship) in making the transitions into, through, and beyond school in the United States?

Culture and cultural context:

1. Is information provided about specific customs, expectations, and assumptions related to successfully negotiating transitions (e.g., how to approach an employer and how to present oneself in an interview)?

2. Is information provided about potential differences between such customs, expectations, and assumptions in students' native cultures and U.S. culture?

3. Is every effort made to ensure that comparisons between U.S. culture and other cultures are accurate and unbiased?

4. Is information provided in formats and contexts and through processes that are consistent with customs and expectations of the cultures of students and their families?

5. Is information provided by the people who are most knowledgeable of cultural expectations and assumptions with regard to the content of the information, the format for presenting information, and the appropriate recipients of the information?

Social background and social context:

1. Is information provided that is accessible and useful to students of all socioeconomic backgrounds (e.g., information on student loans)?

2. Is information provided in ways that show respect for immigrants?

3. Does socioeconomic status have an impact on students' access to information (e.g., information that requires students to use computers to gain access)?

Principle 3: Cultivate Human Relationships

"The need to find a place in a valued group that provides a sense of belonging" is a "fundamental human need" (Nightingale & Wolverton, 1993, p. 15). The groups we belong to provide both support as we make decisions and face challenges in our lives and the frame within which we develop our identities and roles. Adolescents, no less than others, need relationships "both to primary groups such as family and friends and to more formal organizations such as schools and human-service agencies" (Price et al., 1993, p. 35). They need "to experience secure relationships with a few human beings [and] to be a valued member of groups that provide mutual aid and caring relationships" (Takanishi, 1993, p. 1). They "need the support of important, meaningful people" (Comer, 1993, p. 203). In other words, relationships are central to healthy adolescent development.

It should be no surprise, then, that relationships are also central to positive schooling experiences for adolescents and especially for adolescents who are not part of the mainstream socioeconomic structures (see Braddock & McPartland, 1993; Lee et al., 1993; MacIver, 1990; Maeroff, 1990; Natriello et al., 1990). A parent who was also a school board member in a suburban school district captured the crucial role that teacher–student relationships can play:

My daughter had a wonderful experience at [the high school]. That experience hinged around a few teachers with whom she was able to go past the normal student–teacher relationship and develop a friendship that transcended what they were supposed to be teaching. They provided a refuge for her—comfort, support, caring about her as a person. I don't know how to institutionalize that. Those teachers were people who liked and respected kids, who didn't see them as problems, worries, threats. If each teacher could have a relationship with 5 to 10 kids, it would be a much better system. It's something to strive for, especially in a big impersonal high school. We need teachers to deal with kids as human beings, just making themselves available outside of class. (personal communication, April 26, 1995)

Our "methods fetish" and our concentration on "technical" issues in discussions of minority student achievement (Bartolomé, 1994) generally preclude the explicit examination of the role of relationships in schooling. When we do give attention to relationships, we seem more likely to focus on the negative impact of peer pressure or the assumed lack of parental support and guidance than on the positive influence relationships can play in the lives of youths. However, methods, programs, subject matter, technology, school structures, decision-making procedures—elements of schooling that receive considerable attention and resources—form the backdrop within which relationships exist and are the vehicles that either impede or support the development of relationships.

Relationships emerged as the dominant issue in a study of four diverse urban and suburban schools in Southern California (Poplin & Weeres, 1992). When participants in various role groups (including custodians, secretaries, and cafeteria workers as well as teachers, administrators, students, and parents) were invited to "articulate the problems of schooling" through an ongoing series of interviews and discussions, they identified "human relationships" as the key element linked to "the crisis inside schools.... No group inside the schools felt adequately respected, connected or affirmed" (Poplin & Weeres, 1992, pp. 11-12). Indeed, "all too often ... schools represent a ... social environment ... in which close ties to teachers are never established, where enduring relationships with peers are difficult to maintain, and where the school represents a setting for failure rather than success" (Price et al., 1993, p. 32). Students "long for more caring classrooms and schools" (Wheelock, 1993, p. 37).

Although relatively little attention is given explicitly to relationships and few program descriptions highlight them as factors in their success, relationships stand out as central to facilitating transitions for immigrant youths, who experience high degrees of cultural, linguistic, and social disconnectedness. Developing relationships means getting to know immigrant students as individuals and learning about the real lives of particular students. When we are ignorant of the past and present experiences of immigrant students, we tend to stereotype them according to generalizations that may or may not apply to individuals.

We need to balance our knowledge of students as individuals and our understanding of them as members of social and cultural groups. Ignorance of students' social and cultural milieus can lead to serious miscommunication in the classroom, while complete reliance on social and cultural facts in interactions with students can lead to equally unproductive stereotyping.... For example, knowing that social interaction and cooperation is highly valued in many Latin cultures may encourage us to use cooperative grouping to good effect in activities involving Latino students. However, if we always use cooperative groups with Latino students, those who prefer to work alone on some tasks may be deprived of success in those activities. (Lucas & Schecter, 1992, p. 90)

If we get to know students as individuals, we will have a clearer and more accurate understanding of their concerns, needs, questions, strengths, and aspirations. We can understand the ways in which each student departs from the assumed norm (i.e., White, middle-class, native-English-speaking, U.S.-born, etc.). We know where to start to provide them with some of the social and cultural capital that they lack for successfully navigating the U.S. educational system. We may not have experienced the stress of a young immigrant woman who wants to go to college in another city while her parents will not even consider the possibility, for example. But if we know that she is struggling with this conflict in roles and expectations, we can try to find ways to support her and her family in the struggle.

In order to provide useful and appropriate assistance to students through their transitions as immigrants into U.S. schools and culture, we need to know where they are starting from. Information obtainable from intake interviews can give teachers, counselors, and bilingual/ESL coordinators a good basis for initial assistance. Other information and understandings come more easily from talking with students over a period of time. Getting to know students and know about them is also essential in helping immigrant students plan for their futures beyond secondary school. Students from economically comfortable families with strong academic backgrounds can realistically aspire to attend competitive universities even if they are not proficient in English when they arrive, while students with the same initial English proficiency but few economic resources and little previous schooling will have more academic difficulty. Maria Escalante, a teacher of the career preparation curriculum at The International High School, recognizes that although they should be encouraged to have high aspirations, students need to be realistic in their planning. Students not literate in some language—either their own or English—when they enter high school cannot realistically expect to become pediatricians, at least not within the usual time frame in an English-based curriculum. Counselors, teachers, bilingual/ESL coordinators, career education teachers, and anyone else who is in a position to advise immigrant students about their future plans should know each student's background, including strengths, weaknesses, obstacles, and resources. With that information, they can help the students to plan realistically and to seek assistance and support in those areas in which they need them.

Figure 6 presents the human relationships that are of most importance for helping secondary immigrant students make the transitions into, through, and beyond school.

Figure 6. Human Relationships Essential to Facilitating Transitions

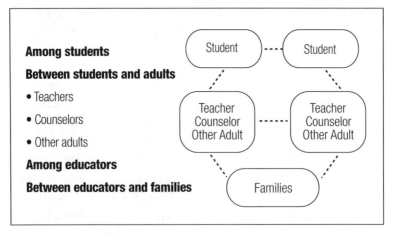

Relationships Between Immigrant Students and Adults

"It seems clear that all youth need to develop strong one-on-one relationships with adults in their communities, schools, and work environments" (Nightingale & Wolverton, 1993, p. 24). When adolescent immigrant students leave their home countries and enter U.S. schools and culture, they experience linguistic and cultural displacement and disorientation. Language shock and culture shock, to varying degrees, interfere with their learning. They must use so much energy trying to maintain, adapt, and develop their identities in their new cultural and linguistic contexts that their concentration, efficiency, and in some cases motivation to learn in school are diminished. One of the best ways to support students through this difficult period of adjustment is to cultivate personal relationships with them. Teachers and others in the school setting need to interact with students and with each other, which means that structures and forums must be in place to allow time and opportunities for the development of human relationships.

Immigrant students also need the support and assistance of adults and more experienced peers who can help them successfully negotiate the transition from high school to beyond. All youths in the United States need better guidance through this period than they receive, and especially so immigrant youths, who, along with poor and minority students, "have access to few resources or information networks to obtain mainstream jobs that lead to meaningful careers" (Glover & Marshall, 1993, p. 135). If immigrant students plan to go to college, most also need guidance through the unfamiliar system of selection, application, and matriculation. Without caring and committed adults to see them through this period, many of them get lost along the way.

Adults need to know about immigrant students' languages, linguistic contexts, educational backgrounds, experiences of immigration, cultures, cultural contexts, social backgrounds, and social contexts in order to fully understand students' behavior, to facilitate their adjustment to their new culture, and to assist them in moving into, through, and beyond school. While adults in schools already know the answers to many of the questions presented in Figure 7 for U.S.-born, middle-class students, they must ask them of immigrant students.

Figure 7. What Adults Need to Know About Immigrant Students

A. Language and Linguistic Context

1. What is the student's native language?
2. To what extent is the student proficient in his or her native language (considering both oral and literate proficiency)?
3. To what extent is the student proficient in English (considering both oral and literate proficiency)?
4. What characterizes the linguistic context in the student's family?
   (a) Which languages are used? By whom?
   (b) What functions do different languages serve (e.g., interpersonal communication, religious activities, work)?
5. What characterizes the larger linguistic context in which the student lives?
   (a) Does the student live within a larger community where the native language is spoken? Written?
   (b) What attitudes toward non-English languages is the student likely to encounter?
   (c) What attitudes toward the native language is the student likely to encounter?

B. Educational Background

1. How many years of schooling has the student had
   (a) in the native country?
   (b) in the United States?
2. Has the student's schooling been interrupted at any point(s)?
3. What has been the quality of the student's schooling
   (a) in the native country?
   (b) in the United States?
4. How did the student's schooling in the native country compare with schooling in the United States in terms of
   (a) content and subjects taught?
   (b) instructional strategies used?
   (c) roles and relationships of teachers and students?
   (d) expectations of girls and boys?

Figure 7. What Adults Need to Know About Immigrant Students (continued)

5. What is the educational and literacy background of the student's parents?
6. What is the tradition of schooling and literacy in the social and cultural group of which the student is a member?

C. Immigration Experience

1. At what age did the student arrive in the United States?
2. Where is the student from?
3. What was life like in the native country?
4. Why did the student come to the United States?
5. Has the student suffered from trauma or violence?
6. Did the student leave loved ones behind in the native country?

D. Culture and Cultural Context

1. What are key norms, customs, expectations, and assumptions of the student's culture?
2. How do those norms, customs, expectations, and assumptions differ from those of U.S. culture?
3. Given those differences, what information does the student need in order to navigate successfully the transitions he or she is facing?

E. Social Background and Social Context

1. What is the socioeconomic situation of the student and family?
2. With whom does the student live?
3. What roles does the student play in the family (e.g., caring for younger siblings on a regular basis)?
4. What work did the parents do in their home countries?
5. Does the student have adult responsibilities?
6. What are the attitudes toward immigrants in the U.S. context in which the student lives?
7. What are the attitudes toward immigrants from the student's particular country or culture in the U.S. context in which the student lives?
8. Does the student live within a larger community of people from the same country or culture?
9. What support services for immigrants are available in the locale where the student lives?

Relationships With Teachers

In schools, teachers are the most important adults for students. In the study of California schools mentioned above, the relationship between students and teachers "dominated the students' feelings about school"; students reported that they liked school when teachers showed that they cared (Poplin & Weeres, 1992, p. 19; see also Lucas et al., 1990). Indeed, the student–teacher relationship is the central relationship in schooling. When teachers take the time to build relationships with students, when they develop personal knowledge of and connections with students, when they show respect for and interest in students, they help to humanize the secondary school experience, mitigating against the impersonal, alienating relationships that characterize traditional secondary schools. These teachers' efforts do not go unnoticed by students, who acknowledge them by such comments as, "The teachers here don't just teach; they care about you" (Lucas et al., 1990, p. 336).

Teachers act as mentors and advisors for students, both formally and informally. The role of George Castellanos in the WISE (WISE Individualized Senior Experience) program at New Rochelle (New York) High School illustrates the profound impact that access to a formal mentor can have on immigrant students' experiences. In two years, he mentored 20 Spanish-speaking students as they developed, carried out, and made presentations on independent senior year projects, including internships, creative projects, and research projects (see the description of the WISE program in chapter 6 under *Adapting School-to-Work Pathways for Immigrant Students*). At Central Park East School in Manhattan, not only do students in the middle and high school "stay with the same small cluster of teachers for at least two years," but each student also "has a principal advisor who knows him or her and his or her family well" (Meier, 1993, p. 201). At Nogales (Arizona) High School, teachers who receive special training volunteer to act as mentors for students who are having academic and attendance problems.

Teachers who share students' cultural and linguistic backgrounds are more likely than others to have the commitment, sensitivity, and knowledge to develop successful relationships with the students. In addition, "the personal insight that teachers of color have about racial and ethnic inequalities in the United States allows them to establish special relationships with students from non-dominant groups" (Villegas, in press, p. 310). Some schools and districts have made it a priority to recruit and hire such teachers, even if it means seeking them in distant states and providing extra incentives (see Lucas, 1992).

Some structures support the development of these kinds of relationships more than others. Teams, clusters, schools-within-schools, advisories, and other organizational innovations in secondary schools allow the time and contact required for student–teacher relationships to develop. Many secondary schools are altering the school structure to decrease the number of students that each teacher interacts with and to increase the amount of time students spend with each teacher. They are, in effect, decreasing the size of the educational unit for students and teachers. In some cases, these smaller units have their own administrators, functioning more independently of the larger school (e.g., at Central Park East in Manhattan and South Shore High School in Brooklyn), and in some cases they function as groups of teachers, still within the larger school administrative structure (e.g., The International High School).

At The International High School, for example, groups of approximately 75 students stay together the whole day and work with the same four to eight staff members throughout a trimester. This minischool design is "very comforting." It provides a "family atmosphere" for students and allows "closer relationships" between teachers and students. "Teachers feel very responsible for the students, and students feel responsible for themselves and each other." This approach "takes the kids who come in very frightened from all over the world with all sorts of varying baggage and experiences" and helps them feel comfortable and ready to learn (C. Glassman, teacher, personal communication, October 28, 1994). The prototype of the clusters at International is the *Motion Program*, which combines a literature course, a combined math and physics course, and an indoor version of Outward Bound called

Project Adventure, all focused on the theme of motion (Ancess & Darling-Hammond, 1994). Besides the greater opportunities for relationships resulting from the high teacher-to-student ratio, the program itself fosters relationships among students.

Many of the activities involve students working in groups on experiments that reveal and test the laws of motion.... In literature, students create a science fiction story that demonstrates … their understanding of key concepts from … physics and mathematics.... Project Adventure allows physical expressions of the laws of motion and emotion … while building trust and teamwork among students. (Ancess & Darling-Hammond, 1994, pp. 7-8)

Some organizational structures designed specifically for bilingual students support the development of relationships. In some schools, bilingual students have a home base where they have access to bilingual teachers (McDonnell & Hill, 1993, p. 66). This may take the form of a bilingual home room, a bilingual house within a larger school, or a program or office designed specifically for bilingual students and staffed with bilingual personnel. These arrangements are especially helpful to students making the transition into a new culture and school system. They provide a temporal and spatial buffer between newly arrived immigrant students and the larger school population, which may not respond with great sensitivity to newcomers. At the same time, they separate immigrant students from the rest of the school, increasing their isolation and reducing their exposure to native-English-speaking models. Therefore, opportunities should be provided outside the cluster or house structure for the development of relationships with other students. Seward Park High School in Manhattan is divided into "houses" of approximately 300 students each. Similar to The International High School's "clusters," they give students greater access to teachers and, in effect, decrease the size of the educational unit. At Seward Park, three houses are designated for bilingual/ESL students who require ESL and content classes in Chinese or specially designed academic instruction in English. Horace Mann Middle School in San Francisco uses the designation "families" for the small groupings of students and teachers providing integrated thematic instruction. There are Spanish and Chinese bilingual families where students receive support and instruction in their native languages.

O'Farrell Community School: Center for Advanced Academic Studies in San Diego (described in Olsen et al., 1994, pp. 154-158), a multiethnic, multilingual middle school, comprises 9 educational families, each with 6 teachers and approximately 150 students. Though this arrangement already provides small groupings that allow for the development of relationships, the school has added another forum for personal interaction and for "addressing the social and emotional needs of students ... : the home-base classroom where each student spends the first 25 minutes and the last 10 minutes of the school day" (p. 155). Each student's home-base teacher acts as the "primary adult advocate" (p. 155), providing counseling and facilitating the development of personal skills. One teacher said, "Home-base allows me to be much closer to the kids" (quoted in Olsen et al., 1994, p. 156).

Student Relationships With Counselors

The relationship between secondary students and counselors is also a central one. Counselors function as gatekeepers (Erickson & Schultz, 1982) for secondary students with regard both to the classes they are allowed and encouraged to take in high school and to the options they pursue beyond high school—which, of course, are intricately related. Given the power they have to limit or expand students' future horizons, counselors need to know and care about students in order to help them make carefully considered decisions about course selection, activities, and future plans. They could also help immigrant students make the adjustment into a new culture, if they had the time and knowledge to do so. Unfortunately, the student-to-counselor ratio and the multitude of responsibilities that counselors have make it impossible for them to develop relationships with students in most schools.

There is approximately one counselor for every 600 students in U.S. public schools, and indications are that students do not develop relationships with them (Dryfoos, 1993, p. 83). With regard to postsecondary planning, counselors spend most of their time and energy helping students select and apply to college; relatively little attention is given to assisting students who are not going directly to college (see Barton, 1990, pp. 23-24). More time and attention also goes to students closer to graduation than to younger students, though the groundwork must be laid early if students are to achieve their full potential (see Wheelock, 1993, pp. 32-35).

In a study of secondary schools that were "taking identifiable, positive steps to educate l[anguage] m[inority] students" (Lucas et al., 1990, p. 320), we found that the counselors were described as "key to [students'] adjustment to the new environment and to their clarification of future goals" (pp. 331-332). Language minority students were given access to counselors who spoke their languages and were either from the same cultural backgrounds or were knowledgeable of those backgrounds. These counselors developed relationships with students and, in many cases, with their families as well. Counselors also play a central role in Project Adelante at Kean College in New Jersey, established to increase Latino students' graduation rates (Vaznaugh, 1995; see description of Project Adelante in chapter 6 under *Pathways to Higher Education*). Counselors who are Latino themselves spend considerable time with students in group and individual settings addressing personal and academic issues.

One particular context—the newcomer school—does offer counselors more opportunities to get to know students and to provide personal counseling than does the comprehensive secondary school. Designed to provide a temporary "safe haven" for recently arrived immigrants (Chang, 1990, p. 9) before they enter regular schools, newcomer schools concentrate on helping students learn English, learn about U.S. culture and schooling, and gain access to health and social services as well as continue their academic development (see description of newcomer schools in chapter 6 under *Pathways Into U.S. Schooling and Culture*). Because the curriculum is generally more limited and standardized for all students and because students go from the newcomer school to a regular high school, course selection and college counseling are not the counselors' major responsibilities. Instead, they can spend more time getting to know students and helping them with social and psychological adjustment to the new culture and schools. A counselor at Newcomer High School in San Francisco said, "I wear many hats; at times I'm a mother, a referral service to agencies, and I may have to be a comedian when needed" (Lucas et al., 1990, p. 334).

Student Relationships With Other Adults

Adults other than teachers and counselors can and do provide "the support of meaningful, important adults" that youths need (Comer, 1993, p. 203). These other adults include instructional assistants (Weiss, 1994), bilingual/ESL coordinators (Lucas, 1992), coordinators and directors of various student activities and programs (such as Malula González, director of the Pace Hispanic Outreach Program at White Plains High School, described below; the staff and coordinator of the AVID program, described in chapter 6 under *Pathways to Higher Education*; see also Lucas et al., 1990; National Coalition of Advocates for Students, 1994), community agency and social service agency personnel (Price et al., 1993), community liaisons (such as George Castellanos, the Hispanic Liaison in New Rochelle High School, described in chapter 6 under *Pathways to the World of Work*), workplace supervisors in apprenticeships and internships (such as those with whom The International High School students work), college students, and community members (such as the resource people who sponsor student projects in the WISE program, described in detail in chapter 6 under *Pathways to the World of Work*). Many of these adults act as mentors for youths, each participating in

a supportive relationship between a youth or young adult and someone more senior in age and experience, who offers support, guidance, and concrete assistance as the younger partner goes through a difficult period, enters a new area of experience, takes on an important task, or corrects an earlier problem. (Flaxman, Ascher, & Harrington, 1988, p. ii)

Such relationships occur naturally between adults and students in a school context and through planned structures that establish opportunities and expectations for mentoring (see Flaxman et al., 1988; Flaxman & Ascher, 1992; Gallimore, Tharp, & John-Steiner, 1992, for discussions of "natural" vs. "planned" mentoring). Youths in transition are especially in need of such relationships. Indeed, "the heart of natural or spontaneous mentoring has always been assistance during a period of transition—from childhood into adolescence, from adolescence into young adulthood, or from novice into expert in the world of work" (Flaxman & Ascher, 1992, p. 4). Planned relationships with older people, such as tutoring, internships, advising, and student clubs and organizations, provide structures through which such assistance can be provided even if it does not take place naturally.

At many secondary schools, bilingual and immigrant students cluster around one office at lunch time, during breaks, and before and after school. This office is usually staffed by someone who is bilingual, but it may also be an ESL teacher or ESL program coordinator. During the 10 minutes I was in George Castellanos' office in the basement of New Rochelle (New York) High School in November 1994, three Latina students came by to say hello. While I was talking to Malula González at White Plains (New York) High School about the Pace Hispanic Outreach Program, I could hear students talking quietly in Spanish in the small room next door. When I was talking with Katharine Sid at Seward Park High School in Manhattan in the Title VII program office, several Chinese students were there. A few years ago when I visited the bilingual office at Gilroy (California) High School, several students came and went and hung around, apparently because they felt at home there. I can think of numerous other occasions when I have observed students hanging around bilingual/ESL offices and resource centers in secondary schools, another version of the "home base." *Ahora: A Bridge to the Future* (described in National Coalition of Advocates for Students, 1994, p. 53ff) is one such place, a "multifaceted resource center" for Latino students at Cambridge (Massachusetts) Rindge and Latin High School. Housed in a large room in the school, the center offers substance abuse counseling, general counseling, higher education counseling, tutoring, mentorship, recreational activities, and cultural activities.

The fact that many immigrant students cluster together around such places indicates that they feel welcomed by the adults who work there. It can also signal an invisibility in and isolation from the rest of the school (Olsen, in press). Mainstream teachers do not always welcome immigrant and ESL students in their classes, and many actively seek to avoid teaching them. U.S.-born students do not always make an effort to interact with immigrant students, which increases their segregation. Therefore, while immigrant students should not be discouraged from frequenting the places where adults do welcome them, schools should make conscious and concerted efforts to help connect immigrant students to the broader school community.

Relationships with adults outside of school can provide a window into the world of work that many immigrant students have no way of opening otherwise. A "community-based mentoring support program" (Price et al., 1993, pp. 53-54) called *Las Madrinas* (the godmothers) provides one example, also building on the power of mentoring relationships. The program brings professional Hispanic women together with young Hispanic women for purposes of leadership development and academic support. The program "combines the development of intense personal bonds with structured group activities" (p. 53). Pairs of *madrinas* and *ahijadas* (goddaughters) meet for a minimum of two hours every two weeks for thirty weeks. Project Adelante at Kean College in New Jersey, established to increase Hispanic students' graduation rates, brings in Hispanic professionals who work at AT&T as mentors for students (Vaznaugh, 1995; see description of Project Adelante in chapter 6 under *Pathways to Higher Education*). In addition to working with them on school assignments and helping them fill out college applications, the mentors take the students to their offices, giving them an orientation to work and careers.

Student-to-Student Relationships

Relationships With Peers

Young people need positive peer relationships as well as connections with adults. Unfortunately, conflict and even violence between and among students have become common features of U.S. schools. The study of California schools conducted by the Claremont Graduate School found that "student-to-student relationships are plagued by lack of knowledge, misunderstandings, racism, cultural conflicts and concomitant fear of one another" (Poplin & Weeres, 1992, p. 21). Immigrants increasingly suffer discrimination and harassment from their peers of all ethnic groups, as students themselves report:

A lot of American kids make fun of immigrant kids. They say: "Go back to your own country." There are fights between Mexican and Asian students. (Vietnamese student in San Francisco, quoted in National Coalition of Advocates for Students, 1988, p. 60)

I like school, but I don't like how other American students call me names. I don't like it when the Americans say: "You dumb Haitian, go back to Haiti." (Haitian student in Cambridge, Massachusetts, quoted in National Coalition of Advocates for Students, 1988, p. 60)

Despite the problems, students in the Claremont study "strongly expressed the desire to know one another" (p. 19), as did a Vietnamese student interviewed by National Coalition of Advocates for Students in Cambridge, Massachusetts, who said: "I like school here. But wish there would be more friendship among immigrant students and American students" (National Coalition of Advocates for Students, 1988, p. 60). New conceptions of teaching and learning support the role of collaboration and social interaction in learning. Peers can diminish the difficulty of the transition into a new school and culture for immigrant students by making them feel welcome and valued as well as by passing on student-to-student information about the less explicit norms and expectations of the school and student culture. It is up to educators to design and nurture learning environments that support the development of relationships among students.

Collaboration on learning activities provides rich possibilities for student relationships to develop within the instructional context, as a teacher at The International High School describes:

In my classroom … students work collaboratively as a whole class, in groups, or in pairs. Sometimes the collaboration consists of helping each other, but it also involves working in groups in which each member has a role and a special contribution to make to a project. When students work alone on individual projects, or in group projects, they present their work in progress to the entire class, and receive feedback and input from all their classmates. Thus, the whole class has a stake in everybody's work. (Dunetz, 1990, p. 4)

Projects engage students in collaboration to accomplish a common goal. Students in a second grade Chinese bilingual class in Oakland, California, in which the teacher was applying the Foxfire approach, collaborated on a community project (Beard, 1994). They spent three weeks carrying out a project in which they visited a community residence for elderly women, interviewed residents about their lives, then wrote books about it. The project involved 25 students who, working in groups, (1) prepared questions; (2) went to the residence and interviewed women there; (3) developed vocabulary lists in English and in Chinese of new words they had learned during their visits; (4) made drawings and wrote descriptions of the women's rooms in English; (5) compiled these into a book; (6) rewrote the descriptions in Chinese; and (7) made another book. Such a project would be just as appropriate for high school students as it was for these second graders.

While the emphasis on collaboration within the classroom context reflects relatively recent views of teaching and learning, students can develop relationships through their participation in school activities beyond the classroom even in the most traditional schools. Activities that engage immigrant students, however, may be different from those that engage other students. Basketball and football, school (English language) newspapers, academic clubs, social clubs dominated by native-born students, and other common extracurricular activities do not generally welcome immigrant students or offer them ways to participate meaningfully. Activities that do attract the participation of immigrant students include bilingual student newspapers, *baile folklórico* groups, mural projects, soccer teams, and ethnic clubs. Educators should not make assumptions about which activities will attract immigrant youths. They should ask the youths themselves, their families, and other community members, then offer those activities along with the more traditional ones.

Relationships With Younger and Older Youths

Teenagers may hear a suggestion or comment from an adult differently than they hear it from someone only a few years older than they are. Older youths can serve as examples, role models, confidantes, and friends in ways that adults cannot. At the same time, older youths can develop responsibility, interpersonal skills, and pride through relationships with younger people. Many programs capitalize on this special relationship, including Project Adelante and the AVID program, which are described in chapter 6 under *Pathways to Higher Education.*

The relationship that develops between a student and an older or younger peer within a particular program or activity may become as important as, or even more important than the ostensible reason for which they are meeting. This appears to be the case with tutors in the Pace Hispanic Outreach Program in White Plains, New York. The program brings students from Pace University, almost all of whom are bilingual Latinos themselves, to White Plains High School to work with recently arrived bilingual Latino students who have been referred for extra help from their teachers and the school's guidance counselors (three of the latter of which are bilingual). Program director Malula González describes the tutors as "very dedicated" and elaborates on the benefits of the program for the high school students:

The relationship between tutors and students is unbelievable. When they see another Hispanic student in college doing something for them, they feel very special. A group of tutors went with me to the graduations of students who had been in the program since 9th grade, and it was very special for the students....

To me, the most important role that the tutors play is being a role model. Knowing there is somebody who was in their position a few years before who has made it gives [students] a sense that they can do it too. A lot of them work after school; they have to work hard. Seeing the tutors helps them know that it's worth it, that they can make it if they keep trying.

There is no generation gap between tutors and students. If I tell [the students] something, it sounds like a mother, [but] they listen to the tutors because they're more the same age. (M. González, personal communication, November 10, 1994)

The director's relationships with the students are also more important to her than her job of coordinating program administration. She says, "I call this a club. I display copies of papers they did well on, good grades. It gives them a sense of belonging. It helps their self-esteem."

The Coca-Cola Valued Youth Program also makes the most of the potential for cross-age relationships while providing support for the development of work-related knowledge and skills among the older students (Cárdenas, Montecel, Supik, & Harris, 1992; National Coalition of Advocates for Students, 1994; Robledo & Rivera, 1990). Secondary students who have been determined to be at risk of dropping out of school are recruited to tutor elementary students. Implemented in 38 schools in seven states, the program provides a structure for bringing together students of different ages and for supporting the development of relationships between them. Tutors attend a weekly one-hour class in which they develop "tutoring skills, self-awareness, pride, and literacy skills" (National Coalition of Advocates for Students, 1994, p. 50). They are guided by the faculty coordinator, who also acts as an advocate and mentor for the tutors, in analyzing and evaluating how their tutees learn and how they teach, which helps them to develop critical thinking skills. The program also includes three field trips per year "to expose students to the economic and cultural opportunities in the community" (p. 51). They explore "real life professional settings" and build self-esteem when the trips highlight cultural contributions of the students' communities. The secondary students teach elementary students 4 hours per week, acting as mentors and role models for the younger students. Because the tutoring is structured and treated as an internship for which they are paid, it helps students develop an awareness of expectations and responsibilities of working in a real job. Tutors prepare for and participate in mock job interviews, including filling out forms in which they describe their past experiences.

Relationships Among School Staff

Adults as well as youths need relationships for support. Indeed, if schools are to be learning communities, the adults in them must be in relationships with each other as well as with students. The isolation and specialization in typical secondary schools diminishes the possibility for interaction and communication among educators and renders their relationships "equally bleak" as those between students and others (Wheelock, 1993, p. 38).

Opportunities are few and conditions poor in which to develop relationships among staff members inside schools. Indeed, schools are not structured to make dialogues between teachers necessary. This is heightened in middle and high schools where schedules are fragmented and academic and/or grade level departments are separated from one another. (Poplin & Weeres, 1992, p. 21)

Like youths, adults learn from interaction and collaboration, and if the adults in a school are not learning, then the students are probably not learning as much as they could be either. Especially given most educators' lack of experience with immigrant students, they need to share ideas, understandings, and strategies in order to develop more successful educational approaches. The collaboration that is integral to new conceptions of teaching and learning and the new school structures discussed throughout this volume provide opportunities for educators to develop the relationships that can help them grow and better serve their students.

The nonteaching staff in schools often have more contact with and knowledge of immigrant students and their families than teachers, administrators, and counselors. "Secretaries, food service workers, daycare workers, security personnel, maintenance and grounds staff, and aides are often the staff members inside schools who live in the communities with the students" (Poplin & Weeres, 1992, p. 24; see also Lucas, 1992; Olsen, 1989; Weiss, 1994). Such support staff members provide a bridge between the school and the community, but this role is rarely given official recognition or support. The hierarchical structure of schools results in "very disconnected relationships" between these staff members and "other professional school staff members." They do not have opportunities to "offer [the] valuable and insightful information" that they could provide (Poplin & Weeres, 1992, p. 24). This information could be used by all members of a school community to support immigrant students' transitions into and beyond secondary school if the relationships between teaching and nonteaching staff allowed for regular and meaningful communication.

New structures like those at The International High School described above, which promote teacher collaboration through teaming and interdisciplinary instruction and which build time into the day for joint planning, provide a framework within which school staff as well as students can develop relationships. Participants in such structures must take concrete steps to ensure that their colleagues in various roles (including support staff members) who are most knowledgeable of immigrant students and immigrant education are part of the team. Too often, ESL and bilingual staff remain peripheral to core planning groups, making it less likely that strategies for addressing the needs and strengths of immigrant students will be integrated into curriculum and instruction.

Relationships with colleagues outside of one's own school and school district can also provide support for adult learning and community building. For example, in Hayward, California, teachers from the district's comprehensive high schools and English Language Center meet four times a year for a full day. All language arts, social studies, math, and science teachers who have at least one bilingual (Spanish/English) or sheltered content class are included. They review data on student progress; read research articles; interact with speakers from outside the district; share curricula, lessons, and instructional strategies; and visit the classes of teachers in other schools in the district and in neighboring districts. This cross-site collaboration has allowed important decisions to be made at the district level. For example, as a result of these meetings, a group of students who were not progressing through the ESL sequence as expected were identified, and a district-wide program was designed specifically for them. Another outcome was the creation of a district-wide sequence of ESL courses with placement criteria, a mastery test, and exit criteria for each level.

In contexts where the overall climate is unwelcoming to immigrants and where immigrant populations are relatively new, such connections with colleagues can be a primary source of collegiality. Professional organizations such as Teachers of English to Speakers of Other Languages (TESOL), the National Association for Bilingual Education (NABE), and their state affiliates provide opportunities for educators of immigrant students to build such relationships. Networks of educators associated with particular educational philosophies, programs, or issues provide another avenue—e.g., the Coalition of Essential Schools (organized around Ted Sizer's principles of schooling), Project Zero (organized around Howard Gardner's theories of multiple intelligences), the Foxfire Teacher Network, the National Writing Project, and the National Mathematics Project. The Four Seasons Network, coordinated by the National Center for Restructuring Education, Schools, and Teaching (NCREST) at Teachers College, Columbia University, is a network of networks that brings together teachers throughout the country who are involved in developing and using authentic assessments as part of their participation in the Coalition of Essential Schools, the Foxfire Network, and Project Zero.

Another educational network coordinated by NCREST focuses more specifically on issues related to student diversity, including immigrant education. The DEWEY (Diversity and Excellence Working for the Education of Youth) Network brings together eight school districts in suburban New York City that are characterized by increasing ethnic and linguistic diversity, and it supports them in working toward systemic reform. The districts are committed to shaping programs that

- investigate and utilize previous academic and life experiences that students bring to the learning process;
- use multicultural and global perspectives as sources of enrichment and knowledge for living in an increasingly global economy;
- offer learning about the world, cultures, and languages to all students;
- take concrete steps to actively value all students' cultures and languages; and
- do so in environments where all stakeholders have engaged in developing shared visions about the education of their children.

To accomplish such sweeping transformations, these schools and communities need to create new learning environments and use different organizational structures that model the spirit of inquiry, inclusiveness, excellence, interdependence, and equity.

The DEWEY Network provides a structure that can promote the substantial changes that these schools and districts are striving for. The central component of the Network is the creation and ongoing support of networking opportunities among the various groups of stakeholders in the schools and communities—that is, structures that bring people together (physically and electronically) and engage them in substantive interaction. Sharing visions, goals, knowledge, and resources strengthens educators' abilities to provide a challenging and appropriate education for all their students. But for such sharing to occur, educators must have forums that allow and encourage it. The DEWEY Network sponsors meetings and problem-solving sessions, ongoing study and networking groups, within- and across-district visitations, the DEWEY Network newsletter, and an electronic network.

Electronic networking offers a relatively new and certainly under-used means through which educators can develop relationships. While many university faculty members use electronic communication, fewer K-12 educators have access to the hardware required. Benefits of electronic communication are that (1) it can be done at whatever time is convenient for both the sender and the receiver of a message; (2) it is faster than other forms of communication; (3) it can connect people in geographically separate locations; and (4) it can encourage participation by those who might not speak out in a face-to-face conversation. It can also support the development of "a culture of inquiry that questions existing assumptions about teaching and learning" (Szecsy, 1995b, p. 7). Electronic networking offers opportunities for busy colleagues within schools and districts to connect, even when the daily schedule has not been reconfigured to allow them to meet face to face.

The Four Seasons Network, mentioned above, uses an electronic network to connect teachers involved in the Coalition of Essential Schools, the Foxfire Network, and Harvard University's Project Zero. Teachers meet face to face during summer Assessment Fairs, but the principal vehicle through which they communicate throughout the year is an electronic network that has "enabled teachers to share current stories of practice, discuss their struggles related to the creation of portfolios and exhibitions of student work, and give each other support and encouragement for taking risks" (Lieberman, 1995, p. 595). The DEWEY Network also promotes electronic communication among participants by providing e-mail accounts through Columbia University. "Scattered throughout the eight DEWEY districts are over 60 DEWEY Electronic Networkers who are extending their conversations with each other via email and making their own discoveries about the richness of this resource" (Szecsy, 1995a, p. 6). Students, teachers, administrators, graduate students, and university personnel communicate on-line about both the practical issues involved in networking (e.g., meeting dates, times, and places) and the substantive issues of the Network (e.g., the benefits of cultural and linguistic diversity in U.S. schools).

Relationships Between Educators and Families

Central among the multiple facets of immigrant students' lives, as of all students' lives, are their families. Many benefits accrue for schools, educators, students, and their families from the nurturing of a reciprocal relationship between families and schools. Immigrant families want their children to succeed in school, but many of them do not know how they can help (see National Coalition of Advocates for Students, 1988, 1994; Olsen, 1988, 1989; Violand-Sánchez et al., 1991). Poplin and Weeres (1992) found that parents in the schools they studied in Southern California felt "isolated and not respected by participants inside school communities," that they "desire and appreciate sincere dialogue between themselves and schools" (p. 24). When immigrant families and educators communicate with each other in a reciprocal relationship, families can help educators understand the different expectations and assumptions that students bring to school from their cultures and experiences, and educators can help families understand the schools' expectations and assumptions. Thus, families can better support their children in adjusting to U.S. schools and in preparing for life beyond high school while they teach them to value their own cultural, linguistic, and personal heritage.

When the families of immigrant youths have no contact with and therefore no understanding of the educational system and the process of socialization that their children are experiencing, they may feel that they are losing their children to the large, unknown world to which their children belong but they themselves do not. They may become confused, bewildered, frightened, desperate, and defeated in their efforts to maintain contact with their children, even as their children become more and more foreign to them. These conflicts and misunderstandings can destroy a family. The schools can play a role in preventing such tragedies by helping family members become part of the school process rather than remaining peripheral to it.

Once schools find ways to inform and engage families in schooling, their involvement can build home–school links that help to reduce the impact of the inevitable cultural clashes that immigrant students experience as they make the transition into U.S. culture. When families understand ways in which they can support their children's educational progress, and when schools understand ways in which they can incorporate families and elements of students' cultures into schooling and support immigrant students' participation in schools, then both groups can contribute to narrowing the gulf between the two worlds that students must negotiate.

Unfortunately, there are many barriers to, and few supports for, the development of relationships between educators and immigrant families. Immigrants have different understandings of the roles of families in their children's education. They may not understand the impact that parents can have by participating in schooling in the United States or the various opportunities for participating. They may not be fluent in English and may have to depend on their children to translate written and oral communications in English. They may have little formal schooling and few literacy skills in their native language or in English and therefore may not understand written communications from the school or be able to help their children with school work. Many of them work long hours and may hold two jobs, making it difficult for them to attend meetings.

Educators cannot rely on the strategies they use to connect with U.S. parents if they want to reach immigrant parents. Given the importance of relationships, "people who live and work in the community, or have close ties to the community often are best situated to connect with parents" (National Coalition of Advocates for Students, 1994, p. 95). As discussed above, staff from the communities—both teachers and support staff—are in the best position to overcome the barriers between school and home, between educators and families. With their inside knowledge, they can translate culturally, socially, and linguistically for both groups.

In order to design strategies for involving parents of immigrant students in schooling, educators need to consider several factors that can influence the nature and extent of their involvement and that are often overlooked because they are not of relevance to U.S.-born parents: (1) length of residence in the United States; (2) English language proficiency; (3) availability of support groups and bilingual staff; (4) prior experience with parental involvement in schooling (Violand-Sánchez et al., 1991, pp. 7-8). Immigrants who have been in the United States for longer periods of time are more likely to have the time, understanding of the system, and resources to participate in more ways than recent arrivals.

Recent immigrants require some orientation to U.S. schooling. As discussed above, intake centers "can provide multilingual assistance in registration, placement, testing, and information services," as well as translation (Violand-Sánchez et al., 1991, pp. 8). The Parent Information Center in White Plains, New York, established in 1989, assists parents in registering their children in kindergartens through a choice program designed to achieve a racial balance in the elementary schools. The first point of contact for parents with the school system, it also functions as a center for other types of counseling, information, and assistance. A Spanish-speaking counselor at the Center works with Spanish-speaking families and has translated all materials into Spanish. Home–school liaisons can also offer information to newly arrived parents, bridging the gap between home and school and forging relationships between educators and immigrant families. A home–school liaison in Elgin, Illinois, said:

The home/school liaisons and the aides know the needs. We came from the people who need the services. We're in contact with the people in the community. We have children enrolled in the programs [for language minority students]. So we know the needs that way. (Lucas, 1992, p. 59)

Those who are not familiar with the home lives of their students must find ways to learn about them in order to be able to build relationships with families. A group of teachers and university researchers involved in an ethnographic study of the "funds of knowledge" of their students' families in Tucson, Arizona, "have found that pivotal and transformative shifts take place in teachers and in relations between households and schools and between parents and teachers" as a result of this effort (National Center for Research on Cultural Diversity and Second Language Learning, 1994a, p. 1; see also González et al., 1993; Moll, Amanti, Neff, & González, 1992; Moll & Greenberg, 1990). Teachers go into the homes of some of their students to learn about the "historically developed and accumulated strategies ... or bodies of knowledge that are essential to a household's functioning and well-being" (p. 1). Finding rich funds of knowledge, teachers come to see their students and their students' families differently, and they incorporate their new perceptions and knowledge into academic content. One teacher, for example, was able to develop an interdisciplinary lesson around candy making after she learned that one of her students had experience selling Mexican candy in the United States and that a parent knew how to make it.

When teachers and other school and district staff visit students' homes and attend community events and celebrations (Freeman & Freeman, 1994; Lucas, 1992), they make connections that can have far-reaching impacts on themselves, the families, and the children, as illustrated by the work in Tucson. Freeman and Freeman describe the discoveries teachers have made about their students' home lives and responsibilities, the respect their parents have for education, and the skills family members have that can later be incorporated into the classroom (e.g., playing musical instruments, carving wood). Educators can also show respect for and learn about their students' families and cultures by attending cultural events and celebrations in their communities. Families are more open to coming to school if a teacher or other educator has reached out to them in these ways.

Another way to build relationships with families is to bring them into the classroom—which requires getting to know something about them beforehand. A teacher applying the Foxfire approach in a sixth-grade class in Richmond, California, asked the father of one of her Lao students to teach the class to make a traditional Lao wooden top. He came to the class several times, first bringing in a piece of wood, then carving the top, then carving a piece of wood to make the top spin, and finally teaching the students how to make it spin. Similarly, the teacher in Tucson who used the candy-making skills of a parent in building an interdisciplinary lesson brought that parent into the class to teach.

Schools can also offer classes for family members to provide access to information and skills that they need. Many schools offer ESL classes for immigrant parents, and some offer native language literacy classes as well. The Freemans (1994) describe an ESL class for adults in which the teacher applied Freire's "problem posing" approach, helping them to identify a problem they were having and then to come up with solutions for themselves and each other (pp. 296-297). Other classes and workshops provide information to parents about school policies and expectations and parents' rights (see Roos, 1994).

Family literacy projects, some of which are funded by Title VII (Family English Literacy Projects [FELP]) of the Elementary and Secondary Education Act (now Improving America's Schools Act), assist parents who have children enrolled in schools and whose native language is not English. In addition to providing ESL and literacy instruction (in some programs, in native languages as well as English), FELPs also include parent–child instructional activities and parenting components to help parents learn about and adapt to U.S. culture and schooling (see Freeman & Freeman, 1994, p. 298ff; Holt, 1994; Rioux & Berla, 1993). Because FELPs involve parents in ongoing activities centered around the school, they promote the development of relationships between parents and school staff involved in the programs.

Families Together, a FELP administered by ARC Associates and the Oakland (California) Unified School District, served Spanish, Cambodian, Mien, Lao, and Vietnamese families through literacy development in English and their primary languages, the recounting and publishing of family stories, the enhancement of parenting skills, and the development of cross-cultural communication and understanding (see Barra, 1994; Rioux & Berla, 1993). Like the ESL class described above, the ESL instruction provided through Families Together was organized around themes identified by the parents themselves as important. In addition, parents read children's literature in their own classes, then read the same books to their children. Participants also shared their personal stories through the exploration of themes such as ancestors, first memories, falling in love, marriage, coming to the United States, and hopes and dreams for the future. They wrote their stories, shared them with other parents in the class, revised favorite selections, edited, and published their writing in English, in their native languages, or in both. The teacher of the family stories class helped with the literacy tasks as needed. Some parents dictated their stories to someone who wrote them in the parents' native language and then translated them into English. They were published in whatever language or languages the parents preferred. Three volumes of stories written by parents were published.

The *Bridges to Literacy* (BTL) program at Ridgeway Elementary school in White Plains, New York, not only gives guidance to parents in helping their children develop literacy skills in English and their native languages, it also functions as a learning experience for the teachers. In 1994-95, BTL involved 12 Spanish-speaking families, 2 Haitian Creole families, 1 Chinese-speaking family, and 1 English-speaking family. Teachers at the school participated as part of a practicum in which they attended classes themselves to learn about strategies for teaching language-minority students, then paired up to develop and present lessons to the parents and their children. Thus, instead of just teaching parents, the teacher participants were acknowledged learners as well. This approach has helped to build collegiality among teachers and increased their capacity to teach language-minority students, as well as strengthening the relationships between the school and the parents involved in the program.

Other strategies used to foster effective home–school communication with families of immigrant students include the following (see Lucas et al., 1990; Olsen, 1989, 1994; Villegas, 1992; Violand-Sánchez et al., 1991):

• Translate school documents and communications into parents' home languages.

• Record a call-in message with information about school in parents' languages.

- Ensure that oral communication with parents is conducted by staff who speak their languages, which may involve engaging consultants to communicate with parents of less common languages.

- Have translators at all meetings that parents might attend.

- Hire bilingual staff at all levels of the school system.

- Have bilingual and ESL staff visit homes.

- Find out from parents when, where, and how it would be convenient for them to meet.

- Hold meetings at times and in places where immigrant parents are more likely and able to attend—such as after church on Sunday (as the director of the Pace Hispanic Outreach Program in White Plains, New York, has done), very early in the morning in a community location, or in parents' homes.

- Make provisions for childcare during meetings.

- Cosponsor meetings with local community organizations that involve immigrants.

- Hold events in which immigrant students participate and receive recognition (e.g., student-of-the-month breakfasts, student recognition assemblies).

Site-based management, an increasingly common element of school reform efforts, requires family involvement. In theory, this forum provides the opportunity for a broad base of parents to participate with educators and other community members in making decisions about schooling. In practice, the efforts to involve immigrant parents are rarely very successful. In order to really involve immigrant parents in the reform efforts as in other school-related activities, schools must give priority to "formal mechanisms" like those described above, "which ensure and facilitate the meaningful participation and voice for the parents/family/caregivers of *all* students" (Olsen et al., 1994, p. 104).

Conclusion

Given the central role of human relationships in influencing the nature and success of the schooling experiences for adolescents, schools and educators would do well to give more conscious attention to developing approaches that support relationships and to removing barriers that undermine or prevent them from developing. While we give an abundance of intellectual, physical, and emotional energy to designing programs and strategies and interventions, many adolescents in our schools are languishing from a lack of simple human connectedness with each other and with the adults in the schools. Immersed in a new culture, language, and school system while also undergoing the developmental changes of adolescence and early adulthood, many immigrant students are especially vulnerable to feelings of disconnectedness. They need guidance into and through the system from caring peers and adults. If we concentrate on school structures, curriculum, instructional strategies, assessment approaches, and academic support systems without a recognition that these "technical" aspects of schooling form the backdrop within which relationships are or are not cultivated, we are missing a fundamental element of schooling for all students.

The structures and strategies discussed above, which educators can use for cultivating human relationships to facilitate the transitions of immigrant youths into, through, and beyond secondary school, are summarized in Figure 8.

Figure 8. Structures and Strategies for Cultivating Human Relationships

Structures

Adult–student relationships

- Mentoring programs
- Counseling programs
- Advisories; families; home bases; houses; clusters
- Tutoring
- Teacher teams; interdisciplinary clusters
- Schools-within-schools
- Newcomer schools
- Institutional collaborations (facilitate relationships with adults outside school)
- Internships
- Electronic networking
- Intake centers (and intake processes, including interviews)

Student–student relationships

- Mentoring programs (involving older and younger youths)
- Tutoring (involving older and younger youths)
- Interdisciplinary clusters
- Schools-within-schools
- Club meetings within the school day

- Buddies (pairing of students)
- Cooperative learning
- Electronic networking
- Bilingual student newspapers
- Extracurricular activities of interest to immigrant students (e.g., soccer, *baile folklórico*)

Adult–adult relationships within schools

- Teacher teams; interdisciplinary clusters
- Regular forums (e.g., shared planning time) for teachers to discuss shared immigrant students
- Schools-within-schools
- Collaborations with other agencies
- Electronic networking

School–family relationships

- Family English Literacy Projects
- Intake interviews and processes
- Home–school liaisons
- Parent centers
- Orientation workshops
- Courses for parents (ESL, literacy, immigration issues)

(Figure 8 continues on the next page)

Figure 8. Structures and Strategies for Cultivating Human Relationships (continued)

Strategies for Educators

Adult–student relationships

- Design school structures to allow time for and attention to small groupings of students and adults.
- Develop an intake process through which information is gathered about each student's background and is made available to the student's counselors and teachers.
- Ensure that someone is responsible for gathering information about immigrant students and making it available to the appropriate people.
- Hire and support the hiring of staff members (including community liaisons, bilingual/ESL coordinators, administrators, and teachers) from the language and cultural backgrounds of the students.
- Ensure that immigrant students have access to counselors who can communicate with them and understand them.
- Act as a mentor, advisor, or tutor for immigrant students.
- Sponsor and participate in school-related activities that involve immigrant students.
- Visit students' homes and communities to learn about the funds of knowledge in their families and cultures.
- Participate in community events and celebrations.
- Read fictional and nonfictional literature about students' cultures.
- Make time to talk with students outside of class.

Student–student relationships

- Design school structures to allow time for and attention to small groupings of students and adults.
- Establish peer mentoring and peer tutoring programs.
- Establish a buddy system so that immigrant students have a peer to turn to for assistance.

Adult–adult relationships within schools

- Design school structures that promote communication between support staff (e.g., instructional assistants, janitors, secretaries) and instructional staff as well as between support staff and students and their families.

School–family relationships

- Visit students' homes and communities to learn about the funds of knowledge in their families and cultures.
- Participate in community events and celebrations.
- Develop relationships with adults in the students' communities.
- Bring family members into the classroom.
- Offer classes and other activities for family members.
- Hire and support the hiring of staff members (including community liaisons, bilingual/ESL coordinators, administrators, and teachers) from the language and cultural backgrounds of the students.

The following questions can help to ensure that issues of special relevance to immigrant youths and their families are taken into account in attempts to cultivate relationships among people involved in the education of immigrant students.

Questions to ask in applying Principle 3: Cultivate human relationships.

Language:

1. Do teachers and other school personnel make it a point to find out about the language background and language use of each student and of each student's family?

2. Are there people in the school who can speak immigrant students' languages?

3. Does the school have a commitment to hiring more people who speak students' languages?

4. Does language have a formal (through rules or policies) or informal (through customs, staffing, unconscious behavior) impact on whether immigrant students and their families can participate in school activities (e.g., extracurricular activities; school committees; advisory programs)?

5. Have steps been taken to include immigrants and their families who are not fluent in English in school activities?

6. Do school activities and personnel support youths in using and learning English without placing them in situations in which they will be judged inadequate or, worse, be harassed because they are not yet fully fluent?

7. Do school activities and personnel value and build upon immigrant youths' native language abilities?

8. Is value for bilingualism part of the culture of the school?

9. Do immigrant students have access to counselors who speak their language?

10. Do immigrant youths have opportunities to interact with other students who speak their native languages?

Educational backgrounds of students and families:

1. Do teachers and other school personnel make it a point to find out about the educational background of each student and of each student's family?

2. Has someone in the school learned about the school system in the students' home countries? Has that information been disseminated throughout the school?

3. Does educational background have an impact on whether immigrant students and their families can participate in school activities (e.g., are activities announced only in writing)?

4. Have steps been taken to include in school activities immigrants and their families who have little formal schooling?

Immigration experience:

1. Do teachers and other school personnel make it a point to find out about the immigration experience of each student?

2. Is counseling available to those students who have had traumatic immigration experiences?

3. Do adults in the school openly acknowledge the challenges and opportunities of the immigration experience?

4. Do nonimmigrant students have opportunities to learn about the immigration experience from immigrant students and their families?

Culture and cultural context:

1. Do teachers and other school personnel make it a point to find out about the cultural background of each student?

2. Are there people in the school who are from immigrant students' cultures?

3. Does the school have a commitment to hiring more people from students' cultures?

4. Have steps been taken to include in school activities immigrants and their families who are not familiar with U.S. culture and schooling?

5. Do school activities and personnel value and build upon immigrant youths' native cultures?

6. Is value for multiculturalism part of the culture of the school?

7. Is there evidence in the school that the particular cultures of the students are valued?

8. Do immigrant students have access to counselors who are from or are familiar with their cultures?

9. Do school personnel understand the nature of relationships between students and teachers and between schools and families in students' native cultures?

10. Are there mechanisms for promoting cross-cultural communication and for dealing productively with cross-cultural conflict?

Social background and social context:

1. Do teachers and other school personnel make it a point to find out about the social background and social context of each student?

2. Does social background have an impact on whether immigrant students and their families can participate in school activities (e.g., do activities require that fees be paid)?

3. Have steps been taken to include immigrants and their families who come from social backgrounds or live in social contexts that make participation in school activities difficult (e.g., through scholarships or transportation)?

Principle 4: Provide Multiple and Flexible Pathways

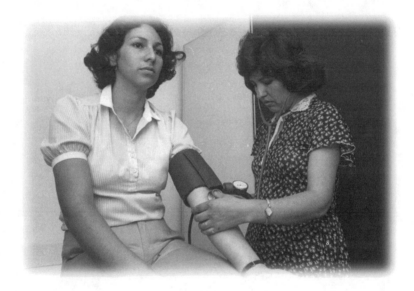

There is no one best path along which all secondary immigrant students should travel to move successfully into and through U.S. schools or beyond secondary school to a life of further education and work. A central theme of this volume is that multiple factors influence immigrants' experiences, strengths, and needs, and that they influence different individuals and families differently. Therefore, as much as we might hope to find the best academic program, the best approach to school restructuring, the best strategy for orienting students to U.S. schools, or the best system for introducing immigrant students to the world of work, we will be frustrated in such efforts.

"Given the right opportunity and support, nearly every child is capable of achieving every worthwhile educational goal, regardless of gender, regardless of skin tone, and regardless of their scores on outmoded measures of intellectual ability" (Oakes, 1995, p. 7). All students should be held to the same high expectations and provided equally challenging curriculum and instruction. All immigrant students should be supported in their efforts to adjust successfully to U.S. culture and schooling and to make a smooth transition beyond secondary school. But "the right opportunity and support" is not the same for every young person. Students must be offered different ways to meet those expectations and to engage in the curriculum, and instruction and different vehicles through which to accomplish their goals. We have to match the immigrant students that we have in our particular schools and classrooms, considering all the complexities that make them who they are, with the pathways into, through, and beyond secondary school that will serve them best. Thus, schools must provide multiple and flexible pathways that address the varied aspects of immigrant students' real lives and that treat them as whole people, not just as learners of English. The pathways described in this chapter are presented as possibilities. Whether they are appropriate and how they should be adapted will vary for each setting and for each set of individuals involved.

Pathways Into U.S. Schooling and Culture

The school is an institution within U.S. culture that plays a central role in the lives of immigrant youths. They and their families must learn new daily routines and functions, new rules and regulations, and new unwritten expectations and assumptions of the school system. In order to be successful in U.S. schools, all students must be skilled in reading, writing, and speaking English. They must acquire the cultural and academic knowledge expected of all adolescents in U.S. schools. Schools take a number of different approaches to assisting secondary immigrant students in their transition into U.S. schooling. I describe these approaches below, focusing on different program configurations. (See the volume in this series by Aída Walqui [in press] addressing curricular and instructional issues within these programs.) Figure 9 maps my discussion of these approaches.

Special Programs for Immigrants and Learners of English as a Second Language

The most common pathways by which immigrant students enter U.S. schools are programs especially for learners of English as a second language, usually within regular schools but sometimes in separate schools staffed by bilingual and ESL professionals. The primary goal of most of these newcomer programs is to teach students English so that they can reasonably enter classes with native-English-speaking students as soon as possible. Another goal of newcomer programs is to provide information and assistance that will prepare recent immigrants for entry into U.S. schools. Because the people who staff these programs tend to be sensitive to the other challenges that immigrant students face, they usually provide personal and academic support that goes beyond English language development. Such support is a formal component of most newcomer schools and programs.

The growing number of immigrants and English language learners in our schools has made it essential that all educators become knowledgeable of and sensitive to students' experiences and that all educators

Figure 9. Pathways Into U.S. Schooling and Culture

Special programs for immigrants and learners of English as a second language:

- Newcomer schools
- Programs for newcomers within comprehensive schools
- Programs for learners of English as a second language within comprehensive schools
  1. *English as a second language programs*
  2. *English-based academic content programs*
  3. *Bilingual programs*

Alternative schools

develop skills for educating them. There is a growing awareness of the deleterious effects of relegating immigrant students to special programs, peripheral to the real life of the school and outside of the education reforms that are taking place (see Haycock, 1995; Olsen et al., 1994). At the same time, simply to assume that innovations are beneficial for all students without thoughtful and knowledgeable consideration of the differences among individuals and groups of students is no more equitable than placing all immigrant students in separate programs. Ideally, all educators should be equipped to give such consideration to student needs and strengths so that separation of immigrant students in special programs is minimized. However, the reality is that teacher education does not prepare teachers to teach all students; it prepares some teachers to teach some types of students. Thus, immigrant students may fair better in separate programs with well-prepared teachers than in mainstream programs with teachers who are ignorant of their experiences, strengths, and needs. Until more educators are better prepared to educate immigrant students, special programs will continue to have a role to play. Nevertheless, they should be carefully examined in every context in which they are implemented to ensure that their benefits are maintained while their weaknesses are minimized.

Newcomer schools

These are special schools for immigrant students from which they move into a regular school setting. Although they are housed in buildings outside the regular school and are called schools, the fact that they are temporary makes them more like programs than like comprehensive high schools. They have been designed in a number of school districts in response to the recognition that "language learning alone is inadequate" to help students make the transition into their new culture (Chang, 1990, p. 9). A major purpose of newcomer schools is to support the adjustment of recent immigrants to their new society and new school system, which includes but is not limited to English language development. Indeed, they offer the most comprehensive contexts within which immigrant students can safely learn about their new culture and can develop relationships with peers, teachers, and other adults who are sensitive to and knowledgeable about their experiences, cultures, and languages, while they are developing English language ability and academic knowledge (see Chang, 1990; Friedlander, 1991; McDonnell & Hill, 1993; Olsen, 1989).

Most newcomer schools "offer students a comprehensive array of academic and support services tailored to their special needs" (Friedlander, 1991, p. 4). Such schools include orientation components that provide needed information to students and their families, offer safety and security for exploration and uncertainty in the initial adjustment period, and address extra-academic concerns and needs that can interfere with adjustment and success in school. Newcomer schools

emphasize safe educational environments, building bridges to U.S. institutions and society, helping children and families get access to needed services, and involving parents in their children's education. They are designed for flexibility, so they can respond directly to students' needs and to the mobility of the student population.... [They feature] the broad integration of academic and nonacademic supports. (Chang, 1990, p. 9)

Newcomer schools vary as to the amount of time students attend (see Chang, 1990; Friedlander, 1991; Lucas, 1993b). Because newcomers are separated from native-born English speakers on the basis of language and national origin when they are in newcomer schools, most districts limit the amount of time they may stay in the program in order to comply with Federal Civil Rights laws, which prohibit discrimination on the basis of race, color, or national origin, and which form the basis for school desegregation. When the U.S. Department of Education's Office for Civil Rights investigated one newcomer school in 1990, it was found in compliance with the law, in part because enrollment was voluntary, the students were from different races, ethnic backgrounds, and language backgrounds, and they attended the school for only one year (see Friedlander, 1991, p. 19). In some districts, students attend the newcomer school for half of the day and a regular secondary school the other half (e.g., the English Language Center in Hayward, California); in others, they attend the newcomer school all day for six months or a year and then enroll in a regular school (e.g., Newcomer High School in San Francisco).

Falls Church Transitional High School in Fairfax, Virginia (described in Mace-Matluck, Alexander-Kasparik, & Queen [in press] in this series and in National Coalition of Advocates for Students, 1994, pp. 83-86), offers another option. This program is designed for young adult English learners with limited literacy in their home language and limited or interrupted schooling, who intend to graduate from high school but who cannot attend school during the day because they have jobs or responsibilities supporting their families. This program is, in effect, an alternative newcomer school. Students can arrange their own schedules, choosing from courses offered from 3:00 to 10:00 p.m. Monday through Thursday and 3:00 to 5:00 p.m. on Friday. Once students have completed the school's curriculum in English, math, science, and social studies, they enroll in the district's alternative high schools to complete requirements for a diploma. If they have not completed high school diploma requirements by the age of 22, they can continue in the adult education program.

The International High School in Queens, New York, is the only example of a newcomer school I know of that students may attend for all four years of high school (see a description later in this chapter under

Alternative Schools). Because the school is on a community college campus and high school students take college courses and share the library and other facilities with college students, they are not completely segregated, as students in other self-contained newcomer schools are.

Many newcomer schools reflect new conceptions of teaching, learning, and schooling, offering smaller, more personalized school settings for those who attend.

[There are] striking contrasts ... between the traditional schools that most immigrant students attend and the newcomer schools available to a minority of students for a short period of time.... Newcomer schools most closely approximate the restructured schools now being advocated by education reformers.... [They tend to have] a strong sense of mission, strong teacher professionalism, active links to other agencies serving children, and instruction customized to the unique needs of their clientele. (McDonnell & Hill, 1993, p. 88)

Newcomer schools are smaller than traditional schools; faculty members are usually "hand-picked, based on their expertise and willingness to work with newcomers;" the schools function "more autonomously" than traditional schools; and staff are more directly involved in school governance (McDonnell & Hill, 1993, pp. 92-93). The greater access to bilingual teachers makes it possible to offer more academic subjects in students' native languages than in most traditional schools. "The emphasis on building student self-esteem also leads teachers to rely more on such techniques as cooperative work groups and portfolio assessments" (p. 97).

These schools reflect the advantages and disadvantages of providing special educational programs for particular groups of students. Designed to give central attention to the needs of immigrant students, they concentrate the expertise and commitment of educators for working with immigrant students in one place. They provide a safe and responsive context for relationships to develop among school staff, support service staff, students, families, and community agencies. Because curricula and support services are designed to address the needs of the whole child, newcomer schools emphasize parent outreach and involvement, links with social service and health agencies, and attention to personal counseling by school-based counselors.

On the other hand, newcomer schools serve only a limited number of immigrants in a district; immigrant students in these schools are separated from nonimmigrant students; students stay in the schools for a limited amount of time (partly because districts do not want them to remain separated); and they are more expensive to operate than traditional schools. In addition, educators in other schools may avoid or postpone developing their understanding of newcomer students as long as they see a place where such students receive special attention, even if it is only for a short period of time. Nevertheless, until all educators are committed and prepared to provide the best of what we know about teaching, learning, and schooling to immigrant students, newcomer schools offer immigrant students a "more focused alternative that ensures recent immigrants fortunate enough to be enrolled in them a richly integrated educational experience, at least for a short time" (McDonnell & Hill, 1993, p. 99).

Programs for newcomers within comprehensive schools

A more common approach to assisting immigrant students through the transition into U.S. society and schooling, "newcomer programs are designed to be transitional educational interventions that enable newcomers to adjust to a different system of schooling and a new society" (Chang, 1990, p. 11). Students generally move from these programs into bilingual or other types of programs for English language learners within the same school, which may include native-born students as well as immigrants. These in-school newcomer programs incorporate many of the features of newcomer schools—formal orientation to U.S. school and culture, family involvement, access to social services, and English language instruction, to name a few. The degree of autonomy of these programs varies; some function as complete schools-within-schools, while others are folded into the larger school administrative structures.

Programs for learners of English as a second language within comprehensive schools

These offer another pathway for facilitating the transition into U.S. schooling for recently arrived immigrant students. The primary goal of such programs is "overcoming language barriers and developing language skills" (Chang, 1990, p. 9)—a central part of the process of adjustment to U.S. culture and schools. These pathways provide a safe environment for the early years of immigrants' schooling in the United States, but they are designed for English language learners rather than immigrants. That is, their primary focus is on English language learning rather than orientation or cultural adjustment, and they may include U.S.-born speakers of other languages as well as newcomers, even at the secondary level. Even within this limited student-as-language-learner paradigm, curriculum can be designed to acknowledge student variation through classes that (1) address different levels of student skills, abilities, and knowledge, (2) offer different degrees of difficulty and sophistication, and (3) use different approaches to teaching academic content (Lucas, 1993c).

The following three types of programs are discussed here: (1) English as a second language programs, (2) English-based academic content programs, and (3) bilingual programs. In their formal structures, these programs generally do not address other aspects of immigrant students' lives besides language learning and (in some) content learning. They may be embedded within a context that provides immigrant students other means for learning about U.S. schools and culture, for gaining access to social and health services, for preparing for the world of work, for overcoming racism and prejudice, for working through intergenerational conflict, and for addressing other issues in their lives.

1. English as a second language (ESL) programs

If schools have any program for immigrant students, they have an ESL program—even when they also have a bilingual program. At the secondary level, such a program usually consists of a series of courses designed for students with varying levels of English proficiency—beginning, intermediate, and advanced. It may also include a special course for preliterate students and a course for "transitional" students—that is, those who are beyond the advanced level of English proficiency but deemed not quite ready to enter the mainstream (see below for a discussion of the transition into mainstream courses). Students may take varying numbers of ESL courses and may be placed in varying numbers of special and mainstream content classes, depending upon their level of English proficiency and the strength of their academic and literacy preparation in their native languages. In most schools, English language learners are placed along a continuum reflecting their English proficiency—from more ESL classes, fewer content classes of any sort, and fewer mainstream classes, to fewer ESL classes, more content classes, and more mainstream classes.

2. English-based academic content programs

Recognizing that English language learners at the secondary level must do more than learn English, many programs go beyond offering ESL classes to include academic content classes taught through specially designed academic instruction in English. (See the volume in this series by Walqui [in press] for an in-depth discussion of such programs and instructional approaches. Terms such as *sheltered instruction, content-based ESL, integrating language and content instruction,* and (in California) *specially designed academic instruction in English* (SDAIE) are used to describe these approaches.) In such programs, students learn English through content, thus contextualizing language learning, and they learn content through English, thus preventing them from falling further behind in their development of content knowledge than would otherwise be the case, especially for older youths whose U.S.-born peers are already learning complex content in school (see Brinton, Snow, & Wesche, 1989; Crandall, 1993; Faltis, 1993; Mohan, 1986, 1990; Short, 1993).

The quality and effectiveness of such programs depends on the preparation of teachers to provide instruction in English that is accessible to English learners without oversimplifying the academic content, as well as on the resources available and the materials and curricula used. Such factors can make the difference between content-based instruction in

English, which uses recognized approaches for making content accessible to English language learners, and "submersion," in which English language learners are simply placed in an English-only environment and expected to learn English and content with little or no support.

Schools and districts take various approaches in designing such programs. In what is usually called *content-based ESL*, ESL teachers use academic content as "the framework for instruction" but "maintain the primary objective of improving the students' skills in reading, writing, speaking, and listening." In this approach, content learning and preparation for mainstream courses are "a secondary agenda" (Short, 1993, p. 3). In the other approach to English-based programs, *sheltered content classes*, content learning is the primary goal. Through participation in professional development activities, content area teachers learn how to adapt their instruction to make academic content accessible to English learners. Such classes may include native English speakers as well as nonnative English speakers, or they may be designed only for nonnative speakers. In a number of programs, core course credit is given for sheltered content clases, if they are taught by teachers certified in the content area. Finally, some programs *integrate language and content instruction*, with equal emphasis on both to attempt to develop students' language proficiency and content knowledge at the same time.

3. Bilingual programs

ESL and English-based programs treat immigrant students primarily as English learners rather than as language learners or speakers of languages other than English. While some English-based programs and schools, such as The International High School, find ways to support the use and development of students' native languages even when instruction is provided primarily or exclusively in English (see also Lucas & Katz, 1994), most tend to ignore or downplay the fact that students speak, communicate in, and often read and write in other languages. Bilingual education programs acknowledge and build upon this fact.

Giving students' native languages a central role in their schooling makes sense for several reasons. First, especially at the secondary level, students cannot wait until they develop academic fluency in English to learn the complex content required to be successful in high school and beyond. By having access to biology, calculus, history, and other academic content courses in their native languages, students can continue to develop their content knowledge even while they are becoming proficient enough in academic English to succeed in English-based courses. Second, students have greater access to their prior knowledge when they can use the language in which they encountered and internalized it. Since we now know that learning involves bringing prior knowledge and experience to bear on new knowledge and experience, it makes sense that we would want to facilitate access to prior knowledge rather than inhibit it by requiring use of a language in which students are not fluent or fully functional. Third, not only does use of the native language provide access to prior knowledge, it also allows students to apply one of their strengths—their native language—to learning rather than depriving them of that strength and forcing them to learn through a medium in which they are weak—English. Fourth, psychological benefits accrue when students know that their languages are valued and respected (see Lucas et al., 1990) and when the stress of performing in a language in which they are not competent is reduced (see Auerbach, 1993). Fifth, continued development of one's native language supports development of second language ability (Cummins, 1981, 1991, 1992). Finally, developing the abilities of U.S. students in as many languages as possible can help to build a future workforce that can participate more effectively in the global community than the overwhelmingly monolingual U.S. workforce of today. It makes no sense to attempt to teach monolingual English-speaking students to speak Spanish, Chinese, and Japanese while discouraging immigrant students who already speak these languages from developing their native language abilities.

Most bilingual programs in the United States are designed to be transitional; that is, students' native languages are used just long enough for them to learn English without falling behind in their learning of content. Very few programs aim to fully develop students' native language abilities over time. However, a growing number of elementary schools offer two-way or dual-language bilingual education (see Christian & Witcher, 1995; Crawford, 1989, 1992; Genesee, 1987; National Center for Research on Cultural Diversity and Second Language Learning, 1994b). In these programs, classes are composed of roughly half native-English-speaking students and half speakers of one other language (usually Spanish). The English-speaking students learn Spanish, and the Spanish-speaking students learn English. Such programs offer benefits to all students: "These programs provide an environment that promotes positive attitudes toward both languages and cultures and is supportive of full bilingual proficiency for both native and nonnative speakers of English" (Christian & Whitcher, 1995, p. vii). However, of the 182 two-way bilingual programs in the United States identified by Christian & Whitcher, only 4 included grades above 8, and only 21 others included Grades 7 and 8.

At the secondary level, bilingual programs (contrasted with English-based programs for bilingual students) include content courses in students' native languages and may also include classes devoted to native language development (most commonly, Spanish for Spanish speakers). Very few schools can offer a full array of native-language courses, even in Spanish, for which there are more teachers and students than any other language. In most cases, the availability of academic content courses in languages other than English depends upon the existence of faculty who are willing and able to teach them (see Minicucci & Olsen, 1991). Thus, students may take some English-based sheltered content courses designed for English learners, some content courses in their native language, some mainstream content courses, ESL, and native language development, if it is available.

Alternative Schools

Besides academic preparation, native language, and proficiency in English, other factors can have a profound effect on the ability of immigrant students to attend and complete school. Some students must "shoulder adult responsibilities" by working to support their families or to care for younger siblings. They "must tend to their own survival before they can consider pursuing or completing a high school education" (National Coalition of Advocates for Students, 1994, p. 87). For these students, providing newcomer programs or offering special curricula within regular schools is not enough. They cannot take advantage of such pathways, which are designed for those with more traditional adolescent and young adult lives. Educators must be more creative in finding alternatives to traditional schooling in order to reach such students.

Manhattan Comprehensive Night High School (described in National Coalition of Advocates for Students, 1994, pp. 87-92) offers one example of a school that has been designed as a result of "shift[ing] the burden of accommodation off students and onto ... schools" (p. 87). (See also the description of Falls Church Transitional High School in the previous section on newcomer schools.) Open to all New York City residents between 17 and 21 years old with a seventh-grade reading level, the school enrolls 500 students, one third of whom are recent immigrants. The school is designed to accommodate the multiple realities of students' lives in its flexible daily and yearly schedule, full academic curriculum, provision of support services, internship placement program, and varied elective offerings and extracurricular activities. A set of elective activities is designed specifically for ESL students: a native language arts course in Chinese, a conversational English course pairing ESL students with native English speakers, and cultural celebrations. The school's Community Coordinator supports students in a multitude of ways, depending, for example, upon their needs—"locating jobs, medical care, housing, and legal assistance" (p. 91). "The first regular academic night high school in the nation" (p. 87), Manhattan Comprehensive illustrates an alternative pathway for immigrants and other students who would probably not be in the educational system without it.

The International High School is also a four-year comprehensive alternative high school, but it is designed specifically for limited English proficient students who have been in the United States for fewer than four years. Designated an alternative high school within the New York

City school system, International differs from newcomer schools in that it is not temporary (students can attend all four years there and graduate) and it does not segregate newcomers from nonnewcomers entirely (high school students interact with community college students and with students from another alternative high school on the same campus in classes, activities, and informal settings). In 1994, the school enrolled 450 students from 50 countries, speaking 34 languages and ranging in age from 14 to 21 years. The school's mission is to enable all students "to develop the linguistic, cognitive and cultural skills necessary for success in high school, college, and beyond" (International High School, n.d., p. 1).

The school facilitates students' adjustment to U.S. schooling and U.S. culture in several ways. Because all of the students in the school are recent immigrants and the faculty are well prepared to teach immigrant students and students who are not native English speakers, immigrant students are central, not peripheral, to everything that happens and every decision that is made at the school. Acknowledgment of and respect for diverse languages and cultures are not special added-on responsibilities of staff; they are the foundation upon which the school is built. Formal orientations for students and faculty in the summer before school starts provide an initial contact and opportunity for information gathering. Multiple opportunities for the development of relationships among students encourage peer support in the process of adjustment.

School organization at International also supports immigrant students' transitions into U.S. schooling and culture through its emphasis on structures and processes that promote the development of relationships within a school community. As discussed previously, the school has been completely restructured into 12 interdisciplinary clusters, each linking four subjects around a theme and involving approximately 75 students and four to eight staff members. Teacher cluster teams design the structure, organization, and activities of each cluster. The organization of school governance actively involves all staff in hiring, designing and developing curriculum and assessment, and developing and implementing the faculty support and evaluation system. The school organization has grown out of the fact that collaboration is a central theme and approach to life at International among students and faculty. Thus, immigrant students are part of a school community with ample opportunities for information and support as they adjust to their lives and to schooling in the United States.

Instruction and assessment at International are squarely centered on the students, reflecting a student–teacher relationship in which teachers are facilitators for student learning and students have choices and make decisions about how and when they learn, including which language they use. This student-centered approach builds a bridge between immigrant students' past and current lives and learning, reducing the disjunctions that can interfere with their successful adjustment to their new lives. It gives immigrant students opportunities to draw upon their previous knowledge and experience. Students rarely sit in a classroom and listen to the teacher; they learn through multiple opportunities for experience and collaboration with other students. They are assessed through a process that emphasizes setting their own goals and standards, demonstrating their learning (rather than taking tests), and being evaluated by peers, teachers, and themselves (see Ancess & Darling-Hammond, 1994, for an in-depth discussion of the assessment practices at International).

Part of this bridge between students' previous and current learning is the attitude toward students' uses of their native languages. Faculty members at International, most of whom speak English exclusively or primarily, view themselves as "teachers of language rather than teachers of English" (Sylvan, 1994, p. 35). They promote language learning in whatever language the students choose for any particular activity or interaction. Beyond the informal uses of their native languages, students can take a course in which native language development is a specific goal. This approach to native language use for learning and explicit development of native language ability reflects International's focus on the student. It also reduces language shock, integrating students' native languages into their learning rather than banishing them altogether or relegating them solely to informal uses.

Conclusion

These programs represent pathways for immigrant students as they make their way into schools and the larger culture in the United States. While a few recent immigrant students have the opportunity to attend a school or a program designed specifically for them or a school designed to respond to their special circumstances along with the special circumstances of other types of students, the great majority of immigrant students make their first contact with schools through programs within regular schools that focus only, or primarily, on their need to learn English. Through collaboration and combined intellectual and financial resources, schools can expand the possibilities for providing multiple pathways that address the varied and various aspects of immigrant students' lives.

Pathways Into the Mainstream

A primary goal of everyone associated with the education of immigrants and English language learners—the students themselves, their parents, teachers, administrators, policy makers, interested community members—is to help them develop English skills strong enough to move into mainstream classes, where they will be integrated with native-born students and where they can participate in the regular curriculum and instruction. Indeed, if immigrant students and other English language learners are to have the best possible opportunities after high school, they must have access to challenging classes that can help them realize their high aspirations. Unfortunately, many English language learners are "mainstreamed" into vocational education, low-track, and remedial classes (see Harklau, 1994b, 1994c) that do not offer them any benefits in the short or long run and may be worse than staying in ESL and bilingual classes, where at least they generally have access to teachers with preparation for working with them. Instead, they are likely to be forever locked into another kind of special program that leads to nowhere after high school (discussed below in *Pathways to Higher Education*). And they may not know enough about the system to recognize that this is happening to them (Harklau, 1994b). The goal, therefore, must be to mainstream immigrant students into classes that will challenge them and prepare them for higher education or for desirable careers.

This transition is more difficult and complex than it may seem at first glance. Ensuring that it occurs smoothly takes careful thought and planning. The complexity is captured by the comments of Joan Kass, district coordinator of foreign language programs and secondary coordinator of English as a second language for White Plains (New York) Public Schools:

The transition is a bigger step for most students than we realize. They are coming out of a protected environment, where the teachers are very caring and sensitive, class sizes are relatively small, instruction is geared to them, and they're not made to feel self-conscious. And they're moving into an environment where not all teachers share the sensitivity of ESL teachers. Classes are generally larger.... There is a jump in terms of the amount of content and work they have to cover. Kids who talk in ESL classes are afraid to speak up in regular classes because they're conscious of their accents. The rate of speech is different. In ESL classes, teachers modify their rate of speaking. In regular classes, speech is coming at them. It's hard for them to understand. (J. Kass, personal communication, July 31, 1995)

Several obstacles must be overcome to smooth the path for students out of special programs and into the mainstream. One is the nature of traditional secondary school instruction, structure, and climate, especially as they contrast with ESL and bilingual classes—a contrast aptly described by Kass above. The teacher-centered, text-centered, individualistic learning environments of traditional secondary classrooms, in which there is no recognition of the immigrant experience and of the process of adjustment to a new culture, are not supportive of recently mainstreamed immigrant students (see Harklau, 1994a). Any students would find it difficult to go from a nurturing environment, where teachers are sensitive to and knowledgeable about their needs and experiences, where instruction is designed to be accessible to them, and where they receive extra support for learning English and academic content, into an environment that is generally not so nurturing and does not take their experiences or learning needs into account.

In fact, like newcomer schools discussed above, special programs often reflect changing conceptions of teaching, learning, and schooling to a greater extent than do regular programs, offering smaller, more personalized school settings. Teachers in those programs may have more familiarity with student-centered instruction and more freedom to apply it than teachers in traditional mainstream programs (Nancy Meyers, staff developer, Phoenix Union High School District, personal communication, August 23, 1995). Students experience a shock when they leave such an environment and encounter the traditional high school structure and climate, which do not provide a nurturing learning environment even for most U.S.-born students. Mainstreaming that allows students to shift gradually to fewer ESL/bilingual classes and more mainstream classes, rather than moving abruptly into the mainstream, can help soften the blow of the change. Ongoing support for immigrant students in mainstream classes, through tutoring, bilingual and bicultural instructional assistants, and mentoring, can also help them meet the challenges of their new environment (Shannon, 1990).

The insufficient preparation of teachers for dealing with the transition is a second obstacle and one of the major differences between ESL or bilingual courses and mainstream courses. Through no fault of their own, many teachers are not prepared for the new types of students they find in their classes. This problem has two faces. On the one hand, most mainstream teachers lack the knowledge to teach immigrant students effectively. Neither their education nor their experience has prepared them to understand what is involved in learning a second language or in adjusting to a new culture. They may assume that if students are in a mainstream class, they are fully acculturated and proficient in academic English and are therefore prepared to participate, just like the U.S.-born students they have been teaching throughout their careers. They may need guidance, for example, in assessing students' content-specific English skills, making English comprehensible, and finding ways to use language-minority students as resources in mainstream classes (Hamayan & Perlman, 1990). On the other hand, most ESL teachers cannot prepare students effectively for the transition to mainstream classes, because they are not thoroughly familiar with the content, expectations, and styles of teaching that characterize them. Their education has prepared them to teach this special population of students, but they may not have had much exposure to the regular high school program.

A third obstacle arises from the fragmentation that characterizes most secondary schools. Faculty members have few opportunities or incentives to communicate with each other, and the gap is especially wide between those who work in special programs and those in the regular program. ESL and bilingual teachers—who have the knowledge and experience for teaching immigrant and ESL students—are often considered peripheral to the life of the school and may not be included in the rare occasions when other faculty members do talk with each other. The experience of an ESL teacher at a middle school in the Northeast, whom I will call "Ted," is familiar to many secondary ESL teachers. As part of a restructuring effort, the school introduced an interdisciplinary cluster in the sixth grade in 1994-95. A team of four teachers (from the English, math, science, and social studies departments) collaborated to provide interdisciplinary instruction to a heterogeneous group of students that included several of the school's substantial number of learners of English as a second language. Ted was their ESL teacher, so he was familiar with their English language proficiency as well as their academic strengths and needs. However, Ted was not included when the teachers met to design the cluster in the summer of 1994, nor was he invited to participate in any of the daily team meetings held by the cluster teachers throughout the year. He was consulted only when the teachers encountered problems with the ESL students, and their questions and requests were narrowly focused on aspects of second language learning. The cluster teachers never asked Ted for input on the cluster concept, design, or implementation. Ted reported that he felt peripheral to the cluster in particular and to the broader reform and restructuring efforts at the school. If Ted had been integrated more effectively into the team, his knowledge of the particular students in the cluster and of strategies for supporting language learning in general could have facilitated the success of the students in the mainstream cluster courses and could have added to the regular classroom teachers' repertoire for working with other learners of English as a second language whom they would encounter in the future. Formal collaborations among ESL/bilingual and mainstream faculty, such as team teaching, as well as less formal ones, through discussions of students and strategies, have great potential for benefiting students in the transition process.

Fourth, there are no clearly agreed-upon criteria for determining when students are ready to be mainstreamed. Test scores measure certain skills and abilities, but what a particular test measures may or may not be a relevant indicator of success in mainstream courses. Teacher perceptions capture some aspects of development and abilities, but personal subjectivity and lack of familiarity of teachers in special programs with mainstream course content, expectations, and teaching styles may limit the accuracy of their opinions. Allowing students themselves to determine when they are ready to move into the mainstream empowers them, reduces their anxiety, and respects their internal perceptions of their abilities, but they lack knowledge of the system and what is needed for success within it. It is advisable for districts to use multiple criteria or measures for determining when to mainstream students. However, deciding how to weigh the criteria and which ones to use requires serious thought and planning.

Figure 10 presents a number of strategies that can facilitate immigrant students' transitions out of special programs and into the mainstream educational program. They are organized according to the time frame within which they need to be applied relative to a student's transition into the mainstream and within broad educational domains. Some of the strategies should be applied in an ongoing way and not tied to specific points in the transition process; others should be applied both before and after a student has made the transition; others should be applied either before or after the transition.

The four obstacles discussed above are reflected in nine domains upon which these strategies have an impact. The domains are

- professional development,
- communication and collaboration among teachers,
- student support services and structures,
- accountability,
- curriculum,
- criteria for transitioning,
- student placement,
- instruction, and
- staffing.

The strategies happen to reflect many of the principles of student-centered learning and school reform. They encourage

- collaboration and communication among teachers across traditional discipline and department lines,
- professional development opportunities to prepare teachers to work well with all students, even those who depart from the traditional norm,
- increased personalization and flexibility of instruction, curriculum, and support services,
- provision of extra support for students who need it in order to meet the high expectations of teachers,
- multiple measures of student abilities,
- rigorous academic instruction and skills development, and
- support for the development of student relationships and collaboration.

Of course, implementing all the strategies in Figure 10 poses a challenge. To implement them optimally, someone must be responsible for coordinating the effort. In many schools, teachers have the best of intentions to do much of what is suggested: to develop a systematic way

Figure 10. Strategies for Facilitating the Transition of Immigrant Students From Special Courses and Programs Into the Mainstream

	STRATEGY	EDUCATIONAL DOMAIN
	Nonspecific Time Frame:	
1.	Provide professional development for all teachers in • second language acquisition, • language development strategies, • cultural differences, • the experiences of immigration, and • cross-cultural communication.	• Professional development
2.	Encourage and facilitate team teaching opportunities for ESL and bilingual teachers* and provide them with joint planning time.	• Professional development • Communication and collaboration
3.	Develop strategies and find opportunities to reduce the separation of ESL/bilingual programs and staff from regular programs and staff. *Examples:* • Joint staff development • Joint meetings on issues of mutual interest and concern • Team teaching with planning time • Joint planning of academic and extra-curricular activities	• Professional development • Communication and collaboration
4.	ESL and bilingual teachers visit mainstream classes to learn more about the content, expectations, and instructional approaches in those classes.	• Professional development • Communication and collaboration
5.	Mainstream teachers visit ESL and bilingual classes (a) to learn more about the content, expectations, and instructional approaches in those classes, and (b) to learn about the students before they come to mainstream classes.	• Professional development • Communication and collaboration
6.	Provide as much personal connection between students and adults as possible. This can lay the foundation for and provide the support that students will need in the transition.	• Student support
7.	Review course offerings regularly to ensure that all students have access to appropriate courses.	• Accountability
8.	Review course offerings regularly to ensure an appropriate sequence of courses for students before and after the transition.	• Accountability
9.	Review staffing regularly to ensure that qualified teachers are teaching the appropriate courses.	• Accountability

*The term "ESL teacher" here includes both teachers of ESL and teachers of sheltered content classes. The term "bilingual teacher" refers to teachers who teach language classes (e.g., Spanish for Spanish speakers) and content classes in students' native languages.

Figure 10. Strategies for Facilitating the Transition of Immigrant Students From Special Courses and Programs Into the Mainstream (continued)

	STRATEGY	EDUCATIONAL DOMAIN
	Before and After the Transition:	
10.	Offer as much extra intensive support as possible. *Examples of structures for support:* • Saturday academies • after-school tutoring • an extra period during the school day • writing labs • summer school courses • a resource center where students can go for extra help as needed	• Student support • Curriculum
11.	Ensure that transitioning students have access to a counselor to help them prepare for the transition and adjust to it once they're in mainstream classes. Make sure they are connected to a person who knows how to assist them.	• Student support
	Before the Transition:	
12.	Design the curriculum to allow students to make the transition gradually. *Examples:* • Students move from native language content class (e.g., social studies) to sheltered content class to mainstream content class. • Offer courses specifically designed to teach students concepts they will be expected to know in mainstream classes (e.g., basic events in U.S. history; how the U.S. government works; information about key U.S. writers). • Offer "transitional" classes that reflect mainstream content, structures, and processes as much as possible.	• Curriculum
13.	Use multiple criteria (e.g., portfolios, grades, standardized tests) and get multiple perspectives (e.g., teachers, counselors, parents, students) to determine when a student should make the transition.	• Criteria for transitioning
14.	Gather information about the effectiveness of mainstream teachers in working with immigrant students through a variety of sources: student reports, observations, and evidence of immigrant student success in their classes (e.g., grades). Then, place transitioning students in classes of teachers who are handpicked as the most supportive, sensitive, knowledgeable, and experienced for working with immigrant students.	• Placement

Figure 10. Strategies for Facilitating the Transition of Immigrant Students From Special Courses and Programs Into the Mainstream (continued)

	STRATEGY	EDUCATIONAL DOMAIN
	Before the Transition (continued):	
15.	Place transitioning students in classes with other transitioning students so they can support each other and so it will be easier for counselors and ESL/bilingual teachers to follow up on them.	• Placement • Student support
16.	Place transitioning students in smaller classes so they can get more personal attention.	• Placement • Student support
17.	Mainstream teachers visit ESL/bilingual classes to talk to the students about what to expect in mainstream classes.	• Student support • Communication and collaboration
18.	Ensure that ESL/bilingual classes emphasize reading and writing skills development and that ESL/bilingual teachers hold high expectations of students.	• Instruction
	After the Transition:	
19.	Establish mechanisms for maintaining regular communication between mainstream teachers and ESL/bilingual teachers and counselors so that the latter can follow up on students' progress and provide assistance to students and to mainstream teachers as needed.	• Communication and collaboration • Student support
20.	ESL and bilingual teachers visit mainstream classes to follow up on transitioning students. They can then provide support for those students as needed and give feedback to the classroom teacher about the students.	• Student support • Communication and collaboration
21.	Continue to offer an extra period for students to get assistance and support as needed, such as tutoring and assistance with homework.	• Student support • Curriculum
22.	Provide extra help for students in those classes they are likely to have most difficulty with. For example, social studies and history assume a lot of basic knowledge about the United States that many immigrants do not have, whereas government is less problematic because it focuses on current events.	• Student support
23.	Encourage teachers to use cooperative learning and student collaboration so students can work with and learn from each other.	• Instruction
24.	Ensure that explicit language development instruction continues for transitioning students in mainstream classes.	• Instruction
25.	Provide bilingual/bicultural instructional assistants in mainstream classes with transitioning students.	• Staffing

to decide when students should be mainstreamed and to follow up afterwards to monitor their progress; to learn more about the education of immigrants and learners of English as a second language; to find out about exactly what goes on in classes taught in other programs and departments; to communicate more regularly with their colleagues; and to find out whether students who are having difficulty in their classes are also having difficulty in others. But they may not manage to follow through on their intentions amid the many demands on their time and attention. Some tutoring and other support may be offered specifically for immigrant students or for all students including immigrants, but the students who need it may not know about it. Some mainstream teachers may be especially sensitive to immigrant students for personal or professional reasons, but those who make placement decisions may not know who those teachers are. This is the nature of life in a busy high school.

The transition process is generally not carefully planned and monitored. Students take available classes that are deemed most appropriate by someone in a position to make placement decisions (a counselor, an assistant principal, an ESL teacher) who may not have expertise in ESL or immigrant education issues. Some of the classes students take during this period of transition address their linguistic needs, and others do not. Without someone responsible for keeping track of the various facets of the transition process for immigrant and ESL students, they may have to rely on luck to make it through. A coordinator of the transition process can ensure that it is a coordinated, rather than piecemeal, effort. While this person will have other responsibilities as well in most schools, explicitly designating responsibility for coordinating the process of transition from ESL to the mainstream can help to ensure that it receives the thoughtful care and planning it requires.

Pathways Beyond Secondary School

Just as immigrant students need access to multiple pathways for making the transition into U.S. schools and culture, they also need various ways to move beyond high school into higher education or work, ultimately aiming for productive and satisfying employment. While useful for purposes of discussion, the distinction between higher education and work is, like most dichotomies, artificial. Many approaches that prepare students for higher education also help smooth the transition to work, and vice versa. Rather than looking for strategies to guide students toward one road or the other, we should strive to open up routes that will lead them to whatever future they want to pursue. This is especially important when developing pathways for immigrant students and others who have traditionally been pushed away from higher education and toward less skilled, lower paying jobs. The challenge is to combine strong academic and career preparation so that young adults have the widest array of choices open to them as they step beyond the high school door. A problem with most of the so-called school-to-work programs and strategies is that they may be seen as simply another form of vocational education that will trap students in nonacademic tracks, and they may indeed do so unless concerted effort is put into preventing this familiar outcome.

To be effective for immigrant students, pathways must be designed and implemented to address their experiences, perspectives, and needs. Just as educational innovations in teaching, learning, and school organization should not be applied thoughtlessly to all students, approaches to preparing immigrant students for life beyond school should be designed to consciously take into account their native language and English language proficiencies, their previous academic preparation, and their family, personal, and cultural expectations, aspirations, contexts, and support.

Pathways to the World of Work

With increased attention at the federal level to the need to prepare youths for the workforce of the future through the School-to-Work Opportunities Act of 1994 and the emphasis on school-to-work readiness in the Goals 2000 legislation, strategies for helping youths through this difficult transition have proliferated at national, state, and local levels. The approaches do not fit into neat categories, but reflect overlapping goals and strategies, which can make it difficult to distinguish one approach from another and to decide which approach is more appropriate for particular students. Figure 11 presents 11 pathways from school to work and some broad features that can help to distinguish them from each other.

As Figure 11 illustrates, some approaches focus students' attention on learning about and preparing for the world of work rather than actually working (career exploration and career guidance). When the pathway does involve actual work, that work may be paid (career academies, cooperative education, youth apprenticeship, school-based enterprises, and entrepreneurship education) or unpaid (internships, youth service and service learning, and mentoring programs). Some approaches are situated entirely or primarily in schools (career exploration, career guidance, school-based enterprises, and entrepreneurship education), while others are situated primarily at worksites with varying degrees of school involvement (internships, youth service, and work-based mentoring programs), and still others take place at both sites (career academies, cooperative education, youth apprenticeship, and service learning). Some are designed to give youths a broad view of an industry or career cluster (career exploration, career academies, school-based enterprises, and entrepreneurship education), while others typically give them experience with a particular job or jobs (cooperative education, youth apprenticeships, internships, youth service, and service learning).

These common pathways for helping youths make the transition from school to work are described below. They are presented as prototypes, with examples to illustrate programs in action when possible. Because the emphasis on the transition from school to work is recent, some of these pathways are still in the process of being shaped; they may not have been implemented at all, or their implementation may not be widespread. None of these program types is designed specifically for immigrant youths, nor do we know much about the participation of immigrants in them. They must be adapted in ways that make them responsive to immigrant youths. For example, undocumented immi-

Figure 11. Pathways to the World of Work

PATHWAY	FEATURES							
	Involves actual work:			Primary location:			Breadth of focus:	
	Yes		No	School	Worksite	Both	Entire industry	One job
	Paid	Unpaid						
Career exploration			✓	✓			✓	
Career guidance			✓	✓			✓	
Career academies	✓					✓	✓	
Cooperative education	✓					✓		✓
Youth apprenticeships	✓					✓		✓
School-based enterprises	✓			✓			✓	
Entrepreneurship education	✓			✓			✓	
Internships		✓			✓			✓
Youth service		✓			✓			✓
Service learning		✓				✓		✓
Work-based mentoring		✓			✓		varies*	

*Mentoring usually constitutes a component of a larger program or pathway and thus can focus more or less broadly, depending upon the nature of the program of which it is a part.

grant students cannot participate in school-to-work pathways that involve payment, because they require documents that these students clearly do not have. To provide access to work experience for such students, schools should offer a range of pathways, including unpaid ones, and should find alternative ways to compensate students that do not require documentation. The questions presented at the end of this chapter provide guidance in making the needed adaptations.

Career exploration

Young people can and should begin to gain a "broad and textured understanding of career options" as early in their schooling as possible (Kazis, 1993, p. 7). Career exploration through workshops, field trips, and other career education activities helps students understand what is possible, what preparation is required for particular careers, and which careers they might want to aim for in their course enrollment and other activities. Adolescent immigrants are in especially great need of such exploration, because they are not familiar with either work and careers or school preparation in the United States. Poor students who live in inner cities, where most adults hold unskilled, low-paying jobs to which youths do not aspire, are especially unlikely to be aware of career possibilities.

Career exploration strategies must take into account students' English proficiency, both for conveying information to them and for helping them consider careers for which their language backgrounds would make them especially suited or unsuited. Project MAINE (Maine Assists Innovators in Nurturing Excellence), a career awareness program for English language learners, provides information and exploration in different languages (as described in chapter 4 under *Information About U.S. Workplaces and Career Preparation*).

Career guidance

Career guidance enhances (1) self-knowledge and self-awareness, (2) educational and occupational exploration, and (3) decision making and career planning (U.S. Department of Labor, 1993, p. 9). As discussed in chapter 4 under *Information About U.S. Workplaces and*

Career Preparation, career guidance includes exploration of and preparation for careers through information about various careers, exploration of personal skills and values with respect to particular careers, and work experience. More comprehensive than career exploration, career guidance may also include counseling, self-assessment and assessment by a career counselor, career and personal planning, placement, referrals, and follow-up. Immigrant students could benefit a great deal from such a program.

Career academies

"At the crossroads between the school-restructuring and the school-to-work movements" (R. J. Ivry, as quoted in Olson, 1994b, p. 29), career academies provide more personal, supportive, and intensive learning environments than traditional high schools because they use a school-within-a-school organization, and they focus students on a single career or industry, providing contextualized learning and the opportunity to apply classroom learning in the real world (see also ASPIRA, 1994; Glover & Marshall, 1993; Kazis, 1993). Career academies, generally designed for students deemed at risk of dropping out of school, combine vocational and academic instruction, the latter drawing content from the former (Manpower Demonstration Research Corporation, 1994). Students develop individual academic and occupational goals. They work for pay in the industry they have selected during the summer after their junior year, and they participate in an internship in their senior year.

About half of the estimated 200 academies nationwide are in California (Olson, 1994b, p. 29). Pasadena Unified School district offers seven different academies housed at the district's four comprehensive high schools—in finance, health care, geospace, high technology, graphic arts, visual arts and design, and computers (described in Olson, 1994b). Approximately 80% of the 700 students enrolled (the latter being 15% of the total student population) in the academies in 1994 were low-income students, special education students, and English language learners. Academic and vocational content is integrated in academy classes, a process that is facilitated by longer blocks of time in the schedule and a common planning period for teachers. Academy courses meet the state high school graduation requirements and admissions requirements for the two California four-year university systems. Students may take courses at the local community college while still in high school, and the district has developed cooperative agreements with several four-year colleges to facilitate the transfer process for academy students into those programs.

Benefits of career academies include the following: (1) The small school-within-a-school approach provides more personal attention and interaction for students. They have greater access to teachers because of the smaller scale of academies as compared to regular schools. (2) The internship gives students the chance to learn about careers first-hand and to develop relationships with mentors in the workforce. (3) Because academies are organized by industry rather than specific occupation, students have more possibilities than in traditional vocational education programs, and academies are less stigmatized since a full array of professions within industries is possible (see Glover & Marshall, 1993, p. 146). (4) A study of 10 academies in California indicated that students in academies "had better attendance, failed fewer courses, earned more credits, got better grades, and were more likely to graduate" than a matched comparison group of students (Olson, 1994b, p. 31). (5) Elements of this pathway that can be particularly beneficial for immigrant students include greater personalization than traditional secondary programs, direct experience in the U.S. workplace, and more focused preparation for employment.

Tensions and obstacles exist as well: (1) Some parents and others believe that academies represent a vocational track and do not want their children to enroll. (2) Some school staff who are not part of the academy resent the fact that class sizes are smaller than in the regular program and perceive that academy faculty have special privileges and that the program pulls out students whom they would like to have in their own classes. (3) The academy seems to reach primarily the students in the middle rather than those "at the ends of the spectrum"—that is, "extremely bright students" and those who might be "loose cannons"

(Olson, 1994b, p. 31). (4) It can be difficult to find internships for students, especially given the economic downturn of recent years.

Cooperative education

The oldest school-to-work strategy, dating from the turn of the century, cooperative education *(co-op)* "combines academic study with paid, monitored and credit-bearing work" (Ascher, 1994, p. 1). Most programs today involve students for a year or less and focus on marketing, trade and industry, or business, providing classes at the school in the morning and placing students at a worksite in a paid job in the afternoon. A co-op coordinator at the school site makes work placements and teaches a course that supports students during their work assignments. Ideally, the worksite supervisor acts as a mentor for the student and works with the co-op coordinator to ensure that students learn on the job rather than just completing job tasks.

Co-op has "been tied to vocational education and [has] not been seen as part of the college-prep curriculum" (Stern, Finkelstein, Stone, Latting, & Dornsife, 1994, p. 17), a fact that has interfered with participation of employers and college-bound students. In fact, students are generally placed in jobs through vocational education programs. Because students are placed in specific jobs, they do not generally have exposure to a wide range of possible jobs within a field, as is the case in well-designed and implemented career academy models. Fewer co-op students go on to postsecondary education than other high school seniors, but more co-op students are working for pay than other seniors (Ascher, 1994, p. 3).

The quality of a co-op program depends on several factors, including (1) student opportunity to "develop new competencies and contribute to the productivity of the organization" (Ascher, 1994, p. 3); (2) knowledgeable and well-prepared co-op coordinators; (3) links between the job and school-based instruction; and (4) clearly established expectations for both the school and the worksite. Clearly, to offer students the real opportunity to go on to higher education as well as to go directly to work, co-op education programs must find ways to make academic courses and college preparation more central.

Youth apprenticeships

Distinguished from more formal apprenticeships for adults, youth apprenticeships provide structured opportunities for high school students to develop on-the-job work-based competencies along with their academic program. While they combine academic and experiential learning, the degree to which the academic component prepares students for higher education, whether students receive certification in a skill area through their work, and how much time they spend in the apprenticeship vary from program to program. In fact, the definition of youth apprenticeship is "still evolving" (Stern et al., 1994, p. 23); "no single model has won general acceptance" (Kazis, 1993, p. 11).

Some elements of youth apprenticeships have been articulated, however (see Kazis, 1993; National Council of La Raza, 1993; Olson, 1994c; Stern et al., 1994), as follows: (1) integration and coordination of vocational and academic learning; (2) integration and coordination of work-based and school-based learning; (3) coordination with postsecondary educational institutions; (4) award of recognized credentials of skill and academic mastery; (5) participation of employers in all facets of the program; and (6) paid work experience for youths.

Benefits of well-designed youth apprenticeship programs include the following: (1) Learning by doing is effective and appealing to youths. (2) Learning in a real job setting with real employers and coworkers realistically prepares youths for the world of work. (3) The program provides academic and job-related preparation. (4) The program provides the incentive of employment for youths to stay in school.

Problems in implementing youth apprenticeship programs include the following: (1) The focus on work-based competencies does not lend itself to preparing students to go on to college, but may perpetuate tracking. (2) Inflexible school schedules and procedures make it difficult to institute apprenticeships in schools. (3) Older workers have concerns that youths will displace them. (4) Some employers are reluctant to participate, because the incentives for businesses are not clear. (5) The lack of nationally recognized skills standards makes it difficult to establish certificates for skills development. (6) It is difficult to make the workplace into a learning environment for youths, because the focus is on production. (7) It is difficult to coordinate and integrate academic and vocational learning.

Apprenticeships are receiving a great deal of attention, especially at the state level, but, like co-op education, youth apprenticeships must incorporate academic learning with work experience to really offer youths the possibility of higher education. Most efforts are too new to yield complete information about the details or their success. Some efforts in place include Boston's Project Pro Tech, Broome County (New York) Youth Apprenticeship Demonstration Project, and the Pennsylvania Youth Apprenticeship Program. Legislation in Arkansas, Oregon, Wisconsin, Georgia, and Maine has established demonstration projects and made youth apprenticeship a central feature of the state school-to-work strategies (see Kazis, 1993; Stern et al., 1994). Maine's three-year youth apprenticeships begin in 11th grade and are coordinated through the technical college system, where students spend their third year (described in Olson, 1994d). By using this approach, the state hopes to encourage more students to pursue postsecondary education.

School-based enterprises

School-based enterprises "engage students in school-based activities that produce goods or services for sale or use to people other than the students involved" (Stern et al., 1994, p. 35). Such enterprises offer a context for students "to apply their classroom knowledge to the real-world problems of real businesses" (Kazis, 1993, p. 10). Because the entire business exists and functions within the school context, students have an opportunity to learn about multiple aspects of the business. Many of these enterprises have grown out of vocational education programs and perspectives, but others grow out of the academic program.

An example of the former is the Montgomery County (Maryland) Students Construction Trades Foundation and Automotive Trades Foundation (described in Kazis, 1993; Stern et al., 1994). In the former program, students participate in all aspects of the design, building, furnishing, and marketing of houses. In the latter program, students recondition and sell used cars. Other enterprises include retail stores inside and outside of schools, restaurants, print shops, farms, and child care centers.

Foxfire is an enterprise that arose out of an academic program. Eliot Wigginton, an English teacher in a Georgia high school, got students engaged in a journalism project that took them out into the local community to interview, tape, and write about local people and customs (Wigginton, 1986). They wrote and published their writings locally at first. From there, the enterprise grew to include books sold nationally, a play that appeared on Broadway, construction projects restoring local buildings and artifacts, and ultimately a corporation supporting nationwide dissemination of Foxfire approaches in schools (see Beard, 1994). Other examples of enterprises within academic programs include a smoked fish export business in a Sitka, Alaska, high school and an environmental improvement project in Oregon in which students "designed and built a trail system, improved a stream habitat, and made hatching boxes and fish runs" (Stern et al., 1994, p. 37).

Benefits of school-based enterprises include the following: (1) Because this approach is situated in the school and directly supports educational goals, it "may be more hospitable than non-school enterprises to activities that are conducive to students' acquisition of knowledge and skill" (Stern et al., 1994, p. 38). (2) Because the enterprise is student-run, students have a greater sense of ownership than in other types of programs. (3) This approach does not require linking with employers in order to implement and maintain the program, a component of other approaches that is time consuming and can be problematic. For immigrant students, the school setting may provide a more accepting, less threatening environment to learn about business than the real world of the workplace.

Disadvantages of school-based enterprises include the following: (1) Lack of employer involvement decreases the carry-over beyond high school. (2) They are generally small-scale initiatives that involve only a small number of students (Smith & Rojewski, 1992; Stern et al., 1994).

Entrepreneurship education

Closely related to and expanding upon school-based enterprises, entrepreneurship education "teaches students to assess their own attitudes, aptitudes, and skills relative to those necessary for developing and running a business" (Smith & Rojewski, 1992, p. 17). Given the growing number of small businesses and the fact that many students will eventually work in them if not own them, such preparation can foster valuable experience and skill, providing a foundation on which students can move into self-employment after graduation. REAL Enterprises, an entrepreneurship program implemented in several Southern communities, takes students through the process of planning, developing, and starting their own businesses (Kazis, 1993; Smith & Rojewski, 1992; Stern et al., 1994). Businesses established in entrepeneurship education programs have included a school day care facility, a delicatessen, and a printing business (Kazis, 1993, p. 10). Given the large number of immigrants who work in service industries such as housecleaning and gardening, the information provided in such a program could work to the advantage of students and their family members in establishing their own businesses.

Internships

A nonpaid strategy for "providing pre-transition work experience to students in authentic work environments is through the use of internships or practicums" (Smith & Rojewski, 1992, p. 18). Common in academic and professional settings, internships pair students with working professionals for a period of time, allowing the student to observe and participate in the work setting first-hand. They tend to involve "one-time, short-term placements" (p. 18), and a student's academic program generally is loosely related to the content of the work. Components of reportedly successful internship programs include

(1) adequate duration of the internship (e.g., whole semester vs. a shorter time); (2) a substantial number of hours each day spent in the internship; (3) "careful attention to pairing interns and professionals"; and (4) periodic or ongoing seminars where interns can discuss their experiences (pp. 19-20).

Two internship programs involving immigrant students are described below, under *Adapting school-to-work pathways for immigrant students*—the WISE (WISE Individualized Senior Experience) program and the career education program at The International High School. In the Coca-Cola Valued Youth Program (described in chapter 5 under *Student-to-Student Relationships*), the tutoring that older students do with younger students is treated as a paid internship, which gives them the experience of working at a real job.

Youth service and service learning

Complementary to youth apprenticeship, youth service also gets "young people out of the classroom and into situations where they take responsibility, learn employability and work skills, and contribute to community development and well-being" (Kazis, 1993, p. 13). While youth apprenticeships generally place students in private for-profit businesses, youth service programs connect students with community and nonprofit organizations and other service groups for nonpaid work that provides "meaningful community service" (Kazis, 1993, p. 13). Service learning takes this approach one step further, integrating academic learning with service activities. Students who visit senior citizens in a nursing home might read about history from the time of the senior citizens' youth or study the physical aspects of the aging process.

Work-based mentoring

Mentoring relationships can serve both psychosocial and instrumental functions (Flaxman, 1992; Flaxman & Ascher, 1992; Flaxman et al., 1988). Mentoring programs designed to help youths make the transition into the world of work primarily serve the instrumental function. Many types of school-to-work programs—co-op, apprenticeship, internship, and career academy models, for example—include a mentoring component. The Quantum Opportunities Program (QOP) in Philadelphia provided academic tutoring, community service projects, summer jobs, career and college preparation, field trips, and even stipends for studying for the four years of the experimental program (Howard, 1995). The mentoring aspect of the program, based on "patience, love, and faith" (p. 1), emerged as the key to its ultimate success: "The key finding: Within a service framework that allows students to bond with their instructors and each other, disadvantaged youths will 'stick with the program,' especially if the adults stick with the teens" (p. 28).

Some programs are specifically designed as mentorship programs. This approach gives students access to a guide in the work world who can "acculturate [them] to a business environment and the world of work," which is the purpose of the *Capital American Stock Exchange's Career Mentoring Program* (Flaxman & Ascher, 1992, p. 12). *Project Step Up*, a mentoring program at Aetna Life and Casualty in Hartford, Connecticut, aims to help disadvantaged teens make the transition from school to work (described in Stern et al., 1994, p. 58). Beginning the program at age 15, students first take classes for five months in business ethics, business writing, basic math, and computer literacy. If they pass the classes, they can work at Aetna, where they are assigned mentors "who are expected to offer personal counseling, to help with homework, and to act as role models" (p. 58).

There are many unanswered questions about the outcomes of mentoring, because little research has been conducted. Tentative guidelines for designing mentoring programs to assist youths through the transition to work include the following (see Stern et al., 1994; Flaxman et al., 1988): (1) Concentrate on youths who need the type of support that mentoring provides. (2) Mentors should have clear goals. (3) Mentors should have continuing support from the program. (4) Mentoring should take place in a context such as a workplace or a school. (5) Ensure that resources provided are specific and relevant to the youth's needs. (6) Pair students with mentors who "are ahead of the mentee[s], but not removed by great social distance" (Flaxman et al., 1988, p. 45).

The WISE program, described below, incorporates a mentoring component into an internship program.

Business–education compacts and partnerships

A final approach to facilitating the transition from school to work is not really a pathway, but rather the foundation for other pathways. Efforts to bring together public schools, institutions of higher education, community agencies, and businesses have been undertaken in some places with the goals of providing incentives for youths to stay in school, supporting their employment readiness, and offering them increased opportunities for employment if they accomplish the first two goals. While collaborations and even effective communication across institutions can be difficult, business–education compacts or partnerships represent a policy-level strategy for improving work readiness of youths.

The first such effort was the Boston Compact, initiated in 1982 and renegotiated in 1988. The schools agreed to make changes to better prepare students, and the business community agreed to offer more job opportunities for city youths. The city reported success in employing youths and in bringing parity to the employment/unemployment levels of African American and White youths (Glover & Marshall, 1993). The Compact itself does not provide any structures or contexts for integrating school and work learning; rather it provides "a base from which to expand toward the integration of school and work and the evolution of the workplace as a learning site for young people" (Kazis, 1993, p. 10). The Los Angeles Area Business/Education Partnership Cooperative (described in chapter 3 under *Businesses*) illustrates a more comprehensive attempt to influence instruction in school and in the workplace.

Adapting school-to-work pathways for immigrant students

Although immigrants undoubtedly participate in many school-to-work programs, research describing these pathways and evaluating their success does not, in general, specifically identify immigrants as participants (e.g., Glover & Marshall, 1993; Olson, 1994a, 1994b, 1994c,

1994d, 1994e; Stern et al., 1994). Any and all of the approaches used in these programs can help to prepare immigrant youths for the transition to work in the United States if they are applied thoughtfully, taking into account immigrants' particular circumstances. One issue of particular relevance to immigrant students is that of payment for work in school-to-work programs. Depending on their status in the United States, immigrant students may not be eligible for paid work. Program developers may need to find other ways to remunerate immigrant students in order to involve them in such programs.

Some concerns about strategies for facilitating the transition to work are relevant to all young people, including immigrant youths. Without a strong academic emphasis, school-to-work pathways may simply perpetuate and further institutionalize tracking (see ASPIRA, 1994; National Council of La Raza, 1993). Many immigrants and other minority youths already fall into the "pool of adults who are 'qualified' to be economically exploited, unemployed, or underemployed" (Spener, 1988, p. 149). Placing 10th graders onto a path that will ultimately offer them few or no options after high school graduation obviously will do nothing to ameliorate this situation, nor will it provide the skilled, educated workers needed by the United States in the coming century. To avoid this outcome, immigrant youths and their families need "career information, counseling, and exploration from an early age" (National Council of La Raza, 1993, p. 53). Student selection for or exclusion from particular programs determines whether the programs are seen as (and therefore become) desirable options or dumping grounds for less-than-promising students. In particular, the fact that "there are few or no existing bilingual school-to-work models ... calls into question the system's ability to reach limited-English-proficient youth" (ASPIRA, 1994, p. 6). Because the special circumstances of immigrant youths have not been given attention in the development of school-to-work programs, it is especially critical that we ask questions about the programs, in order to adapt existing models to make them appropriate for immigrants and English learners.

Detailed descriptions of two different approaches to facilitating the transitions of immigrant students beyond secondary school and toward the world of work illustrate ways in which educators have designed and adapted approaches for immigrant students:

1. The WISE (WISE Individualized Senior Experience) program

The WISE program, begun in 1973 in Woodlands, just north of New York City, "is a transitional program that gives graduating seniors an experience of working independently in the adult world under the guidance of a mentor" (Aronow, 1993). It is in place in 18 schools, most of which are in the New York area, though there is growing interest and awareness in the program across the country. Students in the program actively engage in experiential learning outside the classroom and often in the larger community outside the school, work cooperatively with each other and with a mentor, and make independent decisions about their own learning. Other ways in which the program expands traditional approaches to teaching and learning include the incorporation of portfolio assessment, journal writing, interdisciplinary learning, and a school-to-work bridge.

According to the founder of the program, former social studies teacher Vic Leviatin, the concept upon which the program is built is "bridging"—helping students go "from school to something," whether that is work, college, or lifetime learning. The senior year, and especially the second semester of that year, is the time when preparation for life beyond school is real. The students are *really* going to be on their own in four months, and this gives the experience an authentic purpose that most school-based activities don't have.

In order to begin a WISE program, a school must adhere to four basic principles (quotations are from a WISE Services program flyer):

1. "Each school-based experiential learning program must be designed to meet local needs." Therefore, a task force of parents, teachers, students, and administrators teamed with business, labor, and social

agency leaders must be involved in "collaborative planning, implementation and ongoing evaluation" of the program.

2. Every senior must be given the opportunity to participate. It cannot be offered only to vocational education students or to gifted students.

3. In order to ensure that the experiential learning program becomes equal in educational significance to classroom instruction, students must earn academic credit for their participation. Most often credit is given for English and social studies.

4. Schools must agree to participate in a consortium of schools that have WISE programs to "foster an environment of mutual support, exchange and collaboration."

To put a program in place, the task force forms committees to plan and implement various program elements, such as administration, community relations, and archiving. Each of these committees must be constituted of an approximately equal number of parents, students, and teachers, in addition to the community members and school and district administrators who may also be in the group. The program then comprises the following activities (quotations are from a WISE Services program flyer):

• The task force solicits resource people from the community to act as work-based mentors for students who want to work with them on projects. Many former WISE graduates and people who have participated in various ways continue to act as resources for students and for task forces putting WISE programs together. At later stages in the program, resource people are also solicited in other ways—for example, by the students themselves, by mentors, or by the WISE coordinator for the school.

• Teachers interview all seniors in the high school to tell them about the program and ask about their interests and ideas for independent projects.

• Each student who decides to participate chooses a school-based mentor on the basis of their role as teacher, counselor, or other school-based adult, not on the basis of content expertise. The school-based mentors cannot choose the students.

• During the fall, the students meet with their school-based mentors and explore ideas and interests for a project. They gather data about possible projects from a variety of sources and, if the projects involve an internship, may visit potential internship sites. "The projects include internships with local community agency members or business people, intensive research, or cultural, artistic, craft, performance-based projects." About half of the projects involve internships.

• The students keep journals of the meetings and of their ideas and thoughts as they develop throughout their experiences. The school-based mentors also keep folders of notes and documents.

• Each student, with the help of the school-based mentor, eventually designs a project and negotiates an internship, if that is part of the project.

• During the internship, "students devote significant time to work in their internships, research their topics, maintain written daily journals, discuss their topics with one another, and meet with their [school-based] mentors to explore and reflect upon project issues."

• Students meet with their school-based mentors once a week during the internship to discuss problems, insights, and experiences. "Opportunities must be built-in for shared reflection, mutual support, and community-building."

• Students meet with their peers once a week in "in-school days" to share experiences and exchange ideas and information with other students participating in the program. Sometimes they meet in groups of those involved in similar projects, and sometimes everyone meets together.

• "Upon completion of the project, students submit their daily journals for evaluation and give exhibitions before a panel of students, teachers and community members." These "stand-and-deliver" presentations (V. Leviatin, personal communication, September 30, 1994) last for one hour, are open to the public, and are evaluated by at least one student, one teacher, and one parent, all of whom were on the WISE task force and went through training to become evaluators.

The WISE program offers a rich opportunity for experiential learning that grows out of students' interests and skills and that engages them in collaboration with peers, teachers, and community members. Each student is responsible for selecting, designing, and carrying out a project. Students have the assistance of others as needed and requested, but they are not directed by others; they are the directors of their own projects and determine what they will get out of them. The program offers the same opportunities to all students; no students are excluded, regardless of the labels they may have in other school contexts (e.g., ESL, learning disabled) or the handicaps they are perceived by others to have (e.g., lack of fluency in English). The WISE program puts into action what most educational approaches say, but do not do: It really is for all students.

Immigrant students, like others, benefit from the experiential nature of the program, from the application of school-learned skills to real-life situations, from learning "to deal with adults in an adult environment" (M. Montalto, the New Rochelle High School WISE Coordinator, personal communication, November 7, 1994), from interaction and collaboration, from making their own choices and decisions and dealing with the repercussions of those decisions, from exploring possible careers through internships, from being given the opportunity and support to "dream any dream" (Grosz, 1994), and from sharing the results of their efforts with peers and parents as well as with teachers. The overarching benefit frequently mentioned by students and adults as well is that students learn things about themselves they could not learn in a classroom. Indeed, the WISE program is not like the vast majority of classroom learning experiences; it involves more active, experiential learning, more collaboration for authentic purposes, and more student decision making. In addition, the program involves immigrant students as "complete participants" (V. Leviatin, personal communication, November 22, 1994) who participate in meetings and presentations along with students from all other backgrounds and experiences. They are not separated or treated differently from other students; all students base their project designs on their personal interests, strengths, and dreams.

New Rochelle High School implemented the WISE program in 1993-94. In a suburban district with an increasingly diverse population, the school has a sizable number of immigrant students. In 1994-95, 18% of the students were Hispanic and 3.6% were Asian, mostly recent arrivals. The school does not refer to students as "immigrants" but as "ESL [English as a second language] students." Recruitment efforts for the WISE program were focused on including ESL students, most but not all of whom were immigrants. The following efforts were made to ensure that students who were not fluent in English could participate:

• The central strategy used by the WISE coordinator, Mary Lou Montalto, for informing all seniors about the program was to describe it to all the social studies classes. However, she did not rely only on this method for informing the ESL students, knowing that they might be too shy to ask questions and that they might not understand everything about it from the presentation. Thus, another presentation about the program was done in the ESL classes.

• After the initial presentation about the program, teachers interviewed all seniors about their interest in the program, their plans for the future, and possible WISE projects. To make this process more successful with ESL students, the ESL guidance counselor at the school gave a list of ESL seniors to the WISE coordinator, who asked the ESL teachers to conduct the interviews with the ESL students, because they had relationships with the students and were more sensitive to their language needs. She asked the district liaison to the Hispanic community, George Castellanos, who is also a Spanish teacher at the school and a member of the WISE task force, to interview students who needed to communicate in Spanish.

• Castellanos also made a concerted effort to solicit work-based mentors from the Latino community, so that Spanish-speaking students could do internships and projects within their own community using their own language.

• All of the Spanish-speaking students were placed in contexts where they could use Spanish to some extent. In some cases, all the work was in Spanish, but in most situations students used both Spanish and English. For example, one student who worked for a doctor used Spanish with patients, which was a big help to the doctor, but she used English with the doctor. Students therefore saw how they can use their own language in this country, where it is valued and useful, but they also saw that they have to be fluent in English as well.

• Since students chose their own school-based mentors, having people who knew their language and culture available as mentors helped to encourage immigrant students to participate. Castellanos served as a mentor for 12 of the Spanish-speaking students—at their request, as the program requires. Montalto said, "George really extended himself to be a mentor," and that was one of the key reasons so many Spanish-speaking students participated and had successful experiences.

• Having someone "who knows the culture, someone who has the trust and respect and support of the community, has the respect of the central administration," and who knows the language is crucial, according to Castellanos. Montalto asserted that, "It wouldn't work for ESL kids without someone like George. Other districts who are thinking of doing it should know that." It could be an ESL teacher who has some release time, but someone is needed to give special attention to the ESL students in order to really get them involved.

- Students were allowed to write their journals in Spanish (or whatever language they wanted). Since 1993-94, they have also been required to write an abstract of their journals in English.

- Students were allowed to do their final presentations in Spanish, which several of them did. Some did theirs in both Spanish and English, because their English-speaking friends were in the audience.

The ESL students at New Rochelle High School conducted a variety of projects. One young woman worked with a physical therapist. A young man tutored bilingual middle school students in math. Another young woman worked with a nutritionist at the local hospital. Another young man worked for an architecture firm in New York City and made a model as part of his project. At first, he was shy about presenting and talking about his project in public, but he ended up doing the "model presentation" that "helped sell the program to other people." According to Castellanos, he "dazzled" the community members and parents with what he had done and became "the pride of the Hispanic community."

Three young women decided to work together on a project on tourism. Castellanos introduced them to the owner of Durán Enterprises, an immigrant from Mexico. He took the students to the airport, where they made a video of their tour of a plane and interviews with the pilot and flight attendants. They also worked in the office. One of these girls was very shy, often "nostalgic and sad" before the project, according to Castellanos. During the project, she "blossomed."

A young woman from El Salvador wanted to find out why so many Hispanic students were unhappy with school and why they cut classes. She wanted to do a survey and write a fictional story about Hispanic students in a new environment. As she proceeded with the project, she changed her mind about the medium through which she wanted to explore these issues. She ended up making a video in the well-equipped school film studio of a talk show in which, as the moderator, she interviewed four students and Castellanos—all in Spanish—about the immigrant experience, the differences between students' lives in the United States and in their home countries, and the attitudes of Hispanic students who cut classes. When the young woman's mother saw the videotape, she cried and said, "You have done wonders for my daughter. Thank you." She said that the project helped her daughter mature.

The project was cross-cultural not only for immigrant students. Two English-speaking students who had studied Spanish wanted to work with bilingual students. One worked with an ESL teacher, and the other worked in an elementary bilingual class. Castellanos judged the program to be "a cross-cultural success for every kid" who took the opportunity to make it so.

There are some special benefits of the program for immigrant students. They gain "self-confidence to go on to the college scene," according to Castellanos. They experience success in learning and come to believe that they can make it in college. They also get "to grow in their culture. Many aren't sure of what their own culture offers them here in the U.S. They hear stereotypes, like *mañana, mañana, mañana* for Mexicans." By placing them in contexts where their language and culture are respected, they are "not being suffocated by American culture; they can work in their own culture." At the same time, they see how they and their culture fit into U.S. culture. "It helps them see they can do things in this culture." By writing their journals in Spanish, they develop their native language literacy skills, which is good for their literacy development in English as well, and they get to use their own language for real learning and communicative purposes in the United States.

2. The International High School Career Education Program

Career education is an integral part of the curriculum at The International High School, reflecting two of the eight statements of the school's educational philosophy:

- The carefully planned use of multiple learning contexts in addition to the classroom (e.g., learning centers, career internship sites, field trips) facilitates language acquisition and content area mastery.
- Career education is a significant motivational factor for adolescent learners.

(International High School, n.d., p. 2)

The school's career education program is designed to help students "develop interpersonal skills as they interact with supervisors and employees, examine the culture and organization of their work places, and think about career implications" as well as "develop practical and social work-place competencies" (Ancess & Darling-Hammond, 1994, p. 16). Career education is built into 2 of the school's 12 interdisciplinary clusters. Students who take *The American Dream* must take *The American Reality* afterwards, and those who take *Conflict/Resolution* must then take *It's Your World.* In the first half of these sequences, students prepare for the internships that they will have in the second half. Because these internships take the students outside the sheltered environment of the school, students are encouraged to postpone career courses until at least their second year at the school, when they will have had more experience in the United States.

All students go through the preparation and internship sequence twice during their four years at International. Depending on their needs and interests, they can use the second internship to try out a different career, try a different aspect of the same career, or explore their interests and skills in more depth.

The students' preparation for the internship involves

- reflecting on their values, interests, and abilities;
- getting information about different careers by reading about the career and interviewing someone working in the field;
- getting information about specific internships available by talking with students who have already done internships;
- developing a resume;

- learning about interviews and practicing being interviewed;
- learning about the expectations, norms, and ways of relating in workplaces in the United States; and
- reflecting on obstacles to their careers of interest and on support systems that could help them succeed in those careers.

Once students have decided which careers to explore, the teachers suggest particular placements for their internships and, by the end of the first trimester, the students each choose one. During the internship, they work every afternoon and attend classes in the mornings. They attend weekly seminars in which they discuss and collaboratively solve problems in their internships and reflect on what they do and do not like about their work placements. This approach gives students focused time to gather information about the world of work in the United States and about particular careers as well as the opportunity to put into practice what they have learned.

Students often help each other as they work collaboratively to gather information and make decisions. On a day in late October when I visited the school, I observed a conversation in Spanish between a teacher and a student who had just arrived at the school. After discussing possible options for the student's internship, they decided that working with elementary children was one possibility. Just at that moment, a student walked by the open door and the teacher called him into the room. She introduced the two young men, both Spanish speakers, and told the new student that the other young man had done his internship in a bilingual classroom last year because he, too, spoke very little English at the time. She asked the second student if he had time to tell the new student about his experience to see if it sounded like something the new student would want to do. He said that he did, and the two of them went out together.

According to this teacher, María Escalante, a member of *The American Dream* cluster, "The internship forces them to face reality, linguistically and socially. It's a make-or-break situation for some." They see what they need to do to make the transition beyond high school successfully. They learn the adult responsibilities needed in a career, such as being on time and carrying out duties. Some of them have an "unrealistic idea of the career they choose and their ability." One student wanted to be a pediatrician, although she was not yet literate in her own language. Ms. Escalante suggested to this student that she think about going into health care and exploring the possibilities. The internships help students determine what is and is not realistic.

Some faculty say we should have no limits on our expectations of students. But my experience isn't like that. We set them up to fail if we don't help them see reality. I encourage them to go into the general field they're interested in and see what happens. (M. Escalante, personal communication, October 28, 1994)

I interviewed five students, all of whom had completed two or three internships. (In previous years, students completed three internships during their four years in high school rather than two, which was the plan in 1994. As with everything at International, the career education program is always undergoing scrutiny and revision.) Among them, they had worked at a hospital giving out supplies and filling orders, at a kindergarten, at a pharmacy, in electronics, at the child care center at LaGuardia Community College, as an intern for a teacher, and as office assistants at International. Beyond the fact that they all had wanted to learn in their internships and improve their English, they agreed with one student who said, "People have different priorities. Some want to improve their English; some want to not be shy; some want other things. It depends on the person." This attitude reflects the support for student autonomy at International, which echoes Maxine Greene's call for us to regard youths "as persons with the right to … articulate purposes for themselves" (Greene, 1992, p.41).

Although they had received preparation before their internships, the students weren't fully prepared. One young woman explained, "But the internship is still different than what you did in school. It's just you out there." They reported that their internships were like "regular" jobs where "you have to try to deal with it even if you don't like it." They reported feeling nervous about their English ability but receiving support from their supervisors and from the weekly seminars at International.

When I asked what makes an internship good or bad, one student said, "Yourself. If you really want to learn. It depends on the student." Another said it depends on coworkers and the supervisor, "the people you work with." They reported several benefits from participating in internships:

- "The internship is not about money. It's about you going out there and learning about yourself."
- "It's scary at first, but it helps you learn English and build your confidence."
- "It gives you work experience. You learn more about the subject."
- "It helps you know about real life when you finish college."
- "It's good experience. [It lets you know] how the job really is, how it will be when you finish."

At the end of the interview, one student said, "There are two kinds of education: school education and life education. The internship is a kind of life education."

3. Summary

Little attention has been given to preparing young people in the United States for the transition from high school to the world of work. Now that educators and policy makers have recognized that secondary students need guidance in negotiating this transition, they must be reminded to include immigrant students in program design and evaluation as well as in broader research. The two detailed examples of pathways that support immigrant students in making the transition from school to work provide a glimpse into what is possible. The WISE program shows how an approach developed for nonimmigrant students can be adapted to make it just as relevant and effective for immigrants as for other students. The International High School Career Education Program, designed specifically for recent immigrants, highlights the emphasis that must be placed on preparing students who are not familiar with U.S. workplaces and employer expectations so that their experiences in the work world will be productive. Because the terrain of school-to-work programs is so uncharted, questions like those posed at the end of this chapter can be a useful guide in ensuring that pathways to the world of work are accessible to immigrant youths.

Pathways to Higher Education

All of the issues raised, the suggestions offered, and the questions posed in this volume are relevant to preparing immigrant students for the pursuit of higher education. By applying new conceptions of learning, teaching, and schooling, by cultivating individual and institutional relationships inside and outside of schools, by providing immigrant students with access to information, and by providing multiple pathways into and beyond U.S. schools, we are supporting the development of competent, confident, productive young adults with options for their lives. Many of the pathways to work discussed above aim to provide rigorous academic preparation so that students will aspire to go on to further education after high school and will be academically prepared to do so. Similarly, many of the pathways into U.S. schools and culture provide the foundation for that rigorous education, offer the information and orientation to the U.S. educational system that immigrants need, and support the development of confidence and high aspirations among immigrant students.

In the United States, as in other countries, the option that offers the widest range of possibilities for economic well-being continues to be the attainment of some level of higher education. Future workers will be at a distinct disadvantage without some postsecondary education (see Carnegie Council on Adolescent Development, 1989, for one of many discussions of this phenomenon). Immigrant students who arrive in the United States at adolescence without proficiency in English should not be written off, but they are likely to face many obstacles to a smooth transition to higher education, and to need alternative pathways for reaching higher education.

An overarching obstacle is the failure of the K-12 educational system to adequately prepare students of color for higher education in the United States. Although there are no national data specifically on immigrant students, National Assessment of Educational Progress (NAEP) data have consistently shown discrepancies in performance among White, Black, and Hispanic students (see National Center for Education Statistics, 1994). The data suggest that a disproportionately large number of minority high school students lack the academic preparation needed to carry out the complex mathematics, reading, and writing demands they are likely to encounter in college.

Clearly, schools are not succeeding with students of color. Although this problem is not new, the growing presence of racial and ethnic minorities in the schools is putting added pressure on the educational system to be more responsive to this segment of the student population. (Villegas, in press, p. 298)

Similarly, the K-12 system fails to graduate students of color. Approximately one-third of Hispanics between 19 and 24 years of age and 20% of African Americans did not have a high school diploma in 1992. Thus, disproportionately large numbers of minority students, especially Hispanic youths, are leaving the educational system before reaching the postsecondary level.

What is causing such bleak outcomes for students of color? A number of educational practices and policies diminish the likelihood that youths will be prepared to meet the challenges of higher education or to gain access to it. One of these is tracking—the sorting of students into homogeneous groups on the basis of "perceived differences in needs and ability" (Harklau, 1994c, p. 1). The ostensible purpose of this practice is to make it easier to design instruction for the particular needs and abilities of groups of students so that they will not be lost, if they are less well prepared than others, or will not be bored, if they are more well prepared. Tracking appeals to common sense. However, it works to the definite disadvantage of those in lower tracks (Oakes, 1985, 1986). Once assigned to a track, students tend to remain in it until they graduate. And the instruction that takes place in lower tracks is decidedly inferior to that in higher tracks, relying on memorization, fill-in-the-blank exercises, highly structured and teacher-centered activities, and simplified texts. "Students in the college preparatory program move at a faster rate, have more access to knowledge in subjects such as mathematics and science and are exposed to more higher-order thinking skills than those in lower tracks" (Pallas, Natriello, & McDill, 1995, p. 47). Instruction in low-track classes stands in sharp contrast to all that new conceptions of teaching and learning indicate about how youths learn best.

English language learners are overrepresented in low tracks (Harklau, 1994b, 1994c; Medina, 1988). The reduced opportunities for complex and content-driven interactions and uses of written and oral language decrease the chances that English learners placed in such classes will develop the language skills, much less the academic abilities, to prepare them adequately for higher education. In contrast, students in high-track classes, "in a vivid illustration of self-fulfilling prophecy," are more likely to be given "explicit instruction in valued analytical skills simply because, as high track students, they [are] already assumed to be capable of such analysis" (Harklau, 1994c, p. 15).

The low expectations and watered-down curricula described here are certainly found in designated low-track classes, but they can also be found in general education classes and in bilingual or English-based classes for English learners as well. And they are no less detrimental in these other contexts. The "passive language learning environment, limiting student opportunities to produce language and develop more complex language and thinking skills" found to characterize instruction in a study of 51 elementary schools and 554 classrooms enrolling approximately 2,000 Spanish-speaking English learners did not promote their English learning or their academic learning as much as a more active, language-rich environment would have (see Ramírez, 1992, p. 10; see also Dolson & Mayer, 1992).

Culturally and linguistically insensitive teaching practices can also limit students' potential by denying them access to academic success (Villegas, 1991, in press). When educators are unprepared to act as cultural and linguistic mediators for immigrant students, they may "interpret [students'] behavior … in ways that underestimate [their] academic potential" (Villegas, in press, p. 303), and they may develop low expectations of students' intellectual abilities in response to students' levels of English proficiency.

Inadequate and insensitive counseling in high school is yet another impediment to many immigrant students' progress toward higher education. Many counselors, faced with tracked high schools, the confounding of immigrant students' English abilities with their academic abilities, lack of understanding of the immigrant experience and second language learning, counseling loads of 300 to 700 students, inadequate preparation to assist students with college counseling, and multiple duties from discipline to scheduling, simply are not up to the task of providing sensitive and appropriate course placement or college guidance to immigrant students (see Barton, 1990; Harklau, 1994c; Schmidt, 1994). When students are pushed toward low-track classes or vocational education and away from academic programs, they do not graduate having fulfilled college admissions requirements, and they are likely to score poorly on tests as well. Harklau (1994c) describes the experiences of a young immigrant from Taiwan who "made repeated but ultimately futile attempts to be moved into Advanced Placement classes" by appealing to his counselor, who thought his aspirations were "unrealistic." As Harklau argues, "the counselor's judgment of Eddie's ability was likely to become a self-fulfilling prophecy as Eddie spent more of his high school years in low track classes where he would not learn the skills necessary to function in higher track classes" (p. 27).

Immigrants and other students from non-English-dominant cultural and linguistic backgrounds are seriously affected by such experiences, both because they are more likely to be placed in low-track classes, and because they need more guidance to successfully negotiate the system than more affluent, well-educated students (Schmidt, 1994). Many do not personally know adults who are knowledgeable of the educational system in the United States, and therefore have no access to the informal information and assistance that middle-class students do. They would benefit from basic information about preparing for, selecting, and applying to colleges, which counselors could provide. If they rely on their counselors to provide it, however, most of them will languish in programs that do not lead to college.

Changes in federal financial aid programs, which put more burden on borrowing and less on scholarships, also discourage low-income immigrant students from enrolling in college. Pell Grants, the federal program that provides small grants to low-income families, have been reduced in value "by about 15 percent since 1980 while college tuitions were rising by about 50 percent" ("Tax Deductions," 1995). These and other grant programs are likely to be reduced or eliminated altogether in the current political and economic climate. Loans that leave students and their families with large debts may seem too risky, given the uncertainty of their economic situations and of their completion of college (Chinn, 1988; Hidalgo & Huling-Austin, 1993). Undocumented students face even greater financial obstacles. In many states, including California, they must pay high out-of-state tuition, and federal law prohibits them from receiving financial aid (Stewart, 1993).

If these practices interfere with immigrant students' academic achievement and therefore their access to higher education, then it follows that to promote such achievement and access we should remove these obstacles. We should hold high expectations of immigrant youths and apply curricular and instructional strategies that make our expectations evident. Those strategies should reflect our best thinking about teaching, learning, and schooling, giving immigrant students the benefits of educational change and innovation along with other students. We should eliminate tracking for all students, making all classes high-track classes. We should design strategies for validly assessing immigrant students' knowledge, abilities, and progress (see Ancess & Darling-Hammond, 1994).

This is not to say that we should treat immigrant students exactly like nonimmigrant students. We need to adapt existing strategies and devise new ones for helping all students negotiate the system as they move toward graduation and higher education. Academic support services delivered through such means as tutoring, summer schools, weekend programs, and academies can help improve students' academic abilities and English language skills. Linkages with higher education institutions—especially community colleges—provide direct connections for students who would have no other way to learn about colleges on their own or even to envision themselves attending college. The arrangement at The International High School has this school-community college linkage built in. Because the school is on the campus of LaGuardia Community College in Queens, New York, high school students may take college courses. They also have access to college facilities such as computer labs, the library, and various media production facilities. This offers them access to college-level academics, more sophisticated facilities than most high schools in New York City, possibilities for interacting with a range of diverse college students, the opportunity to gain college credit while still in high school, and the opportunity to experience college before having to make the complete shift beyond high school. In fact, the disjunction between high school and college is much less extreme for International students than for most high school graduates. Similarly, the career preparation and internship program at International (described above) helps to facilitate the transition to the U.S. workplace.

In the remainder of this chapter, I describe two program types and four specific programs designed to help immigrant students through the transition to higher education.

Program types

1. Tech Prep (2+2)

This is an approach to facilitating the school-to-work transition that is built upon the articulation between high school and community college (see ASPIRA, 1994; Glover & Marshall, 1993; Kazis, 1993; Stern et al., 1994). It is called "2+2" Tech Prep, because it involves students in occupationally-specific programs for the last two years of high school and the two years of a community college program. Students concentrate on preparing for technical careers in such fields as engineering, health, business, graphic arts, and agriculture. "Partnerships [between secondary and postsecondary educational institutions, between vocational and academic programs, and among education, business, industry, and labor] are a necessity for full implementation" of Tech Prep programs (Stern et al., 1994, p. 127). Thus, if successful, Tech Prep programs strengthen linkages, not only between schools and colleges, but among various agencies and institutions. While this approach could help to prepare students for future careers as well as to smooth the transition from high school to community college, its full potential for linking school to work has not been met. While work-based learning is theoretically part of Tech Prep programs, in fact its "implementation is essentially school-based at present." It has been called a "school-to-school transition program" (Kazis, 1993, p. 8).

2. Upward Bound

This is another kind of program that is built upon school–university relationships. A college or university with an Upward Bound program identifies and provides special assistance and support to high school students who fit the profile of those at risk of not completing high school and not continuing on into postsecondary education but who have the potential to do so. Programs typically include tutoring, personal and academic counseling, classes during the school year and in the summer to build academic knowledge and skills, orientation to college (e.g., campus visits, talks by college students and faculty), preparation for taking the SAT, and a "bridge" program for high school graduates planning to attend the college or university in the fall (see Legters, McDill, & McPartland, 1993; Natriello et al., 1990). The extent to which the higher education institution collaborates directly with the high school and the number of immigrant students who participate in the program vary. However, Upward Bound is a well-established federally funded program that offers the opportunity for links between higher education and public high schools to promote the college entrance and success of immigrant students.

Specific programs

1. Project Adelante
A program specifically serving many immigrant students, Project Adelante is a joint project of Kean College and three New Jersey school districts. Funded by AT&T, the New Jersey Department of Higher Education, Kean College, and the school districts, the project's goals are "improved high school completion rates, increased college participation, and increased interest in the career of teaching" (Center for Applied Linguistics, 1994, p. 20). Students in Grade 6 or higher are selected to participate in a Saturday Academy throughout the academic year and a five-week residential summer program, both held on the college campus. They also participate in field trips and special activities, such as a science fair, a math olympics, and a bilingual spelling bee. Their parents can take ESL courses offered through the project and participate in seminars on issues they select, facilitated by the counselors. Faculty and counselors from the school districts and from the college teach the courses. Latino college students and juniors and seniors in high school are employed as tutors and mentors for the students in the summer, and Latino professionals serve as mentors. Major components of the program are "English language development workshops; math, science, and computer literacy skills development sessions; music/art/physical education activities; parental involvement activities; career counseling workshops; and field trips" (Villegas, 1992, p. 81).

2. The Hispanic Student Success Program
The Hispanic Student Success Program (described in "HSSP Program Evaluation," 1994) was begun in 1988 by the Hispanic Association of Colleges and Universities (HACU) to improve "the low college going rates of Hispanics" (p. 9). In place in six school districts in San Antonio, the program provides support at elementary, middle, and high school levels to prepare and encourage Hispanic students to go on to

higher education. While we may assume that some of the students in the program are immigrants, the description does not specify whether that is the case or not. Most of the students have little familiarity with higher education, and many "had never seen a college campus and had no idea of the process for getting there" (p. 9). At the high schools, students attend workshops on taking the PSAT and the SAT and visit nearby colleges and universities. Outcomes between 1989 and 1992 showed that PSAT and SAT scores and college-going rates increased among participating students. At the middle schools, a juncture at which many students drop out of school, the program identifies potential leaders among the students, develops their leadership skills, takes them to visit colleges, and exposes them to positive role models. They also try to get students to "understand that they do have choices and that the choices they make now will influence their future" (p. 10). Student attitudes showed that they had come to see college as a possible goal. At the elementary schools, HSSP runs an after-school center where students can come to do homework and receive individual tutoring.

3. AVID (Advancement Via Individual Determination)

AVID is an "untracking" program begun in San Diego in 1980, the goals of which are to "motivate and prepare under-achieving students from linguistic and ethnic minority groups to perform well in high school and to seek a college education" (Mehan et al., 1992, p. 3) and "to restructure secondary school teaching methodologies to allow college preparatory curricula to be accessible to all students" (Swanson et al., 1995, p. 54; see also Mehan et al., 1993; Mehan et al., 1994). It is described as an "untracking" program rather than a "detracking" program, because the goal is not to eliminate tracking but to place more students, especially those who have not achieved highly, "in rigorous academic classes along with their high-achieving peers" (p. 2). By 1995, 115 middle and high schools within San Diego County, more than 200 secondary schools in other California counties, 19 schools in Kentucky, and 10 U.S. Department of Defense Dependents Schools had put AVID programs in place (Swanson et al., 1995, p. 59). While the program is not designed specifically for immigrants, immigrants are among the "high-potential/low-performance" students (Mehan et al., 1992, p. 3) of various ethnic and linguistic backgrounds and English language proficiencies who participate in the program. Written accounts of the program do not, however, specifically discuss adaptations for recent immigrants or how AVID addresses the language needs of students not proficient in English.

AVID students enroll in college preparatory programs and take an AVID course for one period a day. The AVID coordinator teaches this course using "collaborative teaching methods, inquiry approaches, and writing-to-learn techniques" (Mehan et al., 1992, p. 3). In this course, the teacher and aides provide tutoring and other assistance in academic subjects and provide explicit instruction in the skills needed to succeed academically:

> AVID students are taught how to read a book: not simply how to link sounds with letters, but how to interpret and analyze texts ... how to extract the main idea, find supporting evidence, and summarize and synthesize information. They are also taught techniques and strategies for writing essays in English, history, and social studies. Test-taking skills are strongly emphasized. Students are provided explicit instruction about how to eliminate distracting answers on multiple choice questions, and they learn strategies for approximating answers, and probabilities about the success of guessing. (Mehan et al., 1992, p. 12)

They are also taught "strategies for approaching faculty when they are having difficulty in class or need assistance or clarification" (p.12).

In addition to these academic supports, AVID staff and coordinators provide extensive social and personal support as well. They communicate with parents, take students to colleges and universities, bring representatives of colleges and universities into the classes, and help students through the process of selecting and applying for college, including sitting down with them to fill out forms. They provide "a time and a place to study" (Mehan et al., 1993, p. 25). They advocate for students in their other classes and mediate between the students and others when necessary. They counsel students with personal problems.

Graduates of the program enrolled in four-year colleges in 1990-91 in higher proportions than the local or national averages (50% vs. 38% and 39%, respectively). The system of social and academic supports and the "explicit socialization process that parallels the implicit socialization process that occurs in well-to-do families" appear to account for this success (Mehan et al., 1992, p. 12). AVID places underrepresented students in a rigorous academic program and provides them with the system of support and advocacy that sees them successfully through it. Research has suggested that four particular processes are responsible for AVID's success (Swanson et al., 1995):

- Singling out group members for enrollment in special high-status classes and public markers of group identity (such as notebooks, ribbons, and badges with the AVID logo).
- Explicit socialization in the hidden curriculum (for example, note-taking and test-taking strategies and the process of applying to college).
- Teacher advocacy and sponsorship.
- Formation of voluntary associations among students who participate.

4. Step-to-College/Mission-to-College (STC/MTC)

STC/MTC, a collaboration between San Francisco State University (SFSU) and the San Francisco Unified School District (SFUSD), is in place in 10 San Francisco high schools. It shares many features with Upward Bound and includes a component specifically designed for immigrant students, described by Westat (1992). Begun in 1985 and based to some extent on the AVID program, STC/MTC offers underrepresented minority students, including recent immigrants, the opportunity to enroll in a college preparatory program. Features of the program include a core college-prep curriculum beginning in 9th grade, college-level courses taken for college credit in 11th and 12th grades, tutoring, counseling, assistance in applying for college and for financial aid, explicit instruction in study skills development, integration of study skills and writing in all classes, follow-up in college, and professional development for high school teachers and college faculty.

The program's "overriding philosophy is that all students–if given proper training, support, and encouragement–can successfully pursue a college education" (Westat, p. 87). The goal is "to create a culture of college-going" at the participating high schools, all of which are highly diverse inner-city schools, "firmly supported by a program of academic preparation, cultural awareness, skill training, and social support" (p. 87). The students are "predominantly inner-city, economically disadvantaged minorities—primarily African-American, Chicano-Latino, Chinese, and Filipino. A large percentage ... are recent immigrants ... with limited English skills" (p. 89).

STC/MTC began as a collaboration between one professor at SFSU and two administrators at Mission High School with the goal of increasing the number of Chicano-Latino students from that school in college; it included only students who had intermediate English proficiency in their senior year of high school. The response was so positive that the program quickly grew to encompass students of all ethnic groups, including recent immigrants, and to be implemented in other schools. By 1991, STC/MTC had expanded to include five distinct components, as follows:

1. *Step-to-College* recruits students during their junior year and registers them as "transitory" students at SFSU. They take a three-credit Critical Thinking class taught by SFSU instructors on the high school campus for two semesters. They thus earn six college credits while still in high school. They also receive information about college requirements and assistance in filling out application and financial aid forms. This process "demystifies the college experience" and allows them to become "familiar with the format and tone of college courses" (p. 92). Those who are planning to go to SFSU attend orientation sessions, visit the campus, get assistance in matriculating, and take a required STC *College Success Skills* course as freshmen.

2. *Mission-to-College* was designed "to intervene with at-risk students at an earlier point in their school careers" (p. 93) and operates only at Mission High School. Eighth graders in feeder schools are recruited before they enter Mission and, once there, are placed in a college preparatory curriculum, which they follow through 12th grade, when they participate in the Step-to-College component of the program. They receive instruction in study skills throughout all of their courses.

3. The *Academic Fellows Program*, designed to improve the "work habits and attitudes toward school" of second semester freshmen and first semester sophomores at Mission High School, pays students $250 a semester to stay after school and study in the library four days a week for 1¹/2 hours per day (p. 94). Students receive tutoring from SFSU students who were former Mission High School STC participants. The program was designed to provide concentrated study time for students who would otherwise have to work at after-school jobs to earn money.

4. *Bilingual Mission-to-College* (BMTC), originally funded with federal Title VII money, was designed in recognition of the fact that many students in the STC schools who were in need of such assistance were recent immigrants with little proficiency in English. The last year in which this component of STC/MTC was funded was 1993-94. Some of the features of BMTC continue to exist, but it is no longer fully in place. BMTC was similar to the MTC component of the program in its focus on study skills development and college preparatory curriculum. It differed in its attention to students' language backgrounds and proficiency in English. Some courses were taught in English with bilingual tutors, and some were taught using students' native languages and English. Each of the three participating schools (Mission, Wilson, and Balboa High Schools) were assigned two SFSU faculty consultants to work with them in developing curriculum and instructional approaches.

5. *Afrocentric Step-to-College*, in place at Wilson High School, was developed when it became clear that the original STC was not succeeding with African American students. While providing college courses

for juniors and seniors like STC, Afrocentric STC does so through *Introduction to Black Studies* rather than the general Critical Thinking course, and the instruction is more interactive and less lecture oriented than in the general STC classes.

STC/MTC's longevity and apparent success have been attributed to several factors. It is built upon collegial relationships between SFSU faculty and high school teachers. College faculty teach classes at the high schools and high school teachers teach courses at SFSU, and they meet in different configurations in the different schools and at SFSU to participate jointly in various aspects of planning and implementation. The institutional commitment of SFSU, SFUSD, and the schools involved has been carefully nurtured and slowly built by the program director and other staff. In this respect, STC/MTC reflects a successful school/university collaboration built upon working relationships among individuals in both types of settings. Another reason for the program's success is the "caring and personal attention" given to students by instructors (p. 86). As is the case in most innovative programs, many staff members give far more than the time and energy they are contracted for, and it pays off in student engagement and success. A third factor that has served the program well is its adaptability. As described above, it has evolved in response to needs and interests and has been adapted to address the differences among the different groups of students it serves.

Summary of Pathways to Higher Education

In considering which of the various pathways to higher education described above might be most likely to lead immigrant youths toward the goals we all seek, we need to consider the extent to which these pathways are flexible enough to respond to the complexities that characterize real lives. In order to judge accurately whether a particular path can serve immigrant youths well in their transitions into and beyond U.S. schools, we must be knowledgeable of both the students and their experiences and the particulars and realities of the pathways we are considering. The WISE program was shaped so that it engaged and served the immigrant students at New Rochelle High School very effectively, even though the approach was designed for and used with nonimmigrant students for many years before. The shaping took place primarily through the participation of particular people inside and outside the school who took on particular roles and tasks (e.g., interviewing the students, acting as mentors, acting as resource people) and through accommodations to the students' greater proficiency in Spanish than in English. The Step-to-College program was modified to incorporate students who are not proficient in English, though such proficiency was originally a prerequisite for participation. Ensuring that students have options—that is, multiple and flexible pathways available to them—offers the best hope for assisting them through these transitions.

The features of these pathways to higher education for immigrant youths are summarized in Figure 12.

Figure 12. Features of Pathways to Higher Education

Academic Curriculum
- A rigorous, college preparatory curriculum in high school available in bilingual or English-based courses designed for immigrant and ESL students
- Integration of study skills and writing in all courses
- Academic content courses in students' native languages
- College-level courses taken for college credit during high school

Academic Support in High School
- A special course during the school day for academic support and preparation
- Explicit instruction in
  - ... study skills development (notetaking, reading textbooks)
  - ... summarizing and synthesizing information
  - ... writing essays in English and other subjects
  - ... test-taking strategies
  - ... approaching faculty for assistance
- Tutoring before, after, and during the school day (by faculty, adult tutors, and peer tutors)
- Use of bilingual tutors and instructional assistants in classes
- Regular communication between program faculty and faculty of students' other courses to follow students' progress and to provide support and advocacy as needed
- An after-school assistance center
- Saturday classes
- Summer school programs throughout high school
- Summer bridge program before freshman year in college
- Preparation for taking standardized tests (PSAT, SAT)

Personal Support for Students
- Personal counseling—regularly scheduled and on an as-needed basis
- Mentoring by older peers and by professionals from the same ethnic and linguistic backgrounds as students

Figure 12. Features of Pathways to Higher Education (continued)

- Advocacy for students in mainstream classes
- Pay for participation in after-school programs (to allow participation by those who would otherwise have to work)

Personal and Academic Enrichment
- Enrichment courses in computers, dance, art, sports
- Special academic activities (e.g., science fair, math olympics)

Orientation to Higher Education
- Field trips to colleges and universities
- Talks by college students and faculty members
- Information about college requirements
- Assistance selecting, applying to, and filling out financial aid forms for college

Follow-up and Support in College
- A special course during the freshman year of college
- Counselor assigned to follow up on individual students during freshman year of college

Parent Involvement
- Regular and ongoing communication with parents
- Parents' signatures on contracts for student participation in programs
- ESL classes for parents
- Seminars for parents

Formal Links Between High School and College/University
- A formal link between the high school and community college curricula
- University faculty consultants help to develop curriculum and instructional approaches
- University faculty teach courses at the high school
- High school faculty teach courses at the college/university for students in the program

Support for High School and College/University Faculty
- Professional development for high school and college/university faculty members in working with immigrant students

Conclusion

While there are many paths leading to postsecondary education and work, the desired goal for all young adults is to develop the ability and knowledge to make good choices, so that they can be gainfully employed and lead productive, satisfying lives. Immigrant adolescents must have various means and opportunities for achieving this goal, many of which differ from those that work for nonimmigrant students. They need paths that will help them make sense of the assumptions, expectations, and customs of a strange and new country; that will lead them toward proficiency in English no matter where they are starting; that will prepare them for employment in the United States and teach them how to gain access to jobs; and that will prepare them for useful, lifelong education and provide the necessary information and skills needed to gain access to it. These paths may be manifested in what we usually call "programs"—special contexts with their own constituencies, advocates, settings, and even sources of financial support that set them apart from the mainstream. Indeed, most of the examples above take the form of programs. But we should not be limited in our imagination by the program tradition in education. Immigrant students may carve their own paths out of a mainstream context by interacting with it in a unique way.

The following questions can help to ensure that issues of special relevance to immigrant youths and their families are taken into account in designing multiple and flexible pathways for immigrant students moving into, through, and beyond school.

Questions to ask in applying Principle 4: Provide multiple and flexible pathways.

Language:

1. Is explicit attention given to language issues (i.e., the fact that students speak native languages other than English and that their social and academic proficiency in English varies) in the design of the pathways?

2. Does language have a formal (through rules or policies) or informal (through customs, staffing, unconscious behavior) impact on whether immigrant students and their families can participate in the pathways?

3. Are the pathways designed to include immigrants and their families who are not fluent in English?

4. Do the pathways incorporate a philosophy and strategies that support youths in using and learning English without placing them in situations in which they will be judged inadequate or, worse, be harassed because they are not yet fully fluent?

5. Are the pathways designed to value and build upon immigrant youths' native language abilities and to acknowledge that their native language is one of the strengths they bring to learning?

6. Is value for bilingualism built into the design of the pathways?

7. Do the pathways recognize that language is not the only factor that is important for facilitating immigrant students' transitions into, through, and beyond secondary school?

Educational backgrounds of students and families:

1. Are the pathways designed to incorporate participants who have had varied educational experiences?

2. Are assistance and information provided for those who have not had traditional educational experiences?

3. Do the pathways allow different types and degrees of participation to accommodate different degrees of academic preparation?

4. Do staff hold high expectations and provide accessible rigorous academic instruction for all immigrant students, no matter what their previous educational background?

Immigration experience:

1. Do nonimmigrant students in courses and programs with immigrant students have opportunities to learn about the immigration experience from immigrant youths and their families?

2. Do the pathways require participants to show proof of a particular legal status vis-a-vis immigration? If so, is this consistent with the law?

3. Do the pathways take into account the amount of time immigrant students have been in the United States and provide information needed by recent immigrants in order for them to participate?

4. Do the pathways allow different types and degrees of participation to accommodate different degrees of familiarity with the U.S. work world and higher education system?

Culture and cultural context:

1. Are the pathways embedded in a format, context, or processes that assume familiarity with and understanding of particular values (e.g., individual achievement is more important than collective achievement), expectations, assumptions, and ways of thinking and behaving that youths from other cultures might not be aware of?

2. Do the pathways incorporate certain expectations with regard to gender roles, family relationships and expectations, age groups, individuality/collectivity, or other culturally variable roles, relationships, and values?

3. Do the pathways allow flexibility for those who have come from different cultural, linguistic, and educational backgrounds, such as multiple points of entry, various means to and standards for success, and support for diversity of approaches to the tasks at hand?

4. Are different styles of teaching and learning acknowledged and incorporated into the pathways?

Social background and social context:

1. Do the pathways take into account different degrees of access to economic resources (e.g., by not assuming access to computers at home)?

2. Are pathways accessible to students who have to work or who have other responsibilities outside of school?

3. Do pathways value and build on the different social contexts in which the students live (e.g., immigrant communities)?

Conclusion and Recommendations

The complex interplay of individual, collective, and contextual influences on secondary immigrant students' educational experiences and the multiple transitions that permeate their lives can overwhelm us as we strive to envision and establish educational environments that facilitate their transitions into, through, and beyond school. Changing conceptions of learning, teaching, and schooling offer new possibilities for engaging in the process and, at the same time, further complicate what we must bring to the task. Learners can be empowered when they are viewed as active participants in their own learning, as collaborators and as decision makers. Immigrant students can benefit from increased teacher knowledge, personalization of schooling, and direct attention to cultural and linguistic issues when teachers function as learners, collaborators, facilitators, and cultural and linguistic mediators. When schools are organized and conceived as learner-centered communities, as part of a larger situational and chronological context, and as mediators between home and school cultures, immigrant students and their families are more likely to be integrated into the life of the school. However, as educators of immigrant students, we cannot simply apply these changing conceptions—which have arisen out of a European American tradition—without thoughtful consideration of ways in which they are and are not responsive to immigrant students' experiences, perspectives, and needs and without accompanying efforts to adjust those that should be more responsive.

Research and the experiences of students and educators reviewed for this volume suggest four broad principles that can support immigrant students in making these critical transitions. First, by cultivating relationships with other agencies and organizations outside schools, we can combine resources to address the multiple aspects of immigrant students' lives, treating them as whole people rather than solely as learners of English and building upon their strengths rather than seeing them as deficient. Second, by providing access to information about schooling and culture, resources available to them, the world of work, and higher education in the United States, we make explicit a range of expectations, procedures, customs, and values that natives take for granted and that immigrants as well as natives need to make the best decisions and to avoid misunderstandings that can impede student progress. Third, by cultivating relationships among all people involved (students, school staff, families, and other adults), we establish a context that nurtures the crucial "support of important, meaningful people" (Comer, 1993, p. 203) for students as they make decisions and face challenges in their lives, develop their identities, and envision their futures. Fourth, by designing multiple and flexible pathways for immigrant students into, through, and beyond secondary school, we offer various vehicles and opportunities that respond to the complexities of immigrant students' lives, supporting them as they learn about and adjust to U.S. culture and schooling, meet high expectations, engage in challenging curriculum and instruction, and progress through school into young adult lives of further education and work.

Cross-Cutting Themes

Several cross-cutting themes emerge from this work. One of these is **the need to acknowledge, learn about, and frequently remind ourselves of the complexity of it all**: the complex influences on immigrant youths' life experiences and educational experiences; the complexity of the responses called for from educators and from schooling; the layers of possibilities and barriers that immigrant adolescents face from the time of their arrival in the United States, through their interactions with the educational system, and into their lives beyond high school. While all young lives are complex, the facets of immigrant youths' lives carry their own hues and shapes distinct from those of native-born young people in many ways. We show respect for the young people and increase our potential for educating them when we resist the temptation to focus on one or two facets and ignore others, and when we face the realities of their lives and the impact those realities have on individuals rather than acting as if they leave some parts of their lives outside the schoolhouse door when they enter. Acknowledging these complexities also requires us to resist the temptation to fall back on the stereotypes and generalizations that lead us to lump all immigrant students together. It requires us rather to recognize, for example, that refugees' experiences differ from those of immigrants; that Spanish-speaking immigrants in the United States constitute a much larger, more powerful, and more coordinated group than other immigrants; and that the experiences of White immigrants differ from those of ethnic minority groups.

A second and related theme is that **our responses must be flexible and adaptable to these realities.** We must abandon the "one-size-fits-all" approach (Reyes, 1992, p. 435) to education, which is no more appropriate in applying cutting-edge innovations than it is to applying worn-out teaching methods. We must situate our practice within the broader reform movement, but go beyond the "this-is-good-for-all-students" platitudes that too often characterize discussions of how reforms apply to nonmainstream students. Learner-centered education requires that we interrogate potential practices to ensure that they respond to our particular learners before simply applying them. We need to ask the following questions: *Is* this approach, innovation, structure, or strategy appropriate for secondary immigrant students, given the particular and complex influences on their lives and educational experiences? How can we adapt it to make it more appropriate and effective without reducing the potential it presents for student learning? How can we maintain the high expectations built into reforms and, at the same time, provide the support that immigrant adolescents are likely to need to meet those expectations? Even more difficult, how can we reconcile the conceptions of learning that many immigrants bring to U.S. schools when they conflict with the current conceptions in the United States that place great value on individuality and autonomy? How can we create the opportunities, the data, and the expertise to answer these questions as school communities? As we answer these questions, we will identify variations in the responses that are needed to support immigrant students as they make their way successfully into and beyond U.S. secondary schools. With this information, we can then design multiple and expansive options that will support individuals and groups within the larger immigrant population.

A third theme is that the accomplishment of the goals set out above requires **the collaboration of people, perspectives, resources, and**

organizations, rather than the traditional fragmentation and isolation that characterize U.S. education in general, and secondary education in particular. Educators, schools, and school systems must come up with creative ways to build collaborations with health and social service agencies, community-based organizations, businesses, and institutions of higher education as well as with families. Such integration requires the building and nurturing of relationships among people at all levels of engagement inside and outside of schools, which takes time and effort. When people, perspectives, resources, and organizations work together, however, they bring usually disparate elements of youths' lives and experiences together into an educational system that treats immigrant students as whole people, not just as English learners or at-risk students or members of culturally diverse populations.

A fourth theme emerging from this volume—one that also challenges the traditional fragmentation and separation in education—is that immigrant students will make transitions more successfully if they have **greater opportunities for interaction and collaboration with a variety of immigrant and nonimmigrant students.** Many of the structures and strategies described in the volume reflect the view that opportunities for frequent and meaningful interactions with peers of various backgrounds and ability levels as well as with adults promote learning and social development and that all students should be held to high expectations and provided the support to achieve them. The practice of tracking is diametrically opposed to this view, representing an explicit, purposeful plan for the separation of students based on presumed ability levels. Some programs eliminate tracking by grouping students heterogeneously across achievement levels and even ages and grades, while others work to increase the numbers of underrepresented students in high track classes. Whether advocating one approach or the other, many educators and researchers agree that the current system of rigid separation of students through tracking must be abandoned. Similarly, plans for facilitating the transition from school to the world of work now call for an equal emphasis on academic and career preparation so that both traditionally college-bound youths and traditionally non-college-bound youths will participate, and so that both can have the option of going on to higher education. With regard to immigrant students, we are urged to find more ways to integrate special programs for immigrant students and English learners into the broader reforms taking place without losing sight of the necessity to adapt them, as discussed above. We can no longer concentrate our energies on designing and supporting programs that effectively deprive immigrant students of the benefits of the broader education reforms and that allow many educators to avoid developing culturally and linguistically responsive understandings and skills.

A final theme of this volume and one that undergirds all the others is that **educators urgently need more education to increase their sensitivity to and knowledge of their students' cultures and languages.** "Many recent school reform efforts are profoundly flawed by the absence in their design of people who know well the daily lives of children in ethnic, low income, and immigrant communities" (National Coalition of Advocates for Students, 1994, p. 68). In addition to understanding and putting into practice the changing conceptions of teaching and learning and participating in the new structures of schooling, "new and different kinds" of educators (p. 126) are needed who have a positive attitude toward cultural differences, extensive knowledge about students' cultural experiences, and the technical skills to translate this cultural information into pedagogical practice (Villegas, in press) and who have a positive attitude toward linguistic differences, acknowledge the value of bi- and multilingualism, understand language development and second language learning, and possess the skills to guide students in developing bilingual fluency while they learn language and learn through language. Without changes in teacher education programs and extensive professional development for practicing educators, most educators have no way of developing the knowledge and sensitivity that is needed to understand the immigrant experience and its relation to education, to design appropriate educational approaches, or to put into practice the four principles suggested in this volume.

Recommendations

The many messages arising from the examination of the literature and the practices discussed throughout this volume are complex. It is a challenge to distill them into a few recommendations. Nevertheless, I present here key recommendations for policy makers at district and school levels that can increase the effectiveness of schools and educators in facilitating the transitions of secondary immigrant students into, through, and beyond school. The first four recommendations are the four principles discussed in detail in chapters 3 through 6 and are therefore not elaborated here. The other recommendations, each of which is explained briefly, support, undergird, and complement the four central principles.

1. **Cultivate organizational relationships—among schools, health and social service agencies, community-based organizations, businesses, and institutions of higher education.**

2. **Provide access to information about schooling and culture, available resources, the world of work, and higher education in the United States.**

3. **Cultivate human relationships—between students and adults, among students, among educators, and between educators and families.**

4. **Provide multiple and flexible pathways into, through, and beyond school.**

5. **In documents, policies, and practices, do not define immigrant students solely as learners of English. Recognize the reality and complexity of the immigration experience as well as the importance of English language proficiency.**

Immigrant students are not officially recognized as a group in the United States or in most school districts, but are generally identified only through their need to learn English. To be sure, all residents must have a command of English in order to fully participate in U.S. business, government, and education. Thus, English language development must be an educational priority for immigrant students. However, when immigrant students are seen only as learners of English, their special contributions (for example, their proficiency in a language other than English) and their nonlinguistic needs (for example, to learn about the U.S. school system, to develop academic content knowledge and social skills, and to prepare for future work and schooling options) are ignored by the educational system. In addition to rendering them one-dimensional, the characterization of them only as learners of English focuses on an acknowledged deficit rather than on the many other strengths and complexities of their lives.

Immigrants also share the common experience of leaving their native countries and cultures and beginning new lives in a new country. They are influenced by a multitude of factors that can support or interfere with their success in adjusting to those changes. Because of their common experiences, including their need for orientation to their new culture and educational system and their need to learn English, they should be recognized as a distinct group within the educational system. Once educators can see immigrant students as a group, they can respond to their needs and contributions. As long as they are considered only as learners of English as a second language, large parts of their identities are invisible.

6. In documents, policies, and practices, take into account differences among different immigrant groups; do not lump them all together.

To address the real complexities of immigrant students' lives productively and appropriately and thus to assist students in making the transitions into, through, and beyond school, educators must know about those complexities and they must apply what they know with a sensitivity to immigrant students and their experiences. They must avoid stereotypes by recognizing that immigrants are a very diverse group despite what they have in common. Various means are available for developing knowledge and sensitivity of students' lives and experiences: for example, reading fiction and nonfiction, going to films, attending lectures and performances, seeking out knowledgeable people to talk to, making friends with immigrants, and participating in formal professional development activities.

7. Value and support the development of bilingualism and biliteracy among immigrant students in policies and programs; explicitly acknowledge the contributions of bilingual members of the school community, the larger community, and the country as a whole.

When immigrant students see that their languages are valued, they feel less alienated and therefore are likely to adjust more easily to their new culture. When they are encouraged to develop their native language abilities and to learn in their native languages as well as in English, they can (1) learn academic content more quickly than if they have to wait until they are proficient in English; (2) have easier access to prior knowledge that they developed in their native language; and (3) use one of their strengths (their native language) for learning rather than being forced to rely only on an acknowledged weakness (their English language ability). When programs and approaches are adapted so that they can use their native languages, immigrant students can participate in all of the educational opportunities available rather than postponing preparation for future work and higher education.

In addition to the benefits that individual students derive from value and support for bilingualism, communities and the United States as a whole benefit from a bilingual citizenry. Developing the abilities of students in as many languages as possible can help to build a future workforce that can participate more effectively in the global community than the overwhelmingly monolingual workforce of today. It makes no sense to attempt to teach monolingual English-speaking students to speak Spanish, Chinese, and Japanese while discouraging immigrant children who speak these languages from developing their native language abilities.

8. Value and support the development of cross-cultural communication and understanding among all students in policies and programs; explicitly acknowledge the contributions of bicultural members of the school community, the larger community, and the country as a whole.

Although more attention is given to the English language proficiency of immigrant students than to their cultural backgrounds, culture plays a critical role in communication and in adjustment to a new context. Given the increasingly multicultural population, it is imperative that adults and young people learn to communicate effectively across cultures and that they develop respect and value for members of cultural groups other than their own. If immigrant students' new peers and teachers cannot communicate with them or if they feel that their cultures are not valued, they are likely to feel alienated and to have difficulty adjusting to their new culture. This alienation can snowball, leading students to drop out of school. If this happens, not only do the individual young people lose out on life opportunities, but the community and the nation lose out on some of their potential contributions, which would have been nurtured by further education and preparation for careers.

9. Ensure that the education of immigrant students is cohesive and integrated into the larger district program by providing a district-level coordinator of immigrant education.

A mechanism must be put in place to ensure that immigrant students are not forgotten or ignored but are properly integrated into structures and strategies designed for all students. Because immigrant education is understood by so few new and practicing educators and because immigrant students constitute a minority, albeit a growing one, in most schools and school districts, this integration will most certainly not take place unless it is someone's job to see that it does. Someone within school districts must be charged with ensuring that sensitive, informed, explicit thought is given to immigrant students in efforts to design schooling for *all* students. Someone must be responsible for seeing to it that district decision-making incorporates sensitivity to and knowledge of the immigrant experience and immigrant education. Someone with the appropriate professional background and experience must keep track of immigrant students in the educational system; oversee their identification, placement, and movement within the system; and provide leadership in matching the strengths and needs of particular immigrant students with the many possible ways to assist them in succeeding within the educational system and in making the transitions into, through, and beyond secondary school.

A district coordinator of immigrant education, who also functions as the director of an ESL/bilingual education program, can establish avenues of communication among and coordinate professional development for all educators, rather than functioning only within a peripheral program and community that do not interact with those in the mainstream. He or she can build partnerships with social, health, and community agencies and work with those involved in school-to-work efforts to ensure that immigrant students are included in such efforts. In practice, the distinction between an ESL/bilingual program coordinator and a district coordinator of immigrant education may appear minor in contexts where ESL/bilingual programs are in place, but making this distinction sets the stage for continued efforts to truly redesign schooling so that it is responsive to all students.

10. Establish structures and policies that bring together people and programs involved in education reform so that immigrant education is situated within the larger educational context rather than being treated as peripheral to it.

As I have argued throughout this volume, immigrant students must be included in the population of *all* students whom the new approaches to schooling are designed to serve but who, all too often, are not considered when teachers and administrators conceptualize reforms (see

Olsen et al., 1994) partly because educators of immigrant students are seldom included in education reform planning and implementation. We need to situate the education of immigrant students squarely within the education reform movement and provide opportunities for educators of immigrant students and mainstream educators to work together to reform schooling. Unfortunately, school faculty members have few opportunities or incentives to communicate with each other, and the gap is especially wide between those who work in special programs and those in the regular program. Educators of immigrant students need to learn about the principles and practices of education reform and make sure that they are included when their colleagues design and implement new programs and approaches. Mainstream educators need to learn about second language acquisition, the experiences of immigration, and the role of culture in teaching and learning, and make sure that their colleagues who teach immigrant students are included in the design and implementation of new programs and approaches. Formal collaborations among ESL, bilingual, and mainstream faculty, such as team teaching, as well as less formal ones, through discussions of students and strategies, have great potential for benefiting students in the transition process and should be supported by policy makers and administrators.

11. Ensure that practices are adapted and applied by knowledgeable and experienced staff so that they are responsive to immigrant students without compromising high expectations and academic quality.

While we need to bring immigrant students into education reform efforts, a single approach is not appropriate or effective for all students. The more access immigrant students have to educational innovations and the more integrated they are into the broader educational system, the better—provided that the innovations and the system are responsive to their particular experiences, strengths, and needs. Learner-centered education requires that we interrogate potential practices to ensure that they respond to our particular learners before simply applying them, and that we do this without placing students in low-track, no-future classes. New approaches to teaching and schooling must promote academic excellence for all. They should be adapted to incorporate all students, even if they are not fully fluent in English, rather than using students' lack of fluency in English as a reason to exclude them from some educational programs and opportunities. In this process of adaptation, it is critical that those who are making the adaptations are knowledgeable about immigrant students and about educational structures and strategies that support their learning and participation.

12. Provide necessary support and scaffolding to ensure that immigrant students can meet high academic expectations.

While we must ensure that immigrant students are included in education reforms and provided with challenging education, we should not simply place them in mainstream classes—innovative or traditional ones—and abandon them there without special assistance. With extra support, they can succeed; without it, they may fail. The types of support that can make the difference include advice and assistance from bilingual counselors, mentors, and advisors and academic assistance through tutoring, writing labs, special classes during the regular school day, summer school, and Saturday classes. Immigrant students can be made participants in the culture of power that has initiated education reforms by having the purposes of those reforms explained to them— that is to say, they can be empowered to succeed by knowing why they are being asked to make decisions about their own learning. We should not assume that young people from cultures outside the United States are familiar and comfortable with either innovative or traditional practices.

13. Give priority to professional development for all educators to increase their sensitivity to and knowledge of the immigrant experience, including the students' cultures and languages, and to develop their abilities to educate them effectively.

As discussed in several contexts throughout this volume, all educators—administrators, support staff, teachers, and counselors—need to develop their own sensitivity, knowledge, and understanding of what is involved in educating immigrant students as whole people and in assisting secondary immigrant students as they negotiate the many transitions they experience. Decision makers can facilitate this process by making such professional development a priority in hiring, funding, and policy development.

References

Adler, L., & Cragin, J. (1993, April). *How students and programs benefit from business/education partnerships.* Paper presented at the annual meeting of the American Educational Research Association, Atlanta.

American Association of Colleges for Teacher Education. (1994). *Teacher education pipeline III: Schools, colleges, and departments of education enrollments by race, ethnicity, and gender.* Washington, DC: Author.

Ancess, J., & Darling-Hammond, L. (1994). *Authentic teaching, learning, and assessment with new English learners at International High School.* New York: Columbia University, Teachers College, National Center for Restructuring Education, Schools, and Teaching.

Anson, R.J. (Ed.). (1994). *Systemic reform: Perspectives on personalizing education.* Washington, DC: U.S. Department of Education, Office of Educational Research and Improvement.

Apple, M. (1979). *Ideology and curriculum.* London: Routledge and Kegan Paul.

Apple, M. (1982). *Education and power.* London: Routledge and Kegan Paul.

Aronow, I. (1993, June 6). Seniors work plan spreads in schools. *The New York Times.*

Ascher, C. (1988a). *School–college collaborations: A strategy for helping low-income minorities* (Urban Diversity Series No. 98). New York: ERIC Clearinghouse on Urban Education.

Ascher, C. (1988b). *Urban school–community alliances* (Trends and Issues No. 10). New York: ERIC Clearinghouse on Urban Education.

Ascher, C. (1994, January). Cooperative education as a strategy for school-to-work transition. *Centerfocus of the National Clearinghouse on Vocational Education, 3,* 1-4.

Ascher, C., & Schwartz, W. (1989). *School–college alliances: Benefits for low-income minorities* (ERIC Digest No. 53). New York: ERIC Clearinghouse on Urban Education.

ASPIRA Association, Inc. (1994). *School-to-work: Opportunity or barrier?* (Issue Brief). Washington, DC: Author.

Auerbach, E. (1993). Reexamining English Only in the ESL classroom. *TESOL Quarterly, 27,* 9-32.

Barra, A. (1994). *Final performance report: Families together: A family English literacy project.* Oakland, CA: Art, Research, and Curriculum Associates.

Barth, R. (1990). *Improving schools from within: Teachers, parents, and principals can make the difference.* San Francisco: Jossey-Bass.

Bartolomé, L. (1994). Beyond the methods fetish: Toward a humanizing pedagogy. *Harvard Educational Review, 62,* 173-194.

Barton, P. (1990). *From school to work* (Policy Information Report). Princeton, NJ: Educational Testing Service, Policy Information Center.

Barton, P. (1993). A memorandum on the youth transition. In R. Kazis (Ed.), *Improving the transition from school to work in the United States* (pp. 26-31). Washington, DC: American Youth Policy Forum.

Beard, T. (1994). Learning beyond the classroom: Developing the community connection. *CATESOL Journal, 7*(1), 9-17.

Bourdieu, P. (1986). The forms of capital. In J.G. Richardson (Ed.), *Handbook of theory and research for the sociology of education* (pp. 241-258). New York: Greenwood.

Bowles, S., & Gintis, H.I. (1976). *Schooling in capitalist America.* New York: Basic Books.

Boyer, E.L. (1983). *High school: A report on secondary education in America.* New York: Harper & Row.

Braddock, J.H., & McPartland, J.M. (1993). Education of early adolescents. *Review of Research in Education, 19,* 135-170.

Brinton, D.M., Snow, M.A., & Wesche, M.B. (1989). *Content-based second language instruction.* New York: Newbury House.

Burbules, N.C., & Rice, S. (1991). Dialogue across differences: Continuing the conversation. *Harvard Educational Review, 61,* 393-416.

California Department of Education. (1992). *Second to none: A vision of the new California high school.* Sacramento, CA: Author.

Camino, L.A. (1992). *What differences do racial, ethnic, and cultural differences make in youth development programs?* Washington, DC: Carnegie Council on Adolescent Development.

Cárdenas, J.A., Montecel, M.R., Supik, J.D., & Harris, R.J. (1992). The Coca-Cola Valued Youth Program: Dropout prevention strategies for at-risk students. *Texas Researcher, 3,* 111-130.

Carnegie Council on Adolescent Development. (1989). *Turning points: Preparing American youth for the 21st century.* New York: Carnegie Corporation of New York.

Center for Applied Linguistics. (1994). *Project Adelante: Moving onward to a better education.* Union, NJ: Kean College.

Chang, H.N. (1990). *Newcomer programs: Innovative efforts to meet the challenges of immigrant students.* San Francisco: California Tomorrow.

Charner, I., & Fraser, B.S. (1994, April 4). *School-to-work transition: A mosaic in search of a system.* Paper presented at the annual meeting of the American Educational Research Association, New Orleans.

Chinn, S.O. (1988). The ethnic minority educator: Near extinction? *Teacher Education and Practice, 4*(2), 15-17.

Christian, D., & Whitcher, A. (1995). *Directory of two-way bilingual programs in the United States.* Santa Cruz, CA: National Center for Research on Cultural Diversity and Second Language Learning.

Comer, J.P. (1993). The potential effects of community organizations on the future of our youth. In R. Takanishi (Ed.), *Adolescence in the 1990s: Risk and opportunity* (pp. 203-206). New York: Teachers College Press.

Corcoran, T.B. (1990). Schoolwork: Perspectives on workplace reform in public schools. In M.W. McLaughlin, J.E. Talbert, & N. Bascia (Eds.), *The contexts of teaching in secondary schools* (pp. 142-166). New York: Teachers College Press.

Crandall, J.A. (1993). Content-centered learning in the United States. *Annual Review of Applied Linguistics, 13,* 111-126.

Crawford, J. (1989). *Bilingual education: History, politics, theory, and practice.* Trenton, NJ: Crane.

Crawford, J. (1992). *Hold your tongue: Bilingualism and the politics of "English only."* Reading, MA: Addison-Wesley.

Cummins, J. (1981). The role of primary language development in promoting educational success for language minority students. In California Department of Education (Ed.), *Schooling and language minority students: A theoretical framework* (pp. 3-49). Los Angeles: California State University, Evaluation, Dissemination, and Assessment Center.

Cummins, J. (1989). *Empowering minority students.* Sacramento, CA: California Association for Bilingual Education.

Cummins, J. (1991). Interdependence of first- and second-language proficiency in bilingual children. In E. Bialystok (Ed.), *Language processing in bilingual children* (pp. 70-89). Cambridge, England: Cambridge University Press.

Cummins, J. (1992). Bilingual education and English immersion: The Ramírez report in theoretical perspective. *Bilingual Research Journal, 16*(1&2), 91-104.

Darling-Hammond, L. (1992). Building learner-centered schools: Developing professional capacity, policy, and political consensus. In *Building learner-centered schools: Three perspectives* (pp. 17-31). New York: Columbia University, Teachers College, National Center for Restructuring Education, Schools, and Teaching.

Darling-Hammond, L. (1993). Reframing the school reform agenda: Developing the capacity for school transformation. *Phi Delta Kappan, 74,* 753-761.

Delpit, L. (1988). The silenced dialogue: Power and pedagogy in educating other people's children. *Harvard Educational Review, 58,* 280-298.

Delpit, L. (1995). *Other people's children: Cultural conflict in the classroom.* New York: New Press.

Dolson, D., & Mayer, J. (1992). Longitudinal study of three program models for language-minority students: A critical examination of reported findings. *Bilingual Research Journal, 16*(1&2), 105-157.

Drucker, P. (1994, November). The age of social transformation. *The Atlantic Monthly, 27,* 53-80.

Dryfoos, J.G. (1993). Schools as places for health, mental health, and social services. In R. Takanishi (Ed.), *Adolescence in the 1990s: Risk and opportunity* (pp. 82-109). New York: Teachers College Press.

Dunetz, N. (1990). From isolation to collaboration. In *Insights: Thoughts on the process of being International* (pp. 3-5). Long Island City, NY: The International High School.

Dunlap, J.C., & Hutchinson, F. (1994). Health care issues for new Americans. In A. Morse (Ed.), *America's newcomers: An immigrant policy handbook* (pp. 21-33). Washington, DC: National Conference of State Legislatures.

Erickson, F., & Schultz, J. (1982). *The counselor as gatekeeper: Social interaction in interviews.* New York: Academic Press.

Faltis, C. (1993). Critical issues in the use of sheltered content teaching in high school bilingual programs. *Peabody Journal of Education, 69*(1), 136-151.

Fix, M., & Passel, J.S. (1994). *Immigration and immigrants: Setting the record straight.* Washington, DC: The Urban Institute.

Flaxman, E. (1992, August). *The mentoring relationship in action* (Institute for Urban and Minority Education Briefs No. 3). New York: Columbia University, Teachers College, Institute for Urban and Minority Education.

Flaxman, E., & Ascher, C. (1992). *Mentoring in action: The efforts of programs in New York City.* New York: Columbia University, Teachers College, Institute for Urban and Minority Education.

Flaxman, E., Ascher, C., Berryman, S.E., & Unger, M. (1995). Preparation for work: The "forgotten" student. In E. Flaxman & A.H. Passow (Eds.), *Ninety-fourth yearbook of the National Society for the Study of Education: Part II. Changing populations, changing schools* (pp. 143-161). Chicago: University of Chicago Press.

Flaxman, E., Ascher, C., & Harrington, C. (1988). *Youth mentoring: Programs and practices* (Urban Diversity Series No. 97). New York: ERIC Clearinghouse on Urban Education.

Fleischman, H.L., Arterburn, S., & Wiens, E. (1995). *State certification requirements for teachers of LEP students.* Arlington, VA: Development Associates.

Freeman, D.E., & Freeman, Y.S. (1994). *Between worlds: Access to second language acquisition.* Portsmouth, NH: Heinemann.

Freire, P. (1971). *Pedagogy of the oppressed.* New York: Harper and Row.

Freire, P. (1973). *Education for critical consciousness.* New York: Seabury.

Freire, P. (1985). *The politics of education: Culture, power, and liberation.* South Hadley, MA: Bergin and Garvey.

Friedlander, M. (1991). *The newcomer program: Helping immigrant students succeed in U.S. schools* (Program Information Guide No. 8). Washington, DC: National Clearinghouse for Bilingual Education.

Fullan, M.G. (1993). *Change forces: Probing the depths of educational reform.* London: Falmer.

Fullan, M.G. (1994). Coordinating top-down and bottom-up strategies for educational reform. In R.J. Anson (Ed.), *Systemic reform: Perspectives on personalizing education* (pp. 7-22). Washington, DC: U.S. Department of Education.

Fullan, M.G., & Miles, M.B. (1992, June). Getting reform right: What works and what doesn't. *Phi Delta Kappan, 73,* 745-752.

Gallimore, R., Tharp, R.G., & John-Steiner, V. (1992). *The developmental and sociocultural foundations of mentoring.* New York: Columbia University, Teachers College, Institute for Urban and Minority Education.

Genesee, F. (1987). *Learning through two languages: Studies of immersion and bilingual education.* Cambridge, MA: Newbury House.

Giroux, H. (1981). *Ideology, culture and the process of schooling.* Philadelphia: Temple University Press.

Glover, R.W., & Marshall, R. (1993). Improving the school-to-work transition of American adolescents. In R. Takanishi (Ed.), *Adolescence in the 1990s: Risk and opportunity* (pp. 130-152). New York: Teachers College Press.

Gold, N. (1993). Solving the shortage of bilingual teachers: Policy implications of California's staffing initiative for LEP students. In *Proceedings of the Third National Research Symposium on Limited English Proficient Student Issues: Focus on middle and high school Issues* (pp. 223-278). Washington, DC: U.S. Department of Education, Office of Bilingual Education and Minority Languages Affairs.

González, J.M., & Darling-Hammond, L. (in press). *New concepts for new challenges: Professional development for teachers of immigrant youth.* McHenry, IL and Washington, DC: Delta Systems and Center for Applied Linguistics.

González, N., Moll, L.C., Floyd-Tenery, M., Rivera, A., Rendón, P., Gonzales, R., & Amanti, C. (1993). *Teacher research on funds of knowledge: Learning from households.* Santa Cruz, CA: National Center for Research on Cultural Diversity and Second Language Learning.

Goodlad, J. (1984). *A place called school.* New York: McGraw-Hill.

Greene, M. (1992). Restructuring and possibility. In *Building learner-centered schools: Three perspectives* (pp. 35-42). New York: Columbia University, Teachers College, National Center for Restructuring Education, Schools, and Teaching.

Grosz, S. (1994, August 11). Reflections on the CHOOSE Program. *The Gazette* [Croton-on-Hudson, New York].

Hamayan, E.V., & Perlman, R. (1990). *Helping language minority students after they exit from bilingual/ESL programs* (Program Information Guide No. 1). Washington, DC: National Clearinghouse for Bilingual Education.

Harklau, L. (1994a). ESL versus mainstream classes: Contrasting L2 learning environments. *TESOL Quarterly, 28,* 241-272.

Harklau, L. (1994b). "Jumping tracks": How language minority students negotiate evaluations of ability. *Anthropology and Education Quarterly, 25,* 347-363.

Harklau, L. (1994c). Tracking and linguistic minority students: Consequences of ability grouping for second language learners. *Linguistics and Education, 6,* 217-244.

Haycock, K. (1995). Creating new educational communities: Implications for policy. In J. Oakes & K.H. Quartz (Eds.), *Ninety-fourth yearbook of the National Society for the Study of Education: Part I. Creating new educational communities* (pp. 224-239). Chicago: University of Chicago Press.

Heath, S.B., & McLaughlin, M.W. (Eds.). (1994). *Identity and inner-city youth: Beyond ethnicity and gender.* New York: Teachers College Press.

Henze, R., Lucas, T., & Scott, B. (1993, April). *Dancing with the monster: Teachers attempt to discuss power, racism, and privilege in education.* Paper presented at the annual meeting of the American Educational Research Association, Atlanta.

Hidalgo, F., & Huling-Austin, L. (1993). Alternate teacher candidates: A rich source for Latino teachers in the future. In *Reshaping teacher education in the Southwest—A forum: A response to the needs of Latino students and teachers* (pp. 13-34). Claremont, CA: The Tomás Rivera Center.

Hirschy, D. (1990). [Address to the faculty of Grover Cleveland High School, Buffalo, New York]. In *Insights: Thoughts on the process of being International* (pp. 15-19). Long Island City, NY: The International High School.

Holt, D. (Ed.). (1993). *Cooperative learning: A response to linguistic and cultural diversity.* McHenry, IL and Washington, DC: Delta Systems and Center for Applied Linguistics.

Holt, D. (Ed.). (1994). *Assessing success in family literacy projects: Alternative approaches to assessment and evaluation.* McHenry, IL and Washington, DC: Delta Systems and Center for Applied Linguistics.

Howard, B. (1995, January/February). QOP: A "cadillac" job-training program delivers for disadvantaged youth. *Youth Today: The Newspaper on Youth Work, 4*(1), 1, 28-30.

HSSP program evaluation: Hispanic students *can* succeed. (1994, July). *HACU, The Voice of Hispanic Education,* 9-10.

Institute for Educational Leadership. (1994). *Linking schools with health & social services: Perspectives from Thomas Payzant on San Diego's New Beginnings.* Washington, DC: Author.

International High School. (n.d.). *Excerpts from Project PROPEL handbook*. Long Island City, NY: Author.

Johnson, D.W., & Johnson, R. (1987). *Learning together and alone: Cooperation, competition, and individualization* (2nd ed.). Englewood Cliffs, NJ: Prentice Hall.

Kagan, S. (1986). Cooperative learning and sociocultural factors in schooling. In California Department of Education (Ed.), *Beyond language: Social and cultural factors in schooling language minority students* (pp. 231-298). Los Angeles: California State University, Evaluation, Dissemination, and Assessment Center.

Kazis, R. (1993). *Improving the transition from school to work in the United States*. Washington, DC: American Youth Policy Forum.

Kilgore, K., & Webb, R. (1994). Blue Lake Middle School and the dynamics of school reform. In E. Bondy, K. Kilgore, D. Ross, & R. Webb, *Building blocks and stumbling blocks: Three case studies of shared decision making and school restructuring* (pp. 21-37). New York: Columbia University, Teachers College, National Center for Restructuring Education, Schools, and Teaching.

Knoff, L., & Otuya, E. (1995). Who is teaching America's schoolchildren? *American Council on Education Research Briefs, 6*(2).

Lee, V.E., Bryk, A.S., & Smith, J.B. (1993). The organization of effective secondary schools. *Review of Research in Education, 19,* 171-267.

Legters, N., McDill, E., & McPartland, J. (1993). Rising to the challenge: Emerging strategies for educating students at risk. In *Educational reforms and students at risk: A review of the current state of the art* (pp. 49-92). Washington, DC: U.S. Department of Education, Office of Educational Research and Improvement.

Lieberman, A. (1995). Practices that support teacher development: Transforming conceptions of professional learning. *Phi Delta Kappan, 76,* 591-596.

Lieberman, A., Falk, B., & Alexander, L. (1994). *A culture in the making: Leadership in learner-centered schools.* New York: Columbia University, Teachers College, National Center for Restructuring Education, Schools, and Teaching.

Lucas, T. (1992). *Successful capacity building: An analysis of twenty case studies.* Oakland, CA: Art, Research, and Curriculum Associates.

Lucas, T. (1993a). High school restructuring and school reform. In C. Minicucci & L. Olsen (Eds.), *Educating students from immigrant families: Meeting the challenge in secondary schools* (pp. 39-51). Santa Cruz, CA: National Center for Research on Cultural Diversity and Second Language Learning.

Lucas, T. (1993b). Secondary schooling for students becoming bilingual. In B. Arias & U. Casanova (Eds.), *Bilingual education: Politics, practice, and research. Ninety-second yearbook of the National Society for the Study of Education* (pp. 113-143). Chicago: University of Chicago Press.

Lucas, T. (1993c). What have we learned from research on successful secondary programs for LEP students? A synthesis of findings from three studies. In *Proceedings of the Third National Research Symposium on Limited English Proficient Student Issues: Focus on middle and high school issues.* Washington, DC: U.S. Department of Education, Office of Bilingual Education and Minority Languages Affairs.

Lucas, T., Henze, R., & Donato, R. (1990). Promoting the success of Latino language minority students: An exploratory study of six high schools. *Harvard Educational Review, 60,* 315-340.

Lucas, T., & Katz, A. (1994). Reframing the debate: The roles of native languages in English-only programs for language minority students. *TESOL Quarterly, 28,* 537-561.

Lucas, T., & Schecter, S. (1992). Literacy education and diversity: Toward equity in the teaching of reading and writing. *Urban Review, 24*(2), 85-104.

Mace-Matluck, B.J., Alexander-Kasparik, R., & Queen, R.M. (in press). *Through the golden door: Educational approaches for immigrant adolescents with limited schooling.* McHenry, IL and Washington, DC: Delta Systems and Center for Applied Linguistics.

MacIver, D.J. (1990). Meeting the needs of young adolescents: Advisory groups, interdisciplinary teaching teams, and school transition programs. *Phi Delta Kappan, 71,* 458-464.

Maeroff, G.I. (1990). Getting to know a good middle school: Shoreham-Wading River. *Phi Delta Kappan, 71,* 505-511.

Manpower Demonstration Research Corporation. (1994). *Principal conclusions from the school-to-work transition project.* Washington, DC: Author.

Marshall, R., & Glover, R.W. (1996). Education, the economy, and tomorrow's workforce. In L.I. Rendón & R.O. Hope (Eds.), *Educating a new majority: Transforming America's educational system for diversity* (pp. 35-50). San Francisco: Jossey-Bass.

McDonnell, L.M., & Hill, P.T. (1993). *Newcomers in American schools: Meeting the educational needs of immigrant youth.* Santa Monica, CA: Rand.

McGroarty, M. (1986). Educators' responses to sociocultural diversity: Implications for practice. In California Department of Education (Ed.), *Beyond language: Social and cultural factors in schooling language minority students* (pp. 299-343). Los Angeles: California State University, Evaluation, Dissemination, and Assessment Center.

McPartland, J.M. (1990). Staffing decisions in the middle grades: Balancing quality instruction and teacher/student relations. *Phi Delta Kappan, 71,* 465-469.

McPartland, J.M., & Nettles, S.M. (1991). Using community adults as advocates or mentors for at-risk middle school students: A two-year evaluation of Project RAISE. *American Journal of Education, 99,* 568-586.

Medina, M. (1988). Hispanic apartheid in American public education. *Educational Administration Quarterly, 24,* 336-349.

Mehan, H., Datnow, A., Bratton, E., Tellez, C., Friedlaender, D., & Ngo, T. (1992). *Untracking and college enrollment.* Santa Cruz, CA: National Center for Research on Cultural Diversity and Second Language Learning.

Mehan, H., Hubbard, L., Lintz, A., & Villanueva, I. (1994). *Tracking untracking: The consequences of placing low track students in high track classes.* Santa Cruz, CA: National Center for Research on Cultural Diversity and Second Language Learning.

Mehan, H., Hubbard, L., Okamoto, D., & Villanueva, I. (1993, May). *Untracking high school students in preparation for college: Implications for Latino students.* Paper presented at the conference of the University of California's Latino Eligibility Project.

Meier, D. (1993). Transforming schools into powerful communities. In R. Takanishi (Ed.), *Adolescence in the 1990s: Risk and opportunity* (pp. 199-202). New York: Teachers College Press.

Mickelson, R.A. (in press). Opportunity and danger: Understanding the business contribution to public education reform. In K. Borman,

P. Cookson, A. Sadovnik, & J. Spade (Eds.), *Sociological perspectives on school reform.* Norwood, NJ: Ablex.

Minicucci, C., & Olsen, L. (1991). *An exploratory study of secondary LEP programs: Vol. 5. Meeting the challenge of diversity: An evaluation of programs for pupils with limited proficiency in English.* Berkeley, CA: BW Associates.

Mohan, B.A. (1986). *Language and content.* Reading, MA: Addison-Wesley.

Mohan, B.A. (1990). Integration of language and content. In *Proceedings of the First Research Symposium on Limited English Proficient Students' Issues* (pp. 113-160). Washington, DC: U.S. Department of Education, Office of Bilingual Education and Minority Languages Affairs.

Moll, L., Amanti, C., Neff, D., & González, N. (1992). Funds of knowledge for teaching: Using a qualitative approach to connect homes and classrooms. *Theory into Practice, 31*(2), 132-141.

Moll, L., & Greenberg, J. (1990). Creating zones of possibilities: Combining social contexts for instructions. In L.C. Moll (Ed.), *Vygotsky and education* (pp. 319-348). Cambridge: Cambridge University Press.

Morse, A. (1994). Employment and training programs for immigrants and refugees. In A. Morse (Ed.), *America's newcomers: An immigrant policy handbook* (pp. 34-48). Washington, DC: National Conference of State Legislatures.

National Center for Education Statistics. (1994). *Trends in academic progress [NAEP 1992].* Washington, DC: U.S. Government Printing Office.

National Center for Research on Cultural Diversity and Second Language Learning. (1994a, February). *Funds of knowledge: Learning from language minority households. ERIC Digest.* Washington, DC: ERIC Clearinghouse on Languages and Linguistics.

National Center for Research on Cultural Diversity and Second Language Learning. (1994b, December). *Two-way bilingual education programs in practice: A national and local perspective. ERIC Digest.* Washington, DC: ERIC Clearinghouse on Languages and Linguistics.

National Center on Effective Secondary Schools. (1991). *Final report.* Madison, WI: University of Wisconsin, Wisconsin Center for Education Research.

National Coalition of Advocates for Students. (1988). *New voices: Immigrant students in U.S. public schools.* Boston: Author.

National Coalition of Advocates for Students. (1993). *Achieving the dream: How communities and schools can improve education for immigrant students.* Boston: Author.

National Coalition of Advocates for Students. (1994). *Delivering on the promise: Positive practices for immigrant students.* Boston: Author.

National Council of La Raza. (1993). *The forgotten two-thirds: An Hispanic perspective on apprenticeship, European style.* Washington, DC: Author.

Natriello, G., McDill, D.L., & Pallas, A.M. (1990). *Schooling disadvantaged children: Racing against catastrophe.* New York: Teachers College Press.

New York State Department of Education. (1991). *The new compact for learning.* Albany: Author.

Newmann, F.M. (1981). Reducing student alienation in high schools: Implications of theory. *Harvard Educational Review, 51,* 546-564.

Newmann, F.M., & Oliver, D.W. (1967). Education and community. *Harvard Educational Review, 37,* 61-106.

Nightingale, E.O., & Wolverton, L. (1993). Adolescent rolelessness in modern society. In R. Takanishi (Ed.), *Adolescence in the 1990s: Risk and opportunity* (pp. 14-28). New York: Teachers College Press.

Oakes, J. (1985). *Keeping track: How schools structure inequality.* New Haven: Yale University Press.

Oakes, J. (1986). Tracking, inequality, and the rhetoric of school reform: Why schools don't change. *Journal of Education, 168*(1), 60-80.

Oakes, J. (1995). Normative, technical, and political dimensions of creating new educational communities. In J. Oakes & K.H. Quartz (Eds.), *Ninety-fourth yearbook of the National Society for the Study of Education: Part I. Creating new educational communities* (pp. 1-15). Chicago: University of Chicago Press.

Olsen, L. (1988). *Crossing the schoolhouse border: Immigrant students and the California Public Schools.* San Francisco: California Tomorrow.

Olsen, L. (1989). *Bridges: Promising programs for the education of immigrant children.* San Francisco: California Tomorrow.

Olsen, L. (in press). *Learning America: The immigrant experience in U.S. high schools.* New York: New Press.

Olsen, L., Chang, H., Salazar, D., Leong, C., Perez, Z.M., McClain, G., & Raffel, L. (1994). *The unfinished journey: Restructuring schools in a diverse society.* San Francisco: California Tomorrow.

Olson, L. (1994a, January 26). Bridging the gap: The nation's haphazard school-to-work link is getting an overhaul. *Education Week, 13,* 20-26.

Olson, L. (1994b, February 23). On the career track. *Education Week,* *13,* 28-31.

Olson, L. (1994c, March 23). Putting theory into practice. *Education Week, 13,* 25-27.

Olson, L. (1994d, April 20). Technically speaking. *Education Week, 13,* 29-31.

Olson, L. (1994e, May 18). Putting it all together. *Education Week, 13,* 25-29.

Pallas, A.M. (1993). Schooling in the course of human lives: The social context of education and the transition to adulthood in industrial society. *Review of Educational Research, 63,* 409-447.

Pallas, A.M., Natriello, G., & McDill, E.L. (1995). Changing students/ changing needs. In E. Flaxman & A.H. Passow (Eds.), *Ninety-fourth yearbook of the National Society for the Study of Education: Part II. Changing populations, changing schools* (pp. 30-58). Chicago: University of Chicago Press.

Petersen, A.C., & Epstein, J.L. (1991). Development and education across adolescence: An introduction. *American Journal of Education, 99,* 373-378.

Poplin, M., & Weeres, J. (1992). *Voices from the inside: A report on schooling from inside the classroom.* Claremont, CA: The Claremont Graduate School, The Institute for Education in Transformation.

Powell, A., Farrar, E., & Cohen, D. (1985). *The shopping mall high school: Winners and losers in the educational marketplace.* Boston: Houghton Mifflin.

Price, R.H., Cioci, M., Penner, W., & Trautlein, B. (1993). Webs of influence: School and community programs that enhance adolescent health and education. In R. Takanishi (Ed.), *Adolescence in the 1990s: Risk and opportunity* (pp. 29-63). New York: Teachers College Press.

Ramírez, J.D. (1992). Longitudinal study of structured English immersion strategy: Early-exit and late-exit transitional bilingual education programs for language-minority children [Executive summary]. *Bilingual Research Journal, 16*(1&2), 1-62.

Resnick, L.B. (1989). Introduction. In L.B. Resnick (Ed.), *Knowing, learning, and instruction: Essays in honor of Robert Glaser* (pp. 1-42). Hillsdale, NJ: Erlbaum.

Reyes, M.D. (1992). Challenging venerable assumptions: Literacy instruction for linguistically different students. *Harvard Educational Review, 62,* 427-446.

Rioux, J.W., & Berla, N. (1993). *Innovations in parent and family involvement.* Princeton Junction, NJ: Eye on Education.

Robledo, M.R., & Rivera, C. (1990). *Partners for valued youth: Dropout prevention strategies for at-risk language minority students.* San Antonio, TX: Intercultural Development Research Association.

Roos, P. (1994). An overview of the rights of immigrant parents. *CATESOL Journal, 7*(1), 49-52.

Saragoza, M. (1989). *Mexican immigrant children in American schools: A brief sketch.* Berkeley, CA: University Graduate School of Education, Zellerbach Family Fund.

Schmidt, P. (1994, May 11). Indiana study ignites debate over counselors' role. *Education Week, 13,* 10-11.

Shannon, S. (1990). Transition from bilingual programs to all-English programs: Issues about and beyond language. *Linguistics and Education, 2,* 323-345.

Short, D.J. (1993). *Integrating language and culture in middle school American history classes.* Santa Cruz, CA: National Center for Research on Cultural Diversity and Second Language Learning.

Sizer, T. (1992). *Horace's compromise: The dilemma of the American high school* (3rd ed.). Boston: Houghton Mifflin.

Sleeter, C., & Grant, C. (1987). An analysis of multicultural education in the United States. *Harvard Educational Review, 57,* 421-444.

Smith, C.L., & Rojewski, J.W. (1992). *School-to-work transition: Alternatives for educational reform.* Athens, GA: University of Georgia, Department of Occupational Studies. (ERIC Document Reproduction Service No. ED 354 303)

Spener, D. (1988). Transitional bilingual education and the socialization of immigrants. *Harvard Educational Review, 58,* 133-153.

Spenser, M.B., & Dornbusch, S.M. (1990). Challenges in studying minority youths. In S.S. Feldman & G. Elliott (Eds.), *At the threshold: The developing adolescent* (pp. 123-146). Cambridge, MA: Harvard University Press.

Stern, D., Finkelstein, N., Stone, J.R., Latting, J., & Dornsife, C. (1994). *Research on school-to-work transition programs in the United States.* Berkeley, CA: National Center for Research on Vocational Education.

Stewart, D.W. (1993). *Immigration and education: The crisis and the opportunities.* New York: Lexington Books.

Stone, N. (1991, March/April). Does business have any business in education? *Harvard Business Review, 69*(2), 46-62.

Swanson, M.C., Mehan, H., & Hubbard, L. (1995). The AVID classroom: Academic and social support for low-achieving students. In J. Oakes & K.H. Quartz (Eds.), *Ninety-fourth yearbook of the National*

Society for the Study of Education: Part I. Creating new educational communities (pp. 53-69). Chicago: University of Chicago Press.

Sylvan, C. (1994, August 1). Native language development in a multilingual setting. *NABE News, 17,* 35-36.

Szecsy, E.M. (1995a). *Technology and diversity: Partners in networking for systemic change.* Unpublished manuscript, Columbia University, Teachers College, National Center for Restructuring Education, Schools, and Teaching, New York.

Szecsy, E.M. (1995b). *Using technology and being a principal in the restructuring school.* Unpublished manuscript, Columbia University, Teachers College, New York.

Takanishi, R. (1993). Changing views of adolescence in contemporary society. In R. Takanishi (Ed.), *Adolescence in the 1990s: Risk and opportunity* (pp. 1-7). New York: Teachers College Press.

Tatum, B. (1992). Talking about race, learning about racism: The application of racial identity development theory in the classroom. *Harvard Educational Review, 62,* 1-24.

Tax deductions for college. (1995, January 15). *The New York Times,* p. 16.

Tharp, R. (1994). Research knowledge and policy issues in cultural diversity and education. In R.J. Anson (Ed.), *Systemic reform: Perspectives on personalizing education* (pp. 169-200). Washington, DC: U.S. Department of Education, Office of Educational Research and Improvement.

Tharp, R., & Gallimore, R. (1990). *Rousing minds to life: Teaching, learning, and schooling in social context.* Cambridge: Cambridge University Press.

Tikunoff, W., Ward, B.A., von Broekhuizen, D., Romero, M., Castaneda, L.V., Lucas, T., & Katz, A. (1991). *Final report: A descriptive study of significant features of exemplary special alternative instructional programs.* Los Alamitos, CA: Southwest Regional Educational Laboratory.

Tyler, A. (1980). Your place is empty. In D. Danielson, R. Hayden, H. Hinze-Pocher, & D. Glicksberg (Eds.), *Reading in English for students of English as a second language* (pp. 106-128). Englewood Cliffs, NJ: Prentice-Hall. (Originally published in *The New Yorker Magazine*, November 22, 1976)

U.S. Department of Labor, Employment and Training Administration. (1993). *Finding one's way: Career guidance for disadvantaged youth.* Washington, DC: Author.

Vaznaugh, A. (1995, March). *Dropout prevention and language minority youth. ERIC Digest.* Washington, DC: ERIC Clearinghouse on Languages and Linguistics.

Villegas, A.M. (1991). *Culturally responsive pedagogy for the 1990s and beyond.* Princeton, NJ: Educational Testing Service.

Villegas, A.M. (1992). *Immigrant education in New Jersey: Programs, services, and policies: Part II. Case studies of districts and effective program.* Princeton, NJ: Educational Testing Service.

Villegas, A.M. (in press). Increasing the diversity of the U.S. teaching force. In B. Biddle, T. Good, & I. Goodson (Eds.), *The international handbook of teachers and teaching.* The Netherlands: Kluwer Academic.

Violand-Sánchez, E., Sutton, C.P., & Ware, H.W. (1991). *Fostering home–school cooperation: Involving language minority families as partners in education* (Program Information Guide Series No. 6). Washington, DC: National Clearinghouse for Bilingual Education.

Vygotsky, L. (1962). *Thought and language.* Cambridge, MA: Harvard University Press.

Vygotsky, L. (1978). *Mind in society: The development of higher psychological processes.* Cambridge, MA: Harvard University Press.

Walqui, A. (in press). *Access and engagement: Program design and instructional approaches for immigrant students in secondary school.* McHenry, IL and Washington, DC: Delta Systems and Center for Applied Linguistics.

Wang, M.C., Haertel, G.D., & Walberg, H.J. (1995). The effectiveness of collaborative school-linked services. In E. Flaxman & A.H. Passow (Eds.), *Ninety-fourth yearbook of the National Society for the Study of Education: Part II. Changing populations, changing schools* (pp. 253-270). Chicago: University of Chicago Press.

Weiler, K. (1988). *Women teaching for change: Gender, class, and power.* South Hadley, MA: Bergin & Garvey.

Weiss, M.S. (1994). Marginality, cultural brokerage, and school aides: A success story in education. *Anthropology and Education Quarterly, 25,* 336-346.

Westat, Inc. (1992, December). *Reaching for college: Vol. 2. Case studies of college–school partnerships.* Rockville, MD: Author.

Wheelock, A. (1993). *School reform for secondary school students: A case for focusing on the ninth grade.* (Available from The Annie E. Casey Foundation, 701 St. Paul Street, Baltimore MD 21202; 800-222-1099; contact: Tony Cipollone)

Wigginton, E. (1986). *Sometimes a shining moment: The Foxfire experience.* New York: Doubleday.

How to order articles from ERIC

Citations with ED numbers are documents from *Resources in Education*. They can be read at a library with an ERIC microfiche collection or purchased, in microfiche or paper copy, from: ERIC Document Reproduction Service (EDRS), 7420 Fullerton Rd Suite 110, Springfield VA 22143-2852 (Phone: 800-443-3742) (E-mail: service@edrs.com) (World Wide Web: http://www.edrs.com).

For the location of the nearest ERIC collection, contact ERIC Clearinghouse on Languages and Linguistics (ERIC/CLL), 1118 22nd St NW, Washington DC 20037-1214 (Phone: 202-429-9292 ext 200) (Fax: 202-659-5641) (E-mail: eric@cal.org).

List of Organizations and Programs

ACCESS (The Arab Community Center of Economic and Social Services)
Ishmael Ahmed, Executive Director
Arab Community Center of Economic and Social Services
East Office
12740 W Warren
Dearborn MI 48126
(313) 730-3028

Dr. Shereen Arraf, Director
Bilingual Compensatory Education, Chapter 1
Dearborn Public Schools
18700 W Audette
Dearborn MI 48124
(313) 730-3028

Advancement Via Individual Determination (AVID)
Mary Catherine Swanson, AVID
San Diego County Office of Education
6401 Linda Vista Rd
San Diego CA 92111-7399
(619) 292-3500

Ahora: A Bridge to the Future
Silvia Saberta-Keber
Ahora A Bridge to the Future
105 Windsor St
Cambridge MA 02139
(617) 864-0980

Boston Compact, *see* **Project Pro Tech/Boston Compact**

Bridges to Literacy, *see* **Parent Information Center**

Coalition of Essential Schools
Ted Sizer
Coalition of Essential Schools
Box 1969
Brown University
Providence RI 02912
(401) 863-3384
http://www.ces.brown.edu

Coca-Cola Valued Youth Program
Michaela Velasquez, Education Associate
Intercultural Development Research Association
5835 Callaghan Rd Suite 350
San Antonio TX 78228-1190
(210) 684-8180

English Language Center, Hayward Unified School District
Mari Martinez, Director
English Language Center
28000 Calaroga Rd
Hayward CA 94545
(510) 293-8554

Falls Church Transitional High School
Francisco Millet, ESL Coordinator
Theodora Predaris, ESL Program Specialist
Gary Gutmank, Principal
Elizabeth Dovel, Coordinator/Counselor

Falls Church Transitional High School
Department of Instructional Services
3705 Crest Drive
Annandale VA 22003
(703) 846-8632

Families Together
ARC Associates
1212 Broadway Suite 400
Oakland CA
(510) 834-9455
http://www.emf.net/~arc99/

Family English Literacy Projects (FELP)
Office of Bilingual Education and Minority Languages Affairs
U.S. Department of Education
330 C Street NW
Washington DC 20202
(202) 205-5463
http://www.ed.gov/offices/OBEMLA

Foxfire Teacher Network
Sara Hatton
Foxfire Fund
P.O. Box 541
Mountain City GA 30562
(706) 746-5828
http://www.foxfirefnd.com

Horace Mann Middle School in San Francisco
Mr. Murphy
Horace Mann Middle School
3351 23rd Street
San Francisco CA 94310
(415) 695-5881

The International High School at LaGuardia Community College
Eric Nadelstern, Principal
The International High School at LaGuardia Community College
31-10 Thomson Ave
Long Island City NY 11101
(718) 482-5455

JTPA Summer Youth Program Bilingual Summer Academies, Oklahoma City
Mr. Vinh Dang Tran, Administrator
Asian American Student Services
Oklahoma City Public Schools
900 N Klein
Oklahoma City OK 73106

Mr. John Torres, Administrator
Hispanic American Student Services
Oklahoma City Public Schools
900 N Klein
Oklahoma City OK 73106
(405) 297-6522

Los Angeles Area Business/Education Partnership Cooperative
Laurel Adler
Los Angeles Area Business/Education Partnership Cooperative
East San Gabriel Valley Regional Occupational Program
1024 W Workman Ave
West Covina CA 91790
(818) 960-3625

Manhattan Comprehensive Night High School
Howard Friedman, Principal
Manhattan Comprehensive Night High School
240 Second Ave
New York NY 10003
(212) 353-2010

META (Multicultural Education Training and Advocacy)
META Inc
240A Elm St
Somerville MA 02144
(617) 628-2226

west coast office:
225 Bush St Suite 751
San Francisco CA 94104
(415) 398-1977

Multi-Cultural Youth Action Council (MC-YAC), *see* Touchstones

National Association for Bilingual Education
NABE
1220 L St NW Suite 605
Washington DC 20005-4018
(202) 898-1829
http://www.redmundial.com/nabe/first.htm

National Center for Restructuring Education, Schools, and Teaching (NCREST)
NCREST
Box 110
Teachers College Columbia University
New York NY 10027
http://www.tc.columbia.edu/~ncrest/

National Writing Project
James Sterling, Director
University of California, Berkeley
5511 Tolman Hall
Berkeley CA 94720
http://www-gse.berkeley.edu/Research/NWP/nwp.html

New Beginnings
Julie Rosell
2807 Fairmount Ave
San Diego CA 92105
(619) 527-6200

Newcomer High School
Herb Chan
2340 Jackson St
San Francisco CA 94115
(415) 241-6584

O'Farrell Community School—Center for Advanced Academic Studies
6130 Skyline Drive
San Diego CA 92114
(619) 263-3009

Oklahoma City Job Training Partnership Act, *see* **JTPA**

Pace Hispanic Outreach Program
Malula González, Director
White Plains High School
550 North Ave
White Plains NY 10605
(914) 661-8000

Parent Information Center/Bridges to Literacy
Laurette Young, Director
Parent Information Center/Bridges to Literacy
500 North Ave
White Plains NY 10605
(914) 422-2113

Project Adelante
Dr. Ana Maria Schuhman
Dean School of Education
Kean College of New Jersey
1000 Morris Ave
Union NY 07083
(908) 527-2136/2137

Project MAINE
(Maine Assists Innovators in Nurturing Excellence)
Gracye Studley, Director
Multilingual Programs
Portland Public Schools
331 Veranda St
Portland ME 04103
(207) 874-8135

Project Pro Tech/Boston Compact
Lois Ann Porter
The Boston Private Industry Council
2 Oliver St
Boston MA 02109
(617) 423-3755

Project Step Up
Glenn Odenbrett
Case Western Reserve University
10900 Euclid Ave
Cleveland OH 44106
http://www.lerc.nasa.gov/Other_Groups/K-12/csa/step_up_csa.html

Project Zero
Howard Gardner, Co-Director
Project Zero Development Group
Harvard Graduate School of Education
323 Longfellow Hall
Cambridge MA 02138
(617) 495-4342
http://pzweb.harvard.edu/HPZhome.html

REAL (Rural Entrepreneurship Through Action Learning) Enterprises
REAL Enterprises
1160 S Milledge Ave Suite 130
Athens GA 30606
(706) 546-9061

Seward Park High School Project EXCELL
Katherine Sid
Project EXCELL
Seward Park High School/Chinese Bilingual Program
350 Grand St Rm 520
New York NY 10002
(212) 387-9384

Step-to-College/Mission-to-College
Dr. Jacob Perea, Dean
School of Education
San Francisco State University
1600 Holloway Ave
San Francisco CA 94132
(415) 338-1792

Teachers of English to Speakers of Other Languages
TESOL
1600 Cameron St Suite 300
Alexandia VA 22314
(703) 836-0774
http://www.mgi-net.com/mgilists/tesol.htm

Tech Prep
National Center for Research in Vocational Education
University of California at Berkeley
2030 Addison St Suite 500
Berkeley CA 94720-1674
(800) 762-4093
http://ncrve.berkeley.edu

Touchstones/Multi-Cultural Youth Action Council
Joe Garcia, Executive Director
Touchstones
6721 51st Ave S
Seattle WA 98118
(206) 721-0867

Upward Bound
National Council of Educational Opportunity Associations
1025 Vermont Ave NW Suite 1201
Washington DC 20005
(202) 347-7430
http://trio.ume.maine.edu/~nceoa/nceoa.html

WISE Individualized Senior Experience
Vic Leviathan, Executive Director
WISE Program
New Rochelle High School
29 Old Tarrytown Rd
White Plains NY 10603
(914) 428-1968

Index

Fort Worth Independent School District, 36
Four Seasons Network, 130, 132
Foxfire, 125, 136, 183
    Teacher Network, 130, 132, 269
Freeman, D.E., & Freeman, Y.S., 136, 137
Freire, P., 27, 35, 53, 136
Friedlander, M., 152, 153
Fullan, M.G., 34, 65, 71
Fullan, M.G., & Miles, M.B., 53, 71
Funds of knowledge, 135, 136, 142

Gallimore, R., Tharp, R.G., & John-Steiner, V., 122
Gándara, P., x, xiii
Gardner, Howard, 130
GED, 104
Genesee, F., 160
Georgia, 182, 183
Gilroy High School, CA, 121
Giroux, H., 35
Glassman, C., 35, 117
Global perspective, 131
Glover, R.W., & Marshall, R., 30, 77, 113, 178, 179, 187, 206
Gold, N., 45
Goldenberg, C., x
González, J.M., & Darling-Hammond, L., xvii, 36, 44
González, N., Moll, L.C., Floyd-Tenery, M., Rivera, A., Rendón, P., Gonzales, R., & Amanti, C., 135
González, M., 121, 122, 126, 127
Goodlad, J., 47
Graduation rates, 120, 123
Greene, M., 27, 32, 199
Grosz, S., 192

Group
    activities, 123, 125
    differences, ix-xiv, 231, 232
Grouping of students, 118, 142
Guatemala, ix

HACU (Hispanic Association of Colleges and Universities), 208
Haiti, ix, xvi,xvii
Haitian
    Creole families, 138
    students, 124
Hamayan, E.V., & Perlman, R., 167
Hamilton Elementary School, San Diego, CA, 74
Hands-on projects, 29
Harassment, 124
Harklau, L., 90, 100, 164, 165, 202-204
Haycock, K., 56, 58, 151
Hayward, CA, 129, 153, 268
    Unified School District, 268
Health
    care, 207
    clinic, 75
    services, 71-73, 75, 76, 85, 96
Healthy Start, 73
Heath, S.B., & McLaughlin, M.W., 53
Henze, R., Lucas, T., & Scott, B., 35
Heritage, 133
Heterogeneous grouping, 56
Hidalgo, F., & Huling-Austin, L., 205
High expectations, 235, 236
High school
    competency exam, 1
    completion, 2
    –university relationship, 79, 80